The Donnellys

THE DONNELLYS

a trilogy by

JAMES REANEY

with scholarly apparatus by

James Noonan

BEACH HOLME PUBLISHING LIMITED

This edition is published by Beach Holme Publishing,
4252 Commerce Circle, Victoria, British Columbia, V8Z 4M2
with the assistance of The Canada Council.

Originally published in 3 volumes:
Sticks & Stones © 1975 by James Reaney.
St. Nicholas Hotel, Wm Donnelly, Prop. © 1976
by James Reaney.
Handcuffs © 1977 by James Reaney.

Reprinted (with new cover design) 1991, 1993, 1996.

Cover design by Barbara Munzar
Typeset by the Typeworks in 9 pt. Aster.
Printed in Canada by Hignell Printing, Winnipeg Manitoba.

The ballad quoted in *Sticks & Stones* is from Edith Fowke's *Folk Songs of Canada* (Fowke, Waterloo, 1954) to whom acknowledgement is made.

Canadian Cataloguing in Publication Data

Reaney, James, 1926–
The Donnellys

Contents: Stick & stones – The St Nicholas
Hotel – Handcuffs.
ISBN 0-88878-117-2

1. Donnelly family - Drama. I. Title.
II. Title: Sticks & stones. III. Title: The
St Nicholas Hotel. IV. Title: Handcuffs.
PS8535.E12D6 1983 C812'.54 C83-091170-7
PR9199.3.R4D6 1983

This ISBN was originally for *The Donnellys, Part I Sticks & Stones*, which is now out of print.

Contents

Foreword 1

Sticks and Stones 9

The St. Nicholas Hotel 95

Handcuffs 185

Concluding Essay 275

Chronology of Important Dates 289

Glossary 297

Foreword

Sticks and Stones is the first part of James Reaney's trilogy entitled *The Donnellys*. Like the other two parts, *The St. Nicholas Hotel* and *Handcuffs*, it has received wide critical acclaim. Following its premiere at the Tarragon Theatre in Toronto on November 24, 1973, the reviewers seemed to be vying with one another in their praise. Urjo Kareda's review in *The Toronto Star* on November 26 was headlined: 'It's just plain overwhelming.' He went on to say: 'Its premiere at the Tarragon Theatre Saturday night affirmed that theatre's status as the most important source of new plays in this country, just as it reaffirmed Reaney's position in the front ranks of all our imaginative writers... I can't help feeling that it was a landmark evening.' On the same day Herbert Whittaker in *The Globe and Mail* began his review: 'There was a great sense of beginning to the Tarragon Theatre's first showing of *Sticks and Stones*. Here started the poet-dramatist's celebration and conclusions on the province's most favoured folklegend.' Whittaker called the play 'a thoroughly involving theatrical experience.'

The next day *The Globe and Mail* published an interview with Reaney under the heading: 'Canada's own Greek tragedy.' The author was asked why the first play only covers the beginnings of the Donnelly legend. Reaney's reply was: 'Because I discovered the subject was too large for one evening. It is too great a tragedy. It is a story full of levels and generations of people. The closest thing is to the Faulkner novels and the Greek tragedies.' In a letter to *The Globe and Mail* on December 5, Ross Woodman, Professor of English at the University of Western Ontario, continued the comparison of *Sticks and Stones* with other widely recognized literary works saying: 'It is not only the best Canadian play yet written, it is among the best poetic dramas ever written, better, for example, than any of the plays of Yeats, Eliot and Fry. The struggle for survival explored in *Sticks and Stones* assumes, without the slightest verbal or theatrical bombast, epic and tragic proportions. Reaney has dared all and won hands up.' DuBarry Campau in *The Toronto Sun,* November 27, commented: 'James Reaney has reexamined the Donnelly saga with an historian's intent to put the record straight and a poet's fascination with the tragedies they both suffered themselves and inflicted on others... It is an exhausting play to see, in exactly the way all good theatre should be exhausting—it is both draining and releasing, not something to watch but to experience.'

The enthusiasm of the reviewers were not confined to Toronto. Joseph Erdelyi wrote in *The Ottawa Citizen* on December 1: 'It makes a decided impact. *Sticks and Stones* is a theatrical milestone in the recording of the history of Ontario that is certain to generate new interest not only in the Donnellys but in the lives of similar pioneers.' Dave Billington commented in *The Montreal Gazette* on December 6: 'It's taken us a long time, but we are finally beginning to turn our to own history and folk heritage for our cultural raw material... As conceived by Reaney and realized by director Keith Turnbull, the play is not so much a structured three-acter as a trembling, exciting, at times wearying mixture of fact, fiction, poetry and prose... If the succeeding two works are as good as this one, Canada will at last have, in her dramatic repertoire, a trilogy of plays which we can truly point to with pride, not only because they are good plays but because they tell us something about ourselves and our history.'

The success of *Sticks and Stones* proved to be portable to other productions besides that at Tarragon. It was presented at the Banff Festival of Fine Arts in the summer of 1974 under the direction of Thomas Peacocke. Of that production Jamie Portman wrote in *The Calgary Herald* on August 8: 'Reaney has taken the Donnelly story—both the legend and the reality—and has fashioned it into a remarkable and fascinating play called *Sticks and Stones*... The result is an illuminating experience in total theatre.'

From this critical reception of the play it is clear that Reaney has not simply recounted the history of the Donnellys of Lucan, Ontario.

He has transformed that history into a work of art and has created out of the soil of Southerwestern Ontario he knows so well a story that has universal appeal. But Reaney was first of all fascinated by and immersed himself in the history of the Donnellys and their community. As we watch the magic of the plays on stage we keep recalling that these horrendous events actually happened, here, in Canada, in Ontario, in Middlesex County, in the township Biddulph, in and around the small town of Lucan, (present population 1300), eighteen miles north of London, just off the Queen's Highway Number Seven. We wonder why no poet-dramatist has come along earlier to recreate our past in such a way. And we are convinced more than ever, if we needed convincing, that there are many such events in our history waiting for a skilled dramatist or poet or novelist to come and bring them to life for us.

The story of the Donnellys is familiar to many Canadians. It is the story of an Irish family with seven sons and one daughter who lived and struggled and died in and around the largely Irish township of Biddulph in the nineteenth century. The climax of the story is the massacre by a vigilante group made up of some thirty men of four members of that family—the father and mother and two sons, John and Thomas—as well as a niece, Bridget, shortly after midnight on February 4, 1880. In the two trials that followed no one was convicted of the murders, though six people were charged. To this day no one has been brought to justice for these brutal crimes. The story is included as no. VII—'The Biddulph Tragedy'—in a series of Famous Canadian Trials in *The Canadian Magazine* of August, 1915. It is perhaps the most famous unsolved murder in the history of Canadian law.

In his dramatization of their life and death Reaney sees the Donnellys as a family who would not submit to the pressures and prejudices of their society. Of the three plays into which he divides his story, Part One shows us the family establishing themselves in the community of Biddulph, after the migration of their parents to Canada in 1844, up to the year 1867: Part Two focuses on the stagecoach company run by the Donnelly boys and their rivalry with other stages, and brings us into the year 1879; Part Three concludes the saga with events immediately preceding and following the massacre of 1880, the trials, and the vindication of the Donnellys as perceived by Reaney.

The murder of the five Donnellys on February 4, 1880, was the subject of sensational newspaper articles in Canada and elsewhere for months after that fateful night. What was then called simply *The Globe*, in its edition of Thursday, February 5, 1880, featured on its front page a story 'from our own reporter', which had no less than seven headlines, as follows:

Horrible Tragedy at Lucan
Five Persons Murdered by Masked Men
An Entire Household Sacrificed
The House Fired and the Remains Consumed
Result of a Family Feud
The Story as Told by a Child Witness of the Crime
20 Masked Men Engaged in the Bloody Work

The story then began:

Lucan, Feb. 4.—Lucan awoke this morning to shock the country with intelligence of the blackest crime ever committed in the Dominion. The crime consisted of the murder, or rather, butchery, of a family of five—father, mother, two sons and a girl. The victims were named Donnelly, a family that has lived in the neighbourhood for upwards of thirty years. They resided on lot 18, 6th concession of Biddulph. The farm consists of fifty acres. They bore the unenviable reputation of being

THE TERRORS OF THE TOWNSHIP

The above sub-headline (all in capital letters) and much of the newspaper story, with its reliance on hearsay from those who were enemies of the Donnellys, are good examples of the biased attitudes that have permeated so much of the written and spoken accounts of the Donnellys right up to the present day.

After talk of the tragedy had subsided in the early part of this century, the book which revived widespread interest in the Donnellys was significantly called *The Black Donnellys*, by Thomas P. Kelley. It was subtitled 'The true story of Canada's most barbaric feud.' This immensely popular book, first published in 1954, has gone through over twenty reprintings, and is still prominent on newsstands. Its cover shows a picture of the original Donnelly gravestone with the word 'Murdered' under the names of the five victims. Kelley's book is a sensational, melodramatic account of the lives of the Donnellys and goes out of its way to paint them as black as possible. In 1962 Kelley wrote an even more fictionalized sequel entitled *Vengeance of the Black Donnellys*, which purports to give an account of the terrible retribution meted out by the ghosts of the Donnellys on those involved in the massacre.

Unfortunately most people today have gained their knowledge of the Donnellys from Kelley's books. Part of James Reaney's intention in his trilogy is to correct the false impressions created by Kelley. He was able to use the more carefully researched and documented book by Orlo Miller, *The Donnellys Must Die*, which was published in 1962 with the stated intention of contradicting Kelley's view of the Donnellys. Reaney has also done much research on his own and may soon publish his findings in a book of documents relating to the Donnellys and their times.

One of Reaney's methods in discounting Kelley's books is derision. Kelley's *The Black Donnellys* becomes the model of the travelling medicine show in *Sticks and Stones* and is the source of much humour and satire in the play. Showman Murphy is clearly the writer Kelley; the performance by his Shamrock Concert Company is called 'The Black Donnellys', which Reaney describes in an aside in the play as a 'viciously biased melodrama, also the title of the book everyone reads about the Donnellys.' As Showman Murphy sells his East India Tiger Fat and Banyan Tree of Life pills as the price of admission to the show, he recites verses from the 'Old Song' that introduces each chapter of Kelley's book. The Medicine Show begins with the first stanza from the Introduction of the book:

So hurry to your homes, good folks
Lock doors and windows tight.
And pray for dawn, The Black Donnellys
Will be abroad tonight.

The last appearance of the show in *Sticks and Stones* ends with the final verses of the song from the Kelley book, to the accompaniment of the banjo or fiddle:

Oh all young folks take warning,
Never live a life of hate,
Or wickedness or violence, lest
You share the Donnellys' fate.
Their murdered bodies lie today,
A mile from Lucan town.
But the memories of the awful feud,
Time never will live down.

It has been suggested that this 'Old Song', from which Reaney mercilessly quotes several times, was composed by Kelley himself.

There is a certain appropriateness in turning Thomas Kelley into Showman Murphy in the play. The writer's own father, Thomas P.

'Doc' Kelley, was a medicine showman and is celebrated by his son in a recent book. *The Fabulous Kelley*. Born on a farm near Newboro, Ontario, he was known as the King of the Medicine Men, and made more than two million dollars at his trade. He died in 1931 at the age of sixty-six.

Reaney goes to great pains in the play to emphasize the inaccuracies in Kelley's books. He uses the date of the logging bee at which Donnelly killed Patrick Farrell in 1857 as an example. The showman announces that it took place on June 29th; the 'real' Mr. Donnelly corrects him by insisting it was June 25th. In the play the 'real' Mr. Donnelly demands that the showman 'Show me the scene where I kill Farl,' and then corrects him again by saying that the killing was done 'not with an iron bar, but with a wooden handspike.' This incident is an indication of the extent of Reaney's own research on the Donnellys, for here he contradicts both the Kelley and the Miller books. Kelley says Donnelly struck Farrell with an iron bar; Miller says he struck him with an iron, not a wooden, handspike, Miller, also inaccurately, gives the date of the fatal fight as June 27th.

In this scene, as so often in the play, precise historical fact becomes the occasion of moving drama. There is a striking contrast between the huckster Murphy and Mr. Donnelly, who, with great dignity and disdain, forces 'the living (to) obey the dead.' A further indication of Reaney's art is the way he is able to make these scenes deriding Kelley into some of the funniest in the play and to use them both to dispel some of the misconceptions passed on by Kelley and to create sympathy for the 'real Donnellys'. It is worth recalling here that in the *Dictionary of Canadian Biography*, volume x (1972), the article on 'James Donnelly, farmer' was written by James Reaney.

Although Reaney has immersed himself in the history of the Donnellys and their times, he has done much more in *Sticks and Stones* than simply write a documentary drama. He has created a vision in dramatic terms of a family who would not bow to the pressures and threats of the local community. Even if some of the historical details are altered, even if he does not give us a complete picture of the 'real' Donnellys, we must remember that the play's importance lies in its dramatic, not in its historical qualities. The greatest achievement of *Sticks and Stones* is what Reaney as a poet-dramatist has made out of the bare bones of history that he has dug up, as he says, 'from the attics of the local courthouses' and elsewhere.

Reaney's vision comes fully alive only on the stage, as it has so magnificently in the Tarragon Theatre productions of all three parts and on the many stages across Canada where the plays were presented in their national tour in the fall of 1975. Those who have had the privilege of attending one or all of these productions will never forget the experience. Much of the credit for this must go to the sensitive and imaginative direction of Keith Turnbull, who has worked closely with Reaney in the development of all three parts of the trilogy. Several of the same actors have appeared in all three parts and were the nucleus of the NDWT Company, which took the plays on tour. Especially memorable in the Tarragon productions were Gerry Franken and Patricia Ludwick in the roles of Mr. and Mrs. Donnelly. David Ferry, Miriam Greene, Don MacQuarrie, and Rick Gorrie were also seen in all three parts. These and the other five actors in the cast of Part One assume multiple roles in the play. There is no attempt to develop a character in the realistic style of theatre. Amazingly, the eleven actors bring before us some one hundred people. Each of the actors must be flexible enough to shift at times from being a Donnelly to a friend or enemy of the Donnellys. Each must be capable of the enormous energy required by the sometimes dizzying pace at which the play moves. Each must be capable of evoking the verbal and visual imagery that are so entwined in the play. A mark of their and Reaney's success is that while the acting time runs close to three hours, we become so caught in the web of poetry and movement on stage that we hate to see the performance come to an end.

Reaney's technique in *Sticks and Stones* is something quite unique in Canadian drama and perhaps any drama. It is a combination of many things: poetry and prose, realistic action and mime, song and dance, games and ritual, fantasy and dream, past, present, and future. The work has been compared to that of such diverse playwrights as Aeschylus, Shakespeare, Brecht, and the Victorian melodramatists. Time and place frequently dissolve so that the spectator finds himself in 1884 at one moment and 1974 at another, in Tipperary, London, Lucan, or Goderich, in a farmhouse, a barnyard, a church, or a court, on a country road, a wagon, or a train. All these changes are evoked with the help of the simplest of props—ladders, sticks, stones, clotheslines, shirts, wheels, hayforks, barrels, chairs, noise-makers, maps, candles, lanterns. As in his other plays, Reaney's structural approach is to juxtapose many, many sequences of different times, settings and moods. In *Sticks and Stones* he has perfected this method over anything he has ever done before so that one sequence flows easily into another without the separation and numbering of scenes that occurred in his earlier plays such as *Colours in the Dark* and *Listen to the Wind*. He sometimes refers to the sequences in his stage directions as, for example, 'the going-to-Goderich sequence', 'a mass menace sequence', or 'the Donnelly house sequence'. He is always concerned about how one sequence blends into the next, as when he directs, 'The Angelus should bridge between chases's ending and the vesper scene.'

Yet all the sequences in the play are tied to a simple story line. Act One takes us from James Donnelly's settling in Biddulph to his killing of Farrell at the logging bee; Act Two shows the struggles faced by Mrs. Donnelly and her seven children before and after his sentencing until his return from prison seven years later; Act Three features the attempts of neighbours to drive the Donnellys from the township and their final decision never to leave Biddulph. The result of all this complexity in simplicity is an experience that leaves the spectator or reader immesurably enriched though aware there is much he has not absorbed and much to be gained from further viewings and readings of the play. Reaney once said there are a hundred plays in the Donnelly story. He originally wrote one long play about it, and then expanded it into the present three. Of the first of the three, he wrote in the program notes:

The complete story of the Donnelly tragedy is too large for one evening. This play takes you as far as one of those moments after which things will never be the same again. When 'persons unknown' burnt down his barn in 1867 James Donnelly defied this invitation to get out of the neighbourhood. He swore then that he would stay in Biddulph township forever. He is still there. It was at this time that the Donnellys decided to be Donnellys.

Reaney's exciting recreation of how the Donnellys came to be Donnellys is what awaits the reader in *Sticks and Stones.* More than a knowledge of history, what is required is careful attention to the play's poetry and free rein for the visual imagination to 'see' the action on stage as directed by the author within the text. Given these qualities, the reader has an experience awaiting him comparable to that of the reviewers and audiences on that landmark evening of November 24, 1973.

JAMES NOONAN
Associate professor
of English
Carlton University
Ottawa

Sticks and Stones

STICKS AND STONES: The Donnellys, Part I is written by James Reaney and was first performed at the Tarragon Theatre in Toronto on November 24, 1973 with the following cast:

Bob Aarron	Ian Langs
Richard Carson	Carol Lazare
David Ferry	Patricia Ludwick
Jerry Franken	Don MacQuarrie
Rick Gorrie	Fletcher T. Williamson
Miriam Greene	

Directed by Keith Turnbull

Lighting by John Stammers

The play is based on the story of an actual family who came out from Ireland in 1844 to Biddulph Township 18 miles from London, Ontario, and were nearly annihilated by a secret society formed among their neighbours 36 years later. In the text before you, the reader will meet Mr and Mrs Donnelly, their son William and their only daughter Jennie. The other six sons are there, but they appear most clearly in the form of their shirts on Mrs Donnelly's washing line. Watch for friends of the Donnellys—Andrew Keefe, the taverner, and Jim Feeney, the traitor. Their neighbours form a Catholic road of farmers' names and a Protestant road. Then there are enemies: George Stub, a Protestant merchant in the nearby village; and Tom Cassleigh, a neighbour who was tried several times for killing an Englishman named Brimmacombe. Both these gentlemen are also local magistrates! Two more enemies are close neighbours—called here Mr and Mrs Fat; also Pat Farl whom Mr Donnelly killed at a logging bee. There is a Medicine Showman who puts on a rival play to mine about how fiendish the Donnellys were; there are constables, census takers, gaolers, Negro settlers, surveyors, the pyromaniac eight Gallagher boys, Mrs Farl, priests, a bishop and many others.

The complete story of the Donnelly tragedy is too large for one evening. This play gets you started and takes you as far as one of those moments after which things will never be the same again. When 'persons unknown' burnt down his barn in 1867, James Donnelly defied this invitation to get out of the neighbourhood. He swore that he would stay in Biddulph Township forever. He is still there. It was at this time that the Donnellys decided to be Donnellys.

When you immerse yourself in this play, you may find that your experience matches my own when I immersed myself some eight years ago in documents which had lain for years and years in the attics of two local courthouses: after a while I couldn't stop thinking about them.

JAMES REANEY

MRS DONNELLY Now I've reached the borders of Biddulph.

Sticks & Stones

Act One

The room in which the story is presented contains all of the objects and properties required—ladders, barrels, sticks, stones, noise-makers, chairs, etc. The central area is bare except for a pile of sticks on one side and a pile of stones on the other, and possibly a pile of four boulders at the back in the centre. In the distance there is the drunken and rowdy singing of a tavern song.

Oh, three men went to Deroughata
To sell three loads of rye.
They shouted up and they shouted down
The barley grain should die.
(Refrain)
Tiree igery ary ann, Tiree igery ee,
Tiree igery ary ann, The barley grain for me.

Then the farmer came with a big plough,
He ploughed me under the sod.
Then winter it being over
And the summer coming on,
Sure the barley grain shot forth his head
With a beard like any man.

Then the reaper came with a sharp hook;
He made me no reply.

He caught me by the whiskers and
Cut me above the thigh.

Then the binder came with her neat thumb;
She bound me all around
And then they hired a handyman
To stand me on the ground.

Then the pitcher came with a steel fork;
He pierced it through me heart.
And like a rogue or highwayman
They bound me to the cart.

Then they took me to the barn and
Spread me out on the floor.
They left me there for a space of time
And me beard grew through the door.

Then the thresher came with a big flail;
He swore he'd break me bones
But the miller he used me worse
He ground me between two stones.

Then they took me out of that and
Threw me into a well.
They left me there for a space of time,
And me belly began to swell.

Then they sold me to the brewer
And he brewed me on the pan
But, when I got into the jug
I was the strongest man.

Then they drank you in the kitchen
And they drank you in the hall,
(*said, not sung*)
But the drunkard he used you worse;
He pissed you against the wall.

Now the stage turns the deep green of primeval forest; someone imitates the whistle of a deep forest bird—the peewee, and then a boy, Will Donnelly, limps across the stage to sit down on the pile of stones with his catechism book. His mother, a tall woman, enters the forest looking for her son. She comes over to him, accepts his book and says, after refusing his offer of a seat on the stones

MRS DONNELLY Which are the sacraments that can be received only once?

WILL The sacraments that can be received only once are Baptism, Confirmation, and Holy Orders.

MRS DONNELLY Now Will, why can Baptism, Confirmation, and Holy Orders be received only once?

WILL Baptism, Confirmation, and Holy Orders can be received only once because they imprint on the soul—a spiritual mark, called a character, which lasts forever.

OTHERS *at back of theatre, singing softly*
Oh, three men went to Deroughata
To sell three loads of rye.
They shouted up and they shouted down
The barley grain should die.

MRS DONNELLY Now where's your shoes? They were on your feet when we left the chapel.

WILL I know where they are. Mother, I just don't want them to wear out so fast.

MRS DONNELLY Who's making you feel shame of your feet?

WILL Nobody.

MRS DONNELLY Were the boys calling you names in the churchyard then?

WILL Yes. They threw stones at me and they called me—Cripple. I'm used to that, mother, but there was a new boy there and do you want to know what he called me, mother? *she nods* Blackfoot!

MRS DONNELLY Did they call us that then?

WILL Yes. And me myself—the Blackfoot. Cripple, I know. But what do they mean by Blackfoot?

MRS DONNELLY I suppose across the sea even it would come following us.

WILL What come following us, mother? *Enter Mr Donnelly and stands with his back to us far upstage at the centre. The mob moves a step or two closer to the stage. As if made of forest branches and leaves behind them and above them, a silhouette map of Ireland appears towering on the back stage wall.*

OTHERS *a step or two closer*
Then the farmer came with a big plough,
He ploughed me under the sod.
Then winter it being over
And the summer coming on,

Sure the barley grain shot forth his head
With a beard like any man.

Someone in a dress rolls a barrel on stage; "she" covers it with a sheet of rusty tin and then places on top of the tin a model of the Sheas' house. As "she" departs, two men disguised in dresses, bonnets and masks or veils strike matches and burn down the house. The fire makes their shadows grow into the branch map of Ireland. All this proceeds under Mrs Donnelly's speech and illustrates it.

MRS DONNELLY In the old country, Will, where your father and your brother James and your mother were born—you were called a Blackfoot if you wouldn't join the Whitefeet.

WILL Who were the Whitefeet?

MRS DONNELLY Who indeed. They were a faction, they were a secret society, a secret people.

MALE VOICE *from the Others* Six eggs to you Rody, and half a dozen of them rotten.

GIRL'S VOICE The landlords are tyrants—English robbers and murderers that rob the people of their little spots, and turn 'em out to perish. 'Tis justice to punish the bloody robbers!

MRS DONNELLY Oh indeed it was justice and the Whitefeet rode around at night dressed up like ladies, mind you, so they couldn't be recognized. They made it hot for landlords and bailiffs. The trouble was they made it hot for everybody. Will, there was one family—the Sheas—they lived twenty miles off, they said no to the Whitefoot Society, no they wouldn't give up the farm they'd just rented, and a good farm it was in those hard times, just because the Whitefeet wanted nobody ever to rent that farm at all to spite the landlord. So no, says the Sheas. Well, what the Whitefeet did to the Sheas one night is so terrible I'm going to whisper it to you and don't ever talk about it again.

OTHERS

Then the reaper came with a sharp hook;
He made me no reply.
He caught me by the whiskers and
Cut me above the thigh.

WILL Even the baby was dead then?

MRS DONNELLY Despite all the mother did she would have had to drown it altogether to save him from the fire and that baby died, Will, because his father wouldn't join the Secret People, because his father would not do what they done, do what they told him to do. *Men start preparing a barrel for a human occupant by putting thorn branches into it.*

WILL It's better to join them then?

MRS DONNELLY And have to help burn whole families alive in their beds then? Sure, Will, terrible and filthy as the name of Blackfoot is—worse than scab, or leper or nigger or heretic have they made it, they, the clean, just and secret people—I'd rather be called scab, or leper or nigger or heretic or Blackfoot than do what they did to the Sheas. At first they'd ride by and you'd find a note at your doorway that said—"signed by Matthew Midnight."

OTHERS *whispering* Signed by Matthew Midnight.

WILL Who was he?

MRS DONNELLY Oh, the pretend name of their Chief. The Great Chief of the Secret Society and the note would say

MALE VOICE *under and over* Jim Donnelly

OTHERS

Then the binder came with her neat thumb;
She bound me all around.

MALE VOICE Jim Donnelly!

OTHERS

And then they hired a handyman
To stand me on the ground.

MALE VOICE Jim Donnelly!

A man is put into the barrel; they roll it back and forth in time to the singing and the speech. Another man rolls on the floor—back and forth.

MALE VOICE If you don't help us cut off the bailiff's ears tomorrow night you are a Blackfoot and we'll cut off yours an' fill a barrel first with thorns and nails and then—with—you.

MRS DONNELLY Yes. So if you were afraid, Will, you joined them and they made you kneel down and swear and drink—faith to them forever.

BARREL ROLLERS *repeat under* Terry Morgan's in the barrel.

OTHERS *galloping under*

Then the pitcher came with a steel fork;
He pierced it through me heart.
And like a rogue or a highwayman
They bound me to the cart. *knocking*

Mrs Donnelly and Will have climbed a great stepladder at the back of the stage.

MRS DONNELLY One night, Will, your father was up the road visiting a farmer he was to do some work for the next morning. They followed him there. *The barrel rollers join the mob, barrel tumbling down off the stage where Donegan will fall down later, but is hoisted up again; we begin to focus on Mr Donnelly's back.*

OTHERS Come out, Jim Donnelly.

MRS DONNELLY They said to your father

OTHERS Put on you my good fellow and come out till two or three of your neighbours that wish you well gets a sight of your purty face you babe of grace.

MRS DONNELLY You father stood behind the door and he says

MR DONNELLY Who are you that wants me at all?

MRS DONNELLY And they says

OTHERS Come out first avourneen. *Preparing a Bible and candle Donnelly turns to us for the first time. He is a small square chunk of will.*

MRS DONNELLY He opened the door and came out.

OTHERS Oh Jim Donnelly. Jim, the Whitefeet hear that you let one of your mares stand to Johnson's stallion last Monday coming home from the fair.

MRS DONNELLY To which your father replied *he comes towards us and them with affability*

MR DONNELLY It was love at first sight. Shure Johnson's stallion was mounting my one mare before I could stop him. Would you have me break up a pair of true lovers? Would you? And I had my back turned for the merest minute getting the other mare's tail out of a thornbush.

OTHERS Did you not know, Jim Donnelly, that no Whitefoot is to have any dealings with the Protestant and the heretic Johnson?

MR DONNELLY Yes, but it was *They extend two lighted candles to him.*

OTHERS Kneel, Donnelly. Get down on your knees. *But he stands. The barrel is rolled back and forth in front of him.* Swear *striking a book* by the holy evangelists that you will always be joined to this society known as the Whitefeet and that you will forever and forever obey—

MR DONNELLY But you see I won't kneel. And I won't, I will not swear that.

HALF OF OTHERS

Hrump hrumpety bump brump brump
Terry's in the barrel
Hrump hrumpety bump brump brump
Jim Donnelly's in it too
We'll roll you right up Keeper's Hill
it's true, it's true... *repeat under*

This "it's true" with malign stamping of feet goes on under the speech of the Other Half.

HALF OF OTHERS If you refuse, Jim Donnelly—if you refuse, Donnelly, you won't know the day nor the hour nor the night nor the hour when we'll come to

MR DONNELLY No, I'm not! Kneel! No! Swear! No! I will not kneel.

We still hear Terry Morgan in the barrel saying, "It's true, it's true, it's true."

MRS DONNELLY So they cursed your father and called him a

OTHERS Blackfoot! *The barrel is rolled at Donnelly who catches it. As they yell the name at him they turn their backs on him, hiding their eyes as if he's too foul to see. They lie down in two rows on either side of the stage—these will become the "roads" of Biddulph in the next scene.*

MR DONNELLY *singing like one of those John L. McCormack records*

Then they took me to the barn and
Spread me out on the floor.
They left me there for a space of time
And me beard grew through the door.

The shadow map shows Ireland drifting away.

OTHERS *singing into the floor*

Then the thresher came with a big flail;

Mr Donnelly is letting Terry Morgan out of the barrel, rolls it aside where it now becomes a hollow tree and, assisting Morgan, goes straight up stage, then over to stage left where both figures melt into the chorus there.

He swore he'd break me bones
But the miller he used me worse
He ground me between two stones.

MRS DONNELLY What day is it today of all days, William Donnelly?

WILL It's my birthday.

MRS DONNELLY Tell me one wish.

WILL Well, mother, 'tis something other than a prayerbook. I'd like a horse—a black stallion. And a sword. Then I'd ride up and down the line and I'd cut the heads off all those who call me—us—names.

MRS DONNELLY Go over to the old tree the storm fell down, Will. Will, what would you call this big black horse?

WILL Lord Byron. But he wouldn't be lame, you see.

MRS DONNELLY Now see what you find there hidden among the roots. *He searches, crawling into the barrel; searching around it.*

OTHERS *softly and rolling over*
Then they took me out of that and
Threw me into a well.
They left me there for a space of time,
And me belly began to swell.

WILL It's a parcel. *Actually it is just two sticks.*

MRS DONNELLY But it's not likely your father and I would give you a brown paper parcel for your twelfth birthday. What's it a parcel of, Will?

WILL A fiddle. Is it just for today, mother? Just mine for my birthday? But tomorrow will my brothers get at it?

MRS DONNELLY No, Will, it is for you—and only you. To be your music for your entire lifetime. Remember what I've told you today.

Will mimes the fiddle with two sticks; at edge of stage, a real fiddler follows.

WILL *as he tunes* What did happen to father when he wouldn't kneel and he wouldn't swear?

MRS DONNELLY Nothing's happened.

WILL Nothing's happened yet?

MRS DONNELLY Nor ever will.

WILL Are there some of them followed us here then?

MRS DONNELLY Your father outfaced them in the old country, and if they were ever to come after him up the roads of Biddulph he'd do the same to them again. We're not there anymore, Will. We're where **you** were born—not an old country, but a new country these Canadas. Only bullies and blowhards say at you: "You won't know the day nor the hour nor the night when we'll come to—" Aye, yes— come to a tap with our fists on their chests at our gateway that'll send them rolling down the line like ninepins. *She picks up a stone and bowls it down the aisle.* What do your father and mother care if they should follow us—whisper me who called you the name. *he does quickly and*

OTHERS *softly* A high grey hill

MRS DONNELLY Uh, it's his tattletale mother is a fat woman has to be raised in and out and onto her bed with a pulley. No feet at all should be her name and his— the nofeet with all the belly. She's got wind of something and the child has overheard. Will, after this harvest, I'm telling you your father will own this very ground we're standing on and shortly after that we'll own to another heir, not our fifth boy, pray, but our first girl may it please Heaven and when he owns the very ground we stand on and the fields he has made, you'll see they'll never drive us off. We won't be druv!

OTHERS *whistling wind noises* that's Keeper's Hill.

MRS DONNELLY Here we stay.

OTHERS In Ireland. *The map silhouettes the coasts of Iceland, Greenland, Newfoundland, the River, Lake Ontario, Hamilton, the province of Upper Canada where it comes to rest.*

MRS DONNELLY Not in Ireland. No, not there. With old names— Blackfoot, Whitefoot, slavery and fear. Here is a new fiddle, Will, *she takes the fiddle* and we're free as it is to play all the tunes. *She uses the fiddle and speaks this verse, the chorus whistling the tune under.*

Then they sold me to the brewer
And he brewed me on the pan
But, when I got into the jug
I was the strongest man.

If you're afraid you should be— *fills the whole theatre*

OTHERS Ireland *just barely there, but there*

MRS DONNELLY If you're not you'll live. *She turns from us and they leave the forest.*

Then they drank you in the kitchen
And they drank you in the hall,
said, not sung
But the drunkard he used you worse;
He pissed you against the wall.

OTHERS Ten years before this the Township of Biddulph was surveyed.

Surveyor and boy enter with chain, stakes and mallet and book. Two others stretch out blue brook cloth across stage—water music. Rest return to their lines stage right and stage left to make Jacob's ladders, or cats' cradles.

BOY So what's this lot, pa?

SURVEYOR Concession Six Lot Eighteen.

BOY I wonder who'll come to live here. *driving in stakes which indicate the borders of the Donnelly farm*

SURVEYOR You're always wondering about that, aren't you Davie? Well it won't be any more coloured settlers. The Company's tired of them. So it will be Irish squatters more than likely—Big Jim Johnson is bringing over a horde of his relatives from Tipperary and he's bringing every sort evidently so he'll feel at home again.

BOY I wonder what they'll be like.

SURVEYOR Oh, Paddy will fight the coloured folks and drive them out if he can. Then he'll fight his Paddy neighbours and then he'll fight himself and then he'll move on somewhere else and repeat the process.

BOY What'll they fight about, pa? *His father washes his face in the stream.*

SURVEYOR Well, to begin with the way this lot is laid out, there's a small creek enters it from the next farm, crosses it and then flows into the next farm. Farm that is to be. It'll be the subject of a lawsuit, quarrels about water rights, flooding—they'll love that little creek.

BOY Couldn't you stop that?

SURVEYOR Well now, what would you suggest?

BOY Make the farms a different shape?

SURVEYOR I'm not allowed to do that, Davie. The laws of geometry are the laws of geometry. *Looping the chain so as to measure the next lot: we begin to focus on the next scene.* No, people must make do with what right angles and Euclid and we surveyors and measurers provide for them.

BOY *moving on* So what's this lot, pa?

SURVEYOR Concession Six Lot Seventeen.

OTHERS *using ropes and making cats' cradles (Jacob's ladders) out of them and their bodies; fates with string entangling people's lives*

Wild lands wild lands wild lands
Cut into concessions cut into farms
Canada West Canada West
In the New World the new world the new world

Chorus whistles to the "Temple House Reel"; they dance with pieces of wood which they join together into the Donnelly shanty which stands a bit aslant centre stage and behind which appears an early map of Biddulph Township showing the net of concessions, roads, farms with owners' names on them and a feeling that we have come from Ireland to a closer look at what is happening. As if to a tree at the side of the stage someone hammers up a notice with a stone.

A census taker with another big book approaches the Donnelly place and is met by Mr Donnelly. Mrs Donnelly comes out of their shanty with a baby. She puts it down in a cradle and walks over to the tree, takes down the notice.

CENSUS TAKER A fine morning, Jim Donnelly. Now this has nothing to do with taxes. What it is, is this. They're enumerating the population of Canada West in 1848 so what returns will I make for you, Jim Donnelly?

Census taker asks the row of questions on left hand: Donnelly answers with words in right-hand column.

Situation—lot?	Eighteen
Concession?	Six
Religion?	Church of Rome
Natives of Ireland in each family?	Three
Total number of persons resident in the house where the Census is taken?	Four
Lands—Number of acres held by each family?	One hundred
Uncultivated, of wood in wild land?	One hundred
Neat cattle	None
Horses	None
Hogs	Three
Proprietor or Non-Proprietor?	Non-Proprietor
Landlord?	John Grace, carpenter, London Township

CENSUS TAKER You want to keep track of your landlord, Mr Donnelly. Someone was asking Mr Grace about his land up here and he said no one was living on it.

MR DONNELLY It's a funny thing then, Mr Darcy, that he recognizes our money when we go into town to give him his yearly rent then. Does he think it's ghosts that are improving his land for him?

CENSUS TAKER Good day to you, Jim Donnelly. And Mrs Donnelly too.

MRS DONNELLY Good day to you, Mr Darcy. *She comes to her husband with the notice from the tree.*

MR DONNELLY Read it aloud for me, Mrs Donnelly.

OTHERS

Squatters and Trespassers. Notice is hereby given.
Squatters and Trespassers. Notice is hereby given.

MRS DONNELLY Oh, did you know this now, Mr Donnelly. There are now again many people going about the country in search of Improved Lands, occupied by Squatters with the intention of

OTHERS Purchasing over their heads.

MR DONNELLY Over my head is under my feet. Old John Grace is not going to sell it from either over us nor under us till he considers our offer and his promise. He won't even own it himself till eight years from now and if it goes up in value it's my work and yours, Judith, has made it go up. He agreed to that and he's going to stick by it.

A priest interrupts the Donnellys.

PRIEST Who are punished in purgatory?

MR & MRS DONNELLY Those are punished for a time in purgatory who die in state of grace but are guilty of venial sin or have not fully satisfied for the temporal punishment due to their sins.

PRIEST Who are punished in Hell?

MR DONNELLY Not I. No, not James Donnelly. I'm not in Hell though my friends in Biddulph thought to send me there, but after thirty-five years in Biddulph who would find Hell any bigger a fire than that fire I died in. I'm not in Hell for I'm in a play *ladders begin to register on us, poking up behind* and it's my duty to
Name the roads of Biddulph!!

OTHERS

Front Road   Coursey Line   Gulley Road   Sauble Line
Revere Road   Granton Line   Swamp Line   Roman Line

At the back of the stage are raised five ladders. Stage-right ladder is the tallest, then they get smaller to quite a stubby one—their

shadows and patterns matching the map of Biddulph which is a triangle.

MR DONNELLY Yes, those are the roads of Biddulph. I was one of the pathmasters for the Roman Line. My neighbours and myself for three days in the spring and three days in the late summer would dig and pick and scrape and shovel gravel so there'd be a smoother road for my enemies to come and club me, and these roads of Biddulph—you're right to see them as ladders, yes, ladders that we crawled up and down on and up other ladders—up to Goderich for justice, down to London to pay our rent.

The ladders have been laid before Mr Donnelly and he uses their rungs to illustrate.

Why are the roads here rather than here? Why do I live here rather than here? Wild lands cut by surveyors into people—with your chain you decided that it would be here, my farm—that people say I squatted on Concession Six Lot Eighteen—and you decided—

BOY So what's this lot, dad?

MR DONNELLY That's Mulowney's. At his five-acre slashing I should kill Farl and there

SURVEYOR Concession Six Lot Fifteen

MR DONNELLY I should be caught. Caught in the lines and the roads and the farms they made and the quarrels about fences and ditches—the Protestant Line, now who settled that line?

OTHERS *Use a long ladder as the core for this: whistle "Lilliburlero" under—this tune will meet the banjo tune behind the Negro settlers' protest—the chorus forms a double line that faces us with one black in its midst.*

Who settled the third & fourth concessions?
Protestants Johnstons

STICKS HALF CHORUS		STONES HALF CHORUS
Big Jim, Little Jim, Jerry Jim		Johnson
Big John's John's George		Johnson
Big Tom's John's George		Johnson
and	Attery	Stubb
	Armwright	Latchett
	Courcey	Blackwell protestants
and pioneers!	The Guernseys	& the Cobbetts
came with them it appears		And then

BLACK *banjo* What about the Mescoes & the Washingtons
Taylors Runcimans
humming Delkeys & the Bells

MR DONNELLY Yes, the coloured settlers had come to those concessions ten years before any of us came from Ireland and it was their bad luck to have farms just where the new railroad slated to cross the Proof Line Road from London to Goderich. *Burning of house on barrel routine is set up with disguised men. In bowler hat and suspenders, ultra-Protestant George Stub comes forward.*

STUB Darkie, if you don't sell me that corner five acres you've squatted on there I'm going to heat it hotter than hell, and something else so serious might happen that they'll have to erect a gallows for me. *Pinned by a ladder, the Negro cannot prevent them from burning his property.*

ALL Proclamation!

WOMEN Robert Baldwin, Attorney General

MALE VOICE Whereas about midnight of Thursday the 19th day of October now last past, certain Barns the properties of William Bell, Ephraim Taylor, and the Reverend Daniel A. Turner, Coloured Inhabitants of the Township of Biddulph in our Province of Canada were destroyed by fire.

STUB ET AL. *derisively* And whereas there is reason to believe that the said fire was not caused by accident, but was the act of Incendiaries at present unknown. Now Know Ye, that a Reward of

MALE VOICE 50 pounds will be paid to any person

FEMALE VOICES Witness. Our right trusty and right well beloved Cousin Earl of Elgin and Kincardine and Governor General of British North America.

A true copy.

MR DONNELLY Arhh, Stub and his pals got off and it came out that few coloured settlers stayed where they had first settled, but drifted away south to London, down the ladder—Shhh!

The following inserts are like mugshots suddenly cut into the other imagery.

GAOLER	STUB *from behind bars of gaol-ladder*
Name	George Stub
Date When Committed	October 20th, 1848

Height	Six feet
Colour of eyes	Grey
Place of Birth	Tipperary
Religion	Church of England
For what committed	Suspicion of arson, burning the coloured settlers' barns
Occupation	Senator
Mr Stub!	I'm a storekeeper now, but that's what I'll ask Macdonald for in 78 If I get his Catholic candidate all the Orangeman's votes.
Colour of eyes	Grey

MR DONNELLY So the road you lived on could destroy you just like that, and the road you lived on might not turn on you, but decide to have a go at another road. What other road? Why the sixth and seventh concession where I lived. My road. Who settled the Roman Line? Church Line? Chapel Line?

The whistled "Temple House Reel" goes under here; we begin to have a kind of music for each social group.

STICKS:	STONES:
Barry	Trehy
Feeney	O'Halloran
Cahill	Cassleigh
McCann	Flynn
Grace	

Will and Jennie run up and down the ladder that represents the Roman Line.

WILL No, that's wrong now. You should say Donnelly's. Not Grace's farm. John Grace never cleared that farm.

STICKS But John Grace has the deed to this farm, Cripple.

JENNIE When he was my father's landlord, but it was my father cleared the land and made it a farm of value.

STUB Where's your deed, Donnelly?

WILL But don't you see that we had something better than a deed, we had his **word** as a **friend** of my mother and father's over in the old country. Mr Grace told my father he'd get him started on a farm up in Biddulph if Paddy with a hod wasn't good enough for him; he'd pay the taxes, we'd pay him rent and at the end of ten years we'd have the first chance to buy at a fair price.

GRACE *while sawing a stick in two* But how in the devil's name was I to know that at the end of the ten years the War would have driven the price so high and wheat at two dollars a bushel?

STONES Did he get the promise in handwriting?

STICKS Squatters can't read.

WILL When my father was promised that land

WOMEN Concession Six Lot Eighteen

WILL He took a handful of it back to my mother and she said

Mr Donnelly walks down the Roman Line, i.e., the two lines of Sticks *and* Stones *like the line-up of a reel, to Mrs Donnelly at the upstage end. This is one of the most important design images of the story, a man caught between the lines of his neighbours, caught in a ladder, and the big dance at the end of the play will emphasize this quality of the Donnellys being planted in rows of people they can't get away from.*

MRS DONNELLY James. What have you there in your hand?

WILL He said

WILL & MR DONNELLY Mrs Donnelly this is the farm that's going to be ours.

KIDS Concession Six Lot Eighteen

WILL Start again, please. If you walked south down the Roman Line

They say their names with a crouch, and a secret meaning, since most of them are Protestant misunderstandings for Gaelic names. This contrasts the Roman Line with the Protestant Line who are more aggressive and sure of themselves.

	STICKS	STONES
	Barry	Trehy
	Feeney	O'Halloran
	Cahill	Cassleigh
	McCann	Flynn
pause	Donnelly	Mulowney
	Egan	Marksey
	Quinn	Farl
	Gallagher	Duffy
	Clancy	Donovan
bell	and Father Flynn's church	
		and Andy Keefe's tavern
		jug sound

WILL & JENNIE

Brother and sister we walk down the road
We were born on and lived there
The road our father helped build
When his killers were babies.

The road chant can be repeated with variations. Donnellys walk down the line and it is hard to do so; then the line sways out and is wide; then it sprouts perspectives; Mrs Donnelly stands at the end before kneeling; Mr Donnelly then turns to tell us something; actors have been drifting off to view some offstage disturbance.

BOY **The London Inquirer** September 20th 1844.

VOICE The Huron Assizes is to be congratulated on not having a single prisoner stand for trial and aside from

MRS DONNELLY *folding a newspaper* And indeed they were to be congratulated while there was still time because his Lordship never wore a pair of white gloves again, not at least while Biddulph Township was part of Huron County—from 1844 to 1863.

ALL Return of convictions made by her Majesty's Justices of the

The following "Return of Convictions" Sequence needs stone-clicking rhythms, and a chopping block might be brought in to show how they axed out clubs for their battles. The rubrics "Name of Prosecutor," etc. need not be repeated each time but can be represented by a gesture illustrative to each. I see the whole cast drawn up in three files to say and illustrate the three columns. The company should look like an old document which suddenly bristles with stones that hurt as they come zinging through the air.

STONES Peace within the Township of Biddulph

STICKS	STONES	OTHERS
Name of Prosecutor	Name of Defendant	Nature of Charge
George Campbell	Thomas Cain	throwing stones at the premises
William Hogan	James Nugent	evading toll, stealing hoops

Illustrate the crimes with noise and mime and props.

The Queen	Thomas Cassleigh	Murdering an Englishman

as indicated above, but with new variation which the others should carry

STICKS	OTHERS	STONES	OTHERS
Thomas Hogshaw	accuses	William Harleton	of milking a cow —furtively
Dennis Devlin	accuses	Paul Quinlan	of assault & battery

Name of Prosecutor	Name of Defendant	Nature of Charge
Gerald Quinn	Timothy Egan	Tearing down his house

Now the Sticks (*Protestant Line*) *face the* Stones (*Roman Line*) *and whistle "Lilliburlero" at them. The Roman Liners reply with their theme.*

STICKS The Biddulph Riot OTHERS which took place

STONES at Andrew Keefe's tavern

KEEFE *in apron with tray of bottles* A friend of the Donnellys, my name is Andy Keefe and I own the tavern at the first tollgate into Biddulph just across from St Patrick's church. On Christmas Eve, 1857, just after the election in which Mr Holmes defeated Mr Cayley, the Blackmouth Proddies paid me a visit.

STICKS	STONES
ten or twelve sleighs	one hundred persons
Hurrah for the Tips	Hurrah for the Grits
Hurrah for the Tories	Hurrah for Holmes

This choral account of a riot should be counterpointed to a riot mime perhaps in slow motion where the Protestants drive the Catholics off stage with their clubs. But the Catholics secretly return to the stone pile, and throw all the stones offstage at pursuing Protestants. Women take off their black woollen stockings, put a stone in and wave them around their heads. Use sounds from saws on wood, rended wood, sounds of broken glass.

NEGRO WOMAN *with lantern directly in front of us* On the night of December 24th I was at the barn feeding my cattle about six or seven o'clock after night. Heard some sleighs coming up from

A STICKSMAN Strike him strike him

NEGRO WOMAN Bar room door lying on the ground and some men pounding him. I went to the house thinking my children might be frightened, I was all alone, afraid they might molest me.

KEEFE Shame, shame. Have mercy boys.

A STICKSMAN There's a man killed. One of us.

A STICKSMAN Give us a light to find Ryan and Keefe, the bloody Papists.

NEGRO WOMEN *now at ladder behind Donnelly house* Went upstairs in my house, drew out the board in the Gavel end of the house and looked out and saw the moon rising.

KEEFE Did then and there break and destroy all the windows in the lower part of my house

WOMEN Sticks stones and axes. *Repeat under until indicated.*

KEEFE Household furniture, breaking, tearing, burning it, cut down the signpost, cut the spokes of the wagons, cut down the water pump, threw sticks, stones, and the water pail into the house. *Throw a pail of water on the stage floor at this point. Some kneel down to scoop up the liquor.* Broke the taps off my liquor casks, suffered the liquor

A STICKSMAN Don't burn this, his house, he's a good fellow.

STONESMAN Run away.

KEEFE Alex Fraser, John Bell, Peter Cody, my mother, my mother, my two barkeepers, Tim Casey and Bill Ryan.

WOMAN Sticks stones and axes. *end of repeat*

STICKSMEN Hurrah for Holmes—let's go back and kill them all.

KEEFE Hurrah for the Grits! Rushed upstairs to hide for our lives

STICKS Hurrah for Holmes, ye bloody Papists

STONES Hurrah for Cayley

Stones *throw stones at* Sticks—*stones are left covering the stage. This sequence ends with all crawling back on stage groaning and lying down. A man rolls a wheel across the stage. This will soon reappear. Now a sweet-voiced priest drones on about diocesan history. A shuffling friar with staff will eventually meet Tom Cassleigh and his wagon wheel.*

PRIEST The diocese in which the wretched Donnelly family lived had a troubled inception. The first bishop moved the see from London which was but 18 miles away, to a border town some 150 miles away at least. The first bishop built himself a barge in which he planned to visit the hinterland of his diocese, but as it was being launched it sank. Four Dominican friars from Kentucky he left behind to take care of the spiritual affairs of his people in Middlesex and Huron Counties. These friars would tramp the countryside sometimes meeting an old farmer whom they would confess through one of the wheels of his hay wagon.

Cassleigh reaches through the spokes of his wagon wheel to-

wards the wandering friar who comes over to him: this man is young, very sure of himself and violent. His scene with the friar contains both truth and mockery in a mixture for which we can't find a recipe.

CASSLEIGH Bless me, Father, for I have sinned.

FRIAR When did you last confess, my son?

CASSLEIGH Back in the old country, Father.

FRIAR How far away in time would that be now?

CASSLEIGH *pause* I want to confess the sin of murder, Father.

FRIAR Oh, my son, that is a mortal sin.

CASSLEIGH It was, Father, indeed it was mortal to him. But, Father, I didn't kill the man.

FRIAR Oh? Then how are you guilty of the crime?

CASSLEIGH A friend of mine did the deed—for me. It was the Englishman who was killed on our road last February, sure you must have heard about it, caused quite a stir, but I didn't kill him, oh no.

FRIAR Why did you hate the Englishman so much?

With the men of the cast, re-enact the story. Cassleigh goes over and tumbles on the ground with George Armstrong. Use a ladder as a sort of memory curtain. Follow the lead of what action the speeches suggest, but cut to the bone. Candles for the lights in farm houses, paper for snow.

BRIMMACOMBE *directly to us* What have I done to you, man?

CASSLEIGH At your barnraising north of our settlement where you Cornishes live in Usborne Township, Mr Brimmacombe

VOICE He attacked me and was taken away. There was a fight between George Armstrong and Thomas Cassleigh. Brimmacombe and two others of us parted them. Brimmacombe told his hired man to hold Cassleigh down until he'd promise to be quiet. When Cassleigh got up he took off his coat and struck the hired man, saying to Brimmacombe—

CASSLEIGH And you will be marked yet some time between this and the London road.

BRIMMACOMBE Me, man, what have I done to you?

FRIAR What is the fifth commandment of God?

CASSLEIGH The fifth commandment of God is: Thou, Brimmacombe—should not have seen me beaten so badly. *The Roman*

Line forms for Cassleigh to skulk up and down, hiding behind people as if they were houses, shanties, trees and barns. Where are they now? Brimmacombe and his man. I seen them go down the road in the morning. When are they coming back? Perhaps they'll get a knock somewhere when they were not looking for it. *Try a Roman Line formation that goes across the stage rather than up and down it.*

MRS DONNELLY The whole settlement knew several weeks beforehand that if Brimmacombe came back up the Roman Line he would never reach home alive. *There is a flurry of snowflakes, the Roman Line has candles for its thin row of lamps and candles in the winter twilight. We focus on Andrew Keefe and Brimmacombe, perhaps at the end of the name sequence for the Roman Line which can go on softly under*

ALL The sixth of February, 1857.

KEEFE Take my advice, Mr Brimmacombe, cut the bells off your sleigh now that your hired man has gone ahead and you're all alone, not wise, Mr Brimmacombe, not wise. How the devil did your sleigh upset so – och, it's that big snow drift that comes between the church and my tavern – and you've got two cows as companions – take the other road home.

BRIMMACOMBE Andy Keefe, how can I do that. I've sent my hired man ahead of me. He's to meet me at Donnelly's schoolhouse. How can I tell the roads apart in the twilight and the snow? They're just two lines of sparks where the settlers have lit their lamps and candles. Ah – this is the other road that's safe for a Protestant to drive his cattle up.

ALL The snow was on the ground.

The theatre gets very dark; we see two ladders with their shadows.

BRIMMACOMBE What road am I on then?

STICKS *softly* Donovan STONES Clancy

BRIMMACOMBE Not Courcy and Blackwell?

STICKS Gallagher STONES Duffy

BRIMMACOMBE Not Armwright Latchett?

ALL Quinn Marksey

BRIMMACOMBE Then I'm not on the Protestant Road?

MARKSEY Brimmacombe, we told you you'd be marked between your house and the London road and I mark you here. *Silhou-*

ette ladder clubbing and whistle under the Roman Line reel.

WOMAN

whick whack sticks and clubs
crick crack stones they threw
sticks and stones stones and sticks *Whisper this under.*
Lanterns come from all sorts of places in the theatre.

MAN ONE He had a small bit uv a stick in his hand.

MAN TWO Coming home about 8 or 9 o'clock at night I saw his whip and cap beside him where he lay on the road. My wife was with me and sez she

WOMAN Och Paddy, is this a log or a man in the shnow?

MAN TWO An sez she

WOMAN I think he's an Englishman name of Brummygum.

MAN ONE I didn't hear any one say it was Brummygum. Dannelly that's now in the Pinitinshery—was the first man that towld me. *The lanterns converge over the dead body.*

WOMAN It was then just sunset and growing dark—

CHILD A man was dead on the road—

MAN TWO Saw the body lying up the road oh! He must have been killed.

Shadows of people, confessional wheel, then a slow retreat and disappearance of lanterns until we are left with the friar and his penitent in the summer afternoon light.

ALL It's a dangerous thing to find a dead body.

WOMAN Sell your land, Joe.

MAN ONE People moved away if they could.

MRS DONNELLY The Cassleighs and the Markseys were near and dreaded neighbours.

MAN TWO Tom Cassleigh and his great friend, Will Marksey, shortly after this bought up some of the deserted farms.

FRIAR Are you sorry then that you took his life?

CASSLEIGH *pause* I didn't take it, Father.

FRIAR You and your friend must give yourselves up to the magistrates.

CASSLEIGH I'm sworn to my friend, Father.

FRIAR Why is it two years since the deed was done and still they have not caught you? Or was it that you were taken but each time you terrified the constables into letting you go?

CASSLEIGH Why, Father, they've been and tried me for it, but I've got a friend who stole the witness papers from the courthouse and I believe they can't try me again till they get them all sworn and copied out again.

FRIAR What friends are these?

CASSLEIGH Friends of my ribbon, Father.

MAN ONE Did not say I heard Marksey say he had given Brimmacombe a tap.

FRIAR Did not those who saw your friend strike the blow bear witness?

CASSLEIGH They saw him. They saw him seeing them seeing him and they saw me seeing him seeing them seeing them seeing him. Can we help it if they have a mortal fear of us?

FRIAR You are not sorry for what you have done then?

CASSLEIGH Am I not then? I didn't do it. I can't tell on my friend. And he may have hit the Englishman a bit uva tap, but he didn't hate the man.

FRIAR And I cannot absolve you of your mortal sin. But may God soon move you to true repentance for your sins—that you may receive His sacred absolution. In nomine Patris et Filii et Spiritus Sancti.

We watch Cassleigh weaving back and forth behind the wheel as the friar walks up the Roman Line.

GAOLER	CASSLEIGH
Name?	Tom Cassleigh
Number?	551
Age?	27
Height?	5 feet, 8½ inches
Colour of eyes?	Grey
Crime?	Suspicion of murder

As the friar walks up the Roman Line they kneel to him and so reveal the census taker and the Donnellys.

CENSUS TAKER	DONNELLY
How many natives of Canada?	five, five boys
How many acres?	one hundred
In cultivation?	30 in crop, 70 acres of wild land

Wheat?	28 acres, yielded 15 bushels per acre
Potatoes?	2 acres—30 bushels

CENSUS TAKER Good day to you, Jim Donnelly.

MR DONNELLY Good day to you, Mr Hodgins. *A very tinny bell rings the Angelus.*

FRIAR Angelus Domini nuntiavit Mariae

POPULUS Et concepit de Spiritu Sancto. Ave Maria

FRIAR Ecce ancilla Domini

POPULUS Fiat mihi secundum verbum tuum. Ave Maria

FRIAR And the word was made flesh

POPULUS And dwelt among us. Hail Mary.

FRIAR Ora pro nobis, sancta Dei Genitrix

POPULUS That we may be made worthy of the promises of Christ. Gratium tuam

This prayer goes under the scene with the friar: use Latin and English mixed, and swell up when there are chances.

Angelus Domini nuntiavit Mariae Et concepit de Spiritu Sancto Ave Maria...	The Angel of the Lord declared unto Mary And she conceived of the Holy Ghost. Hail Mary...
Ecce ancilla Domini. (Fiat mihi secundum verbum tuum)	Behold the handmaid of the Lord. (Be it done unto me according to Thy word.)
Ave Maria...	Hail Mary...
Et Verbum caro factum est. (Et habitavit in nobis.)	And the Word was made flesh. (And dwelt among us.)
Ave Maria...	Hail Mary...
Ora pro nobis, sancta Dei Genitrix (Ut digni efficiamur promissionibus Christi.)	Pray for us, O Holy Mother of God. (That we may be made worthy of the promises of Christ.)
Oremus:—Gratiam tuam quaesumus Domine, mentibus nostris infunde; ut qui angelo nuntiante, Christi Filii tui incarnationem cognovimus,	Let us pray: Pour forth, we beseech Thee, O Lord, Thy grace into our hearts, that we, to whom the Incarnation of Christ Thy Son was made

per passionem ejus et crucem ad resurrectionis gloriam perducamur.	known by the message of an Angel, may, by His passion and cross, be brought to the glory of His Resurrection.
Per eumdem Christum Dominum nostrum	Through the same Christ Our Lord.
Amen	Amen

FRIAR A letter for you, Mr Donnelly, from Ireland. And one for you, Mrs Donnelly. *They thank him under the continuation of the Angelus prayer.* Do you ever wish sometimes to be where this letter came from, Mrs Donnelly? *They shake their heads and murmur* "No, Father" *under the prayer.* May I purloin one of your five sons for a moment, Mrs Donnelly? William, I have something for you as well as for your parents. William Donnelly, the bishop will visit this mission on the Saturday after St John's Day. Will you be ready for his questions and his presence, do you think? I have with me your confirmation ticket.

They have come down the Roman Line and out into the downstage area where there are trees (ladders) for Will to climb up, swing from as the friar tries to tempt him into the priesthood.

WILL There is a question, Father, I want to ask the bishop.

FRIAR And what is that question, my son?

WILL People call me Cripple, Father. What I want to know is: why was I created lame? I'm going to ask him that.

FRIAR I wonder, Will, if I might try to answer for him. That's a good question, Will, but first let me ask you a question. What is it you want most to give to yourself?

WILL I used to want to give myself a horse—and a sword, Father. For when I'm riding I'm not a cripple then. I used to want to give myself a fiddle. Then I received one for my birthday. Now I want to play my fiddle so well that people will ask me to play at their weddings because when I play or when I dance why then you see, Father, I'm not crippled then.

FRIAR Are you crippled then when you're praying?

WILL *pause* No, Father.

FRIAR What the bishop may say to you is that your lameness is God's marking you for His own. Your condition is a badge of His favour.

WILL Father, if you had been lame could you have confessed as many souls as you have this week?

FRIAR No, my son. No. Will, here is the piece of paper you will need to be able to receive the holy sacrament of confirmation.

WILL Thank you, Father.

FRIAR Will, would you know then how to address the bishop with the proper form of his title if you should decide to ask him this question of yours. *After a pause, Will shakes his head.*

ALL Per eumdem Christum Dominum nostrum. Amen. *The prayer under ends. The missals rustle shut and then the angelus mood is broken by one of the ladders crashing to the floor.*

axes and wood-chopping sounds

CORONER In the year 1847 eight men were accidentally killed, two men were murdered by falling trees.

MR DONNELLY Yes, it got so you didn't have to use knife or club, why a tree would do it for you. There was one farm I was chopping on in the winter of 1855 where an accident happened *all the ladders are lowered by ropes in slow motion on top of Mr Donnelly* to me. I wasn't hurt. I just sat there in the snow thinking for a while as they chopped through the branches to get at me. There's two men here I don't know well at all at all, and they done that. There were two families came to our line that fall, just fresh out from the old country—one of them had a wife who was as broad as she was long, the other was a man who was helping the fat woman's husband get my farm away from me and his name was—Farl.

WILL & JENNIE Why is our father's farm so narrow?

DONNELLY KIDS (STONES) *advancing across the stage picking up stones: the stage is the front field of the Donnelly farm* Picking up stones in our father's front field. Where do we put them, Pa?

MR DONNELLY At the line fence over there and the line fence over there. *Points and illustrates with the extreme edges of the playing area. They toss the smaller stones into these two lines. Use quite big stones for some of the boys to lug. Underline with whistled reel. Now enters the Fat Woman; we never really catch her name, but she is the arch enemy of the Donnellys; her husband is also fairly fat and they have a certain on the ground quality which materializes everything, while with the Donnellys there is just the opposite feeling. She enters carrying a small laundry stove which she crashes down.*

FAT WOMAN Husband. *pause* If you're the boss, prove it. Prove it by putting on your mitts, go out and get me some wood.

MR FAT I asked my old woman where'd I get the kind of wood she wanted.

FAT WOMAN I need some more than dry wood for my little darling of a laundry stove here. Did you really buy that hundred acres Donnelly is squatting on, or who's the boss?

FARL *springs up from nowhere* Shure Mike. You're the boss. We'll get some of the best dried kindling for your old woman she ever seen. Come on. *Out they go.*

FAT WOMAN Now there goes the boss. At last. There goes the boss.

WILL & JENNIE Why is our father's farm so narrow?

JENNIE I remember the census taker came up the road again.

KIDS (STONES) Ten years we picked up the stones.

The two lines of people move towards each other.

STICKS Widening and clearing

STONES Our father and his neighbours slashed and burned, chopping

STICKS 1846 forty-seven forty-eight forty-nine fifty

STONES plowing harrowing sowing harvesting *scythe sounds*

ALL 1851 fifty-two fifty-three fifty-four fifty-five

WILL My mother gave me a violin for my birthday and the landlord's lease was now paid up. Now he would transfer the ownership of the land to us.

GAOLER Colour of prisoner's eyes?

MR DONNELLY Grey.

GAOLER How many years have you lived in Canada?

MR DONNELLY Sixteen years.

CENSUS TAKER How many acres of wild land?

MR DONNELLY Only thirty. All the rest is cleared.

CENSUS TAKER How many children altogether then?

MR DONNELLY Seven. Seven boys.

CENSUS TAKER How many bushels of wheat did you harvest last year?

pause

MR DONNELLY Mr Darcy, why did you not fill in the number when I said my farm was a hundred acres with thirty acres in wild-land?

CENSUS TAKER Ah, Mr Donnelly, if you could read and write you might see where.

MR DONNELLY I know I can't write my name, Mr Darcy, but I know what it looks like and I know what 100 acres looks like. Where did you put that down?

CENSUS TAKER Mr Donnelly, your landlord has been talking to a fellow.

MR DONNELLY What fellow? No one's to buy it but Donnelly. Who then?

CENSUS TAKER That I don't know.

MR DONNELLY By our ancient agreement, I made Mr Grace, our landlord, an offer last week.

CENSUS TAKER Not high enough. This other bid's higher.

MR DONNELLY Am I to get any of my fields at all then?

CENSUS TAKER It's all rumours and whispers as yet, Mr Donnelly. The north half where you live is the most valuable half because of your barns and your cabin. How many bushels of wheat did you

MR DONNELLY *directly to audience, as the Roman Line routine forms* We never cut the tongues out of horses. Never. We loved horses. But the lying tongues of men. Yes. Cut them out. Men, yes. Horses, no. Where are my spectacles so I can see this medicine showman that's coming by tonight *furious search for spectacles* telling the story of how I—who is it who's going to take my farm away from me?

WOMEN

Then the farmer came with a big plough;
He plowed me under the ground.

MR DONNELLY Is it—

Repeat the following names under and over the next four speeches.

CHORUS

Barry	Trehy
Feeney	O'Halloran
Cahill	Cassleigh
McCann	Flynn
Donnelly	Malowney

Egan	Farl *pause*
Quinn	Marksey *pause*
Gallagher	Duffy
Clancy	Donovan *keeping repeating this under and over*

At the top of the Roman Line a ladder is held. Mrs Donnelly climbs up and over this, then comes right down the Roman Line towards us.

WILL Our mother then said she would walk down the roads to the town.

MRS DONNELLY James, I'm walking down to the town to see this landlord of ours. I'll take our fifty pounds and the ring on my finger and my last gold earring and I'll curse him at the pawnshop, him that's forcing me to haggle a pawnbroker and I'll—

WILL She walked all the way to Andy Keefe's tavern, then past Kelly's tollgate, then past Ryan's Tavern at Elginfield, then past all the taverns and tollgates on the Proof Line Road, down, down, down to our landlord's place in the town.

MR DONNELLY Which of you robbers is buying my farm out from under me? Is it you turning me into a squatter—Farl? *He repeats the names and strides up and down the Roman Line of actors. They hum, whistle and sing snatches of the second verse, say their names in turn, turn their backs on him, swing around with him caught in the formation. The bell and jug sound recurs whenever he comes to the south end of the street.*

Bell is rung; tavern mouth plunking noise

end of choral repetition

CHORUS *under* At dark in the night at dark in the night &c.

MR DONNELLY

Is it Cahill Is it Cassleigh
McCann Flynn &c.
Because I loved my land so and stuck to it
I killed and in turn you broke my bones, burnt my home
Harvested me and my sons like sheaves and stood
Us to die upon our ground
Where now nothing will ever grow.

As the line comes around he emerges as if shot out of its gamut and stands in front of us with a handful of dust.

And this earth in my hand, the earth of my farm
That I fought for and was smashed and burnt for

CHORUS *kneeling* Confiteor Deo omnipotenti ... beato Michaeli Archangelo. Aufer a nobis quaesumus, Domine, iniquitates nostras. *repeat under*

MR DONNELLY *but kneeling on only one knee*

Now my body belongs to its dust
Which dust once belonged to me.
As it is blown away, I forget
Concession Six Lot Eighteen
South Half or North Half which was mine?
We are blown away and both lost *prayer stops*
– – – – – – – – – – – – – – –Like actors' words.

The Chorus raggedly rise, confusedly murmur as he melts into their ranks; we begin to hear the sawing sound Grace makes on his sawhorse.

VOICE It's the Medicine Show for Heaven's sakes. He's stopping his wagons at the crossroads. Hey *As the crowd goes offstage after the attraction Mr Donnelly emerges on stage left with a harrow made out of tree branch, to which stones have been tied. He is harrowing the big front field of his farm before division; prominent should be his house just to the left of back centre. Chairs should be ready for the fence sequence and the actors who did the Fat Woman with stove sequence should stand poised to do this all over again—just offstage—so that it glides smoothly into the chaining of the Donnelly house sequence. Built of ladders, this house stands in front of the map of Biddulph. The children are picking up stones as before.*

JENNIE & WILL Why is our father's farm so narrow?

WILL Once it was eighty rods wide as from me to you

JENNIE Until there was a man took 40 rods of it away.

WILL My father was harrowing his wide front field *Mr Donnelly can go through a whole sowing, cultivating and harvesting mime here.*

JENNIE When somebody started to build a fence. *Farl and Mr Fat place six chairs down the centre of the stage. A game develops in which Farl puts up the chairs. Donnelly takes them down again, or charges right through the fence with his harrow, etc.*

MR DONNELLY There's a queer fellow

WILL My father said at this new fence.

MR DONNELLY He keeps planting these sticks down the centre of my spring sowing. Will, will you hand me that axe. This one's a bit stiff.

JENNIE And he said to them that were building the fence

MR DONNELLY An axe is as good as a spade any day, whoever you are. *The fence game boils down to just the two of them, Farl and Donnelly, furiously putting up and upsetting chairs to stick, stone, reel sounds. There should be a menace scene here where all the* Stones *push all the* Sticks *back!*

WILL Until a piece of paper came to our house

CHORUS House! Shanty. Sticks. Sticks and stones which whack click thwonk, Sticks *cross to chair fence centre.*

CHORUS Against James Donnelly. To recover possession of the

BOYS Picking up stones in our father's front field
Where do we put them, pa?

MR DONNELLY At the line fence over there. *Boys drive chair fence, held by sticks, back.*

WILL Half the field is lost to you, father, says the bailiff's paper. South Half of Lot Eighteen Concession Six. A suit of summons in ejectment for

MR DONNELLY No boys. No. Not over there. This is the new line. *He points to the centre of the stage.* Put the stones here. *The line of chairs presses in his family to centre where they put down stones; chairs retreat. Mr Donnelly reaches over it to pluck crop planted on the other side.* They've got half of my farm. *From now on, a line of stones cuts the Donnelly farm and the playing area in half.*

JOHN What happens to the wheat we sowed over there, pa?

MR DONNELLY That wheat is lost. And my scythe never touched it.

While they are dreaming, over the field a huge chain is hooked by Mr Fat to the foundations of the Donnelly house and attached to an imaginary team of oxen offstage.

It was harvested by a piece of paper. I've known men burn their crop rather than have a stranger harvest it. *turns around.* Get that hook out of the rib of my house. *Another hook is attached to the opposite side of the house.*

MR FAT Gee up, Bright. *Use cowbells. We see the chain tighten. As Fat pricks the offfstage oxen with his goad the chain responds.* It's my property now, Donnelly. My wife wants some kindling wood and since you'll be moving somewhere else you won't want this old shanty and these old lean-tos anymore. By Holy Jesus, I'll put this shanty down on top of you if you don't get out of it. *A baby cries.* Gee up, Buck. Gee up, Bright! Haw!

MR DONNELLY Will, go over to Mike Feeney's and tell him there's two-legged visitors I want to get rid of.

STICKS He hawed his oxen round.

MR FAT If you can call it a shanty.

KIDS (STONES) It's not a shanty it's a house.

FARL It's a squatter's hut, you whelps.

STICKS He hitched to both corners of the house

KIDS (STONES) but he could not

STICKS pull it down.

MR FAT I'll bring it to two yoke and pull it to Hell's blazes.

Mr Donnelly succeeds in unlinking one of the chains.

MR DONNELLY Up Bright!

Caught in his chain Mr Fat gets dragged offstage, but runs back and hooks up again. A contest develops where Donnelly unhooks one chain and Farl hooks up the other that Donnelly has just unhooked.

MR DONNELLY Tell me, Mr Farl, just why do you hook up that chain for him?

FARL I didn't hook it up then, Jim. I'm not that fast on my feet.

MR DONNELLY Now you were and there you did it again. What's eating you? What have I done to you that you want to pull down my house?

FARL Not a bloody thing, Jim, only that you're a blackleg back in the old country.

MR DONNELLY What did you call me?

FARL Sure, don't you know what I called you?

MR DONNELLY By your heart cease calling me Blackfoot. You've been calling me and my children that ever since you arrived here two years ago. *The chain unhooking game goes on at a faster pace.*

FARL Didn't call you Blackfoot, called you blackleg, but I'll call you Blackfoot if you like.

MR DONNELLY Don't call me that in front of the others and start all that over again.

FARL But how will they know in this settlement you've come to who the real blackfeet are. Mike, there's other ways than pulling it down, Jim here's so nimble on his feet, take the old axe to it.

KIDS (STONES) Your axe isn't half sharp enough, mister.

MR DONNELLY Raise that axe on my house, you tub

FARL Now who's calling the names.

MR FAT This is my property and I'll use it as I like.

MR DONNELLY Get out of here!

MR FAT What would you say, Donnelly, if I had thirty men here in five minutes with twenty yoke of oxen. *stamping his foot*

MR DONNELLY *stamping his foot* By judas you do and you can't. *Farl mouths something in Donnelly's ear.* Stop calling me that, stop saying that.

FARL Why what'll you do to me, Jim, you old Blackfoot.

MR DONNELLY Stop hooking up that chain. *Will approaches with the gun; Mrs Donnelly approaches with a piece of paper in her hand. The sight of the gun changes the positions and attitudes of the attackers.*

MR FAT *unhooking* I'll be here tomorrow morning. I'll have that shanty—Gee up, Buck. Gee up, Bright. I'll

Donnelly with Mrs Donnelly just beside him, but he doesn't see her.

MRS DONNELLY Mr Donnelly, what I have in my hand is the deed for the north half. For the fifty acres we're standing on and our house is standing on.

Farl mouths something at Donnelly just as he is leaving. Donnelly rushes after Farl and shoots at him.

FARL *howling* Oh, you've done it to me now. Murder. My arm's got a bullet in it. Mike—did you see what he done to me, we'll have to look into the law of this, Jim.

MR DONNELLY *grasping the rungs of a ladder* So what's next. Have I killed him yet?

MRS DONNELLY Mr Donnelly, there's a proverb that sticks and stones may hurt my bones, but words will never harm them.

MR DONNELLY Not true, Mrs Donnelly. Not true at all. If only he'd hit us with a stone or a stick, but ever since that day you told me they'd been calling our son that in the churchyard it's as if a thousand little tinkly pebbles keep batting up against the windows in my mind just when it's a house that's about to sleep. I didn't kill him, this time. It's his tree that came down on me in the woods that time, Judy, he's been after me for some time, next time it's

VOICE There was a man shot in Biddulph

CHORUS

Name of Prosecutor	Name of Defendant	Nature of Charge
Patrick Farl	James Donnelly	Shooting with intent

Mr and Mrs Donnelly stand with their backs to us. Fat Lady comes on with stove.

MRS FAT Well what happened to you? Where's the wood?

MR FAT Here's your wood.

MRS FAT Well you're the boss but I recognize that wood. You were leading me to expect I'd have the Donnelly shanty for kindling. This is from our own woodpile.

MR FAT It is. Missus, do you know—we'll never get them off that place.

MRS FAT Are you trying to tell me you'll let them beat you out of one hundred acres of good—

MR FAT Missus, I've got them off half of it, what more do you want? And poor Farl's got a bullet in his arm. *howl from Farl*

MRS FAT My brother shot in the arm, is he? This won't end yet, mister, you mark me. That family has got to be got rid of. Unless we do something now that family is going to— *quietly turning to us* What happened after he took a shot at poor Pat would never have happened if my man had been the boss and put their shanty in my darling little laundry stove that cold wintry day. *She grabs the stove.*

From the back of the auditorium comes a travelling medicine show, the Shamrock Concert Company, which puts on a viciously biased melodrama called the Black Donnellys, also the title of the book everyone reads about the Donnellys. The Showman is a loud, slick Canadian Irishman with torches & a series of lurid canvas pictures which are attached to a map hanger. He shows some of these as a come-on. His stage wagon can be pushed on from the wings: on it his performers play a small scene. With their backs turned to us for most of this, the Donnellys with great dignity reject this lurid view of themselves. At last, Mr Donnelly will turn on the Showman to correct one of his errors and we must get a chance to compare the "false" Donnelly with the "real" Donnelly.

SHOWMAN Yes, if that poor woman who had to live her life on the fifty acres cheek by jowl to the Donnellys had just succeeded in jamming their filth-ridden shanty into her darling little cook stove the family would have left the neighbourhood and the boys wouldn't have grown up and we wouldn't be singing today!

So hurry to your home, good folks.
Lock doors and windows tight
And pray for dawn, the Black Donnellys
Will be abroad tonight.

In just a little under half an hour, folks, my artists of the Shamrock Concert Company will present you with the Black Donnellys. Tickets are half price to everyone of you who purchases a full tin of my East India Tiger Fat.

By thefts they showed their father's blood
By fights and drunken sprees
Till the countryside, living in dread,
Called them the Black Donnellys.

Buy a bottle of Banyan Tree of Life pills and the price of admission is free. Before my players give you a preview of this evening's drama, let me show you a few scenes which I have had painted on canvas for your historical information.

The canvas presentations are really a big wallpaper sample book, with nothing drawn on its pages.

Here ladies and gents, you see the unsuspecting Donnelly family, notorious as the terrors of the township ever since the father and mother arrived in 1847—here in this canvas you see this family about to go to bed the night of February 3, 1880.

Donnelly was clubbed to death, as was his wife,
Tom & Bridget murdered too.
Then the old house was set on fire
And to the skies its wild flames flew.

CHORUS Five Persons Murdered by a Mob
An Entire Household Sacrificed
Result of a Family Feud
Forty men engaged in the bloody work

SHOWMAN Ladies and gents just one small scene from tonight's attraction The Black Donnellys. A little scene with John Donnelly! His father! His mother! *The False Donnelly actors should be the Grand Guignol persons of folklore—wild cats on hot stoves.*

FALSE JOHN So they say we derailed the train, hunh? What else are they saying we done, eh mither? Eh, fither?

FALSE MR & MRS DONNELLY *alternately* Burning two barns, cutting the tongues out of twenty horses and putting four hundred iron pins in Gallagher's wheat sheaves so's the threshing machine would catch fire.

FALSE JOHN *with a fistful of weapons* Tom, get up! We'll show those blank blank so and so's they can't pin anything on us.

FALSE MR DONNELLY John, what are you going to do, avourneen?

FALSE MRS DONNELLY Shure there's been enough misery and tribulation now, do you want to bring my gray hairs with sorrow to the grave? *sudden manic change in her character* But there's one thing, son, I never hear them saying you done.

FALSE JOHN What's that, mither?

FALSE MRS DONNELLY Killing a man.

FALSE JOHN Couldn't do that, mither.

FALSE MRS DONNELLY Then you're no son of mine. Until you've killed your man the way your darling father did, you're no son of mine.

The actors stop, fall out of character, move off with the stage wagon.

SHOWMAN Tickets are half price to everyone of you who purchases a full tin of my East India Tiger Fat. Come to the Market Square and see

CHORUS

Donnelly squatted on John Farrell's land
Just laughed when ordered to pay
Then with iron bar struck Farrell dead
At a loggin'

MR DONNELLY Show me the scene where I kill Farl; the living must obey the dead. Look, Mr Showman Murphy, you've printed up my blood—was I like him or she like her or my sons like—them? One thing to start with—I didn't murder him. Kill not slay, killed him with a—you ignoramus—not with an iron bar, but with a wooden handspike. *The actors begin to set up the barrels and sticks for the fight scene and Mr Donnelly picks up one of the handspikes.* Like this one. And it happened like this at William Mulowney's but you go ahead first, Showman. Show me.

SHOWMAN Ladies and gents. By special request we also show you: Donnelly's Fight with Farrell at the Logging Bee 29th of June, 1857

MR DONNELLY 25th day of June 1857

SHOWMAN 25th day of June, 1857— *merrily* Donnelly Kills Farrell in a fight at the Loggin' Bee

GROG BOSS

I am a farmer grizzled & gray
Was the grog boss at the bee that day
Step up, boys, for a swig or a sip
The better your handspike neath the big logs to slip.

The Roman Line formation queues up for a drink, then begins to handspike barrels towards the stage centre.

Farl, that's ten times you've drunk
For more work you've got very little spunk
I said corking the bottle and daring his frown
Sure one more drink and he'd roll on the ground.

FARL Am I to have none and Donnelly's to have one?

FALSE MR DONNELLY Faith, Farl, I'll beat you, have yours and mine too. *takes two swigs*

FARL Like you shot me before, and you'll do it again. Your handspike, my handspike—settle you then.

A circle of men closes around the fighters so we can't see beyond the occasional raised stick. A man with whip, on a barrel rolled by another man. "Gee up there! Hey, what's up?" "Farl and Donnelly boxing." *They join the circle of watchers.*

CHORUS *drifting away from fight and back to work* Arhh, they're too drunk to hurt each other much. Both tipsy. Arr, Donnelly's letting on to be a bit high.

INQUEST VOICE Did not see Farrell take up a handspike at all, thinks it Donnelly's intention to pick a quarrel with someone when he came to the bee more than to help to do anything.

CHORUS Leave them be! Hey! They're biting each other. Separate them. Get that handspike away from Farl. *Another handspike rolls behind Donnelly.*

INQUEST VOICE A certain wooden handspike the value of one penny.

FALSE MR DONNELLY Farl—will you say you're beat?

FARL *up and down struggling with man who is wrestling stick away from him* I've had enough and will fight no more. Don't you touch me again. *to wrestling man* Yes, you! *Donnelly trips over a handspike, comes up with it in both hands, winds it over his head and throws it.*

FALSE MR DONNELLY Farl, take this to Hell with you. *Vain at-*

tempts to interpose; Farl is hit, and rolls over.

MAN ONE Donnelly you've murdered the man.

FALSE MR DONNELLY The first one who lays a hand on me gets the same medicine.

MAN TWO AND ONE The man's murdered, Donnelly, you've murdered the man. Saw him wind it over his head. I heard the blow quite plain.

MAN THREE Don't be a fool, Donnelly. You're going with us to the constable.

MAN ONE Throw down that bar or we'll take it away from you.

FALSE MR DONNELLY The first one that tries won't live to tell about it. And when you come for me you'd better come shooting.

Everyone is cowed by this, including audience. Reel music and barrels rolling as transition.

MR DONNELLY Let's have that again. When I came to the logging bee at Mulowney's there were four piles of logs in his five acre field. *four barrels with one man, back turned, at each barrel*

MULOWNEY Jim, I asked you to come to my logging bee and come you have at last, my boy. *He directs men to the piles waiting each with its boss.* Lanigan, who've you got for your boss?

MAN ONE *turning around* He's with me. Carroll.

MULOWNEY Pat Ryan—over there, who's—

MAN TWO *turns around* Dennis Darcy.

MULOWNEY Mike Feeny—over there. You're with—

MAN THREE *turns around* Marty Mackey.

MULOWNEY Jim, now you're needed one man to fill in at that pile and your boss is

FARL *at fourth barrel* Pat Farl, I'm the boss of this team. Mulowney, no! I'll not work with a Blackfoot the likes of him. Where's the grogboss? *With a bottle each, the two men have a drink-at-one-swig contest which Farl loses.*

MR DONNELLY I said I was no worse than the worst of the Farls, and I was good enough for the best of them shoved up in a pile on my plate and I could drink him horizontal at any logging bee, any day. *drinks*

FARL *onlookers laughing* Why Jim, you piss it all away that's why, the rats come out at night and lick it off—the darling pair of black *pause* boots you're wearing to the logging bees these days.

MR DONNELLY I said. Now that's wrong what you're saying

FARL *lightly slapping him* But what have I said, Jim?

The two men fight close to us; farther away the Chorus forms a circle as if it surrounded Farl and Donnelly. This circle shifts as the fight shifts.

CHORUS Bite him, Jim.

MR DONNELLY He kept saying the name at me.

FARL Blackfoot, Blackfoot.

CHORUS He's down, he's up. Here back there, get this over with so we can—Mike, give him a chew uv tobacco. He needs a swig, look at him. At it again. Thwonk! Well struck, Pat Farl. He's down for the clinch and now he's up and—stop them biting. Look at them! Try to stop that if you can.

MR DONNELLY *placing a handspike at centre downstage* He was on my

CHORUS Blackfoot, Jim. Ah, that rouses him! Blackfoot *and on, under*

MR DONNELLY back like this shouting in my ear. We'd been grappling for over an hour and the sun was very hot and there was no lack of whiskey or anything we wanted so long as we kept on fighting. *illustrates* He was on my shoulders with words in my ears and blows—I rolled over and got in a few, then we rolled over again. *laughter* I picked this up and half stood with it in both my hands, he still on my back. *With the handspike he makes a furious upward motion from between his knees to just behind his head. The burden drops off him, he stands straighter and still, then takes off his shirt. Bright sunlight. The circle of men dissolves with*

CHORUS You're dead, Farl. Donnelly, you've murdered the man.

Slowly they and Farl form the Roman Line. Mrs Donnelly, in apron, stands at upstage end of it. Donnelly plods up to her, kneels at her feet after catching up some dirt in his hand. As she speaks all the players kneel.

MRS DONNELLY James, what have you there in your hand?

MR DONNELLY Mrs Donnelly, this is what is left of our farm and I've killed a man for it.

VOICE End of Act One

CHORUS

Oh, three men went to Deroughata
To sell three loads of rye.

They shouted up and they shouted down
The barley grain should die.
    (Refrain)
Tiree igery ary ann, Tiree igery ee,
Tiree igery ary ann, The barley grain for me.

Sticks & Stones

Act Two

In the darkness we see a cluster of lighted lanterns; the roads of Biddulph are held up in the middle of these. Then as the Chorus proceeds with the prelude below, the ladders are placed against the back map wall as before and the lanterns separate, come towards us, disappear into the audience as if we had just been run over by a group of constables on the search. This will leave us with Andrew Keefe and James Donnelly, dressed as a woman, at the front of Keefe's tavern.

CHORUS *Distribute the following phrases with differing textures.*

Constables William Howard and Adam Hodgins
to search for Donnelly the murderer of Farl
12 miles travelled
since James Donnelly has not been taken
May it please your Excellency
the following facts
44 miles travel after James Donnelly for the murder of Patrick Farrell
I hereby certify that Henry Sutton, Constable, did perform the above service
and other houses in that locality and back
James Donnelly five miles and
In the month of June last a most brutal murder was committed

in the Township of Biddulph in open day in the presence of many persons. The Murderer Donnelly has since eluded justice although efforts have been made to arrest him. One night with High Constable Lyster after Donnelly
October 16, 1857 twelve miles and one night (one dollar)
watching in the woods Constable Joseph Lynch
Two nights watching to apprehend James Donnelly
To travelling 18 miles to arrest
Since James Donnelly has not been taken

Constable puts up the notice of reward on a tree in front of Keefe's tavern. Rolling a barrel past a "woman" who sits on his tavern step sharpening a sickle, Andrew Keefe says

KEEFE Which is the last of all occupations? Which is the last of all occupations? Tavernkeeping is the last of all occupations. And I, Andrew Keefe, am a tavernkeeper whose house is a public house and whose very tree is pissed upon by the world.

CONSTABLE Good day to you, Andrew Keefe. You're back from Goderich Gaol, I see, and your old mother is also up and about again I see. Smoking her pipe and sharpening her sickle.

KEEFE Ah, Constable Howard, it makes a mother healthy to have her son at home with her again and so up and about she is, smoking her pipe and sharpening her sickle. She doesn't speak English or she'd give you the time of day.

CONSTABLE Keefe, that's the fifth time I've nailed this notice at your door on your tree. Good day to you. *He mounts his horse and rides off. Keefe tears down the notice and takes it across to Donnelly.*

KEEFE & CHORUS

Rewards!! You warrant two surprise marks, Jim.

$400 and $100

for the apprehension and delivery in the County Gaol, Goderich, of

James Donnelly

MR DONNELLY Oh, what's to become of me, Andy Keefe, when I'm worth so much to anybody but myself. Can't sleep in the Haskett barn anymore. Last night they found the hole in the hay mow where I usually sleep. Old Mrs Haskett persuaded them it was her goose's nest. That's a very large goose you have there, says this constable fellow. She has to be, says Mrs Haskett, to fit the nest. And he believed her! Now he'll be back. Then what, Andy?

KEEFE Jim, I advise this culvert over here. *motioning to empty barrel, Donnelly tries it for size.*

MR DONNELLY Ah, he'll gallop right over me on the road above; it's a snug place to be until there's a flood.

Mrs Donnelly gets up from chair, and walks over to Stub's store where Stub waits for her.

KEEFE *getting jug* I seen Mrs Donnelly walk by this morning, Jim. What does she think now of it all. *He pours two horns of whiskey.*

MR DONNELLY Oh, she's tramped into Lucan to George Stub's store to see him again.

KEEFE And how did she come into the way of asking him?

MRS DONNELLY Father Flynn, Father Flynn says that George Stub is the great new man of standing. Why Andy, he's just been made a Justice of the Peace.

KEEFE Sure and anybody that can burn down the coloured settlers' barns in 1847 and get made a magistrate in 1857 has got to be a very wise Orangeman indeed; not only that, Jim, when the Protestants swept down here last Christmas to riot my tavern apart who was it that whacked down my signpost with an axe and who was it roaring "Hurrah for Holmes" as he did so. Why it was George Stub was that lad and my signpost still falls over at the mere sight of him.

MR DONNELLY You need a strong man for your Justice of the Peace they say.

KEEFE How much stronger can you get? Who'd have guessed that's how you get to be magistrate. Whacking down my signpost with an axe. Well, Jim, and what does law-abiding, high-flying George Stub advise?

Stub says bracketed sequence, along with Mr Donnelly.

MR DONNELLY Oh he says (never fear, Judith. Tell Jim to give himself up. Manslaughter. Self-defence. Just as you say. Light sentence. Happens all the time). But we keep wanting to know—what really went on at the inquest. None of us were there. The jury was Protestant. The witnesses weren't, but have you got any of them to come right out, Andy, and say what the colour of their words were.

KEEFE They tell it the way you tell it, Jim. Those that were at the bee.

MR DONNELLY That they sicced me and Farl on like dogs? Sure in the tavern they'll own up to that but it's all written down what they really said at an inquest and that'll be read in a courtroom.

KEEFE If anybody can fish it out of George Stub, then Mrs Donnelly's the woman to do it. So it's giving yourself up is it?

MR DONNELLY I wish to do it so that not one of those constables makes a penny out of me, but after that ... what's to become of me? Deep in liquor for which Heaven forgive me, I struck out blindly at a man who was biting me, biting me in the feet and the belly and the neck and the heart—horsefly? Do they hang for that? *At "horsefly", Mr Donnelly repeats (with the sickle) the gesture he made on killing Farl.*

KEEFE Ah, did I show you what I found pinned to my door this morning. *Gives Donnelly a look at a note and a drawing.*

MR DONNELLY No, but you can tell it to me.

KEEFE "Andrew Keefe is a Blackfoot." Isn't that the name Farl kept calling you?

MR DONNELLY Yes, that's the name they have for us. Sure the Protestants just attacked you; can't your own Catholic kind leave you alone, Andy?

KEEFE No. People like you and me, Jim, are caught in the middle. We won't join. Except this time, what is it I should have joined?

Constable's horse is heard; Mr Donnelly crawls into a barrel-culvert with his drink.

CONSTABLE Mr Keefe, I just seen your old mother come out of the priest's house. Who was that other old woman sitting here with you?

KEEFE That was her. *pause* Well, I told you she was up and around. She can really travel.

CONSTABLE Oh, Mr. Keefe, I'll have to search your premises. Open up in the Queen's name. *He consults a small book. Kneels down.* Why there's a space under your tavern he could be crouching in. Four hundred dollars could be right there. Just waiting. Or it could be in your stable. *mime* What a great heap of horses you have, Andrew Keefe.

The constable tests hay with a fork.

KEEFE Did you not know, man, that the horses for the stage are kept here? These horses are those that galloped all the way from Goderich yesterday and they're taking a rest.

CONSTABLE What's in those barrels you have in your kitchen, Andy? *lights pipe*

KEEFE Saving your truncheon of authority, Mr Constable Howard, do please not light your pipe here. Those are barrels of blasting powder for all the work at the railway cutting I've got the contract for.

CONSTABLE *a definite spurt of flame from his pipe as he sits on a barrel* Have you got that contract now? Why, Andrew Keefe, you are a brave man!

KEEFE Why am I a brave man?

CONSTABLE Gallagher's eight boys were just telling me that if you *yawns* get the contract to dig that cutting through the knoll on their farm why they'd burn and they'd heat your place here hotter than Hell's corners and dared me to stop them. *The constable moves from barrel to barrel until he lands on the culvert-barrel in which Donnelly is hidden.*

KEEFE *covers his face with his apron and kneels* Oh, cut out my heart. Here, try one of these barrels, constable, that culvert's pretty cold.

CONSTABLE Not a barrel filled with blasting powder, thank you. And I can't seem to get any money out of the authorities for all I do, you know, watching in the woods night after night for the murderer Donnelly.

KEEFE Arrh, man, there might be four hundred dollars there right under your ass.

CONSTABLE Yes, and there might not.

Old Mrs Keefe, back from the priest's house and identical in appearance to Mr Donnelly's silhouette, now appears. The constable chases her; this gives Donnelly a chance to get out of the culvert so that we have a double image which the constable shares. Keefe almost persuades him it is the whiskey; he chooses to pursue old Mrs Keefe who holds him till Donnelly has disappeared. All this is mimed to whistled reel music and when finally the constable discovers his mistake he nails the Reward notice back on the tree and departs. Stick and stone percussion. Sunset and sinister Angelus ends it; the church is right away across the road. The silent film possibilities of two old women, now one, now two, even three, if Keefe gets into the act with something from a clothesline. As the Angelus finishes we have a rest by concentrating on Keefe kneeling in the sunset light of his tavern praying with missal. The Angelus should bridge between chase's end and this vesper scene.

KEEFE *trying to stay awake in his tavern, talking to himself, slowly heading towards sleep on the floor, kneeling, then rising* Oh my poor old mother never ran so fast in her life as she did when the constable thought she was Jim Donnelly. I've put her to bed now, she's snoring like a baby and outside the shadows are all joining each other till they become all one big shadow, even my own shadow joining ... it. *A barrel slowly rolls towards him.* Christ have mercy on me this is a barrel rolling towards me, come here, my darling, and give me sustenance to keep me awake till dawn *yawning* else they'll come and burn the place down. Uh— blasting powder. Where's the whiskey barrels. *Three men indistinctly stand over him.*

MEN Andy Keefe, darling, come. Raise yourself up, put on you, my good fellow, and come out till two or three of us that wish you well give some advice.

KEEFE How'd you get in here, Tony Gallagher. I locked all the doors. No—you're not there. You're in my head from what the constable spoke of.

MAN THREE If you take the contract for cutting the right of way through the knoll on my farm we will visit you at all hours of the night when you least expect it.

KEEFE To hell with you, Gallagher. I'm signing the contract; I've signed it. You're not getting the work away on me. *The men fade.* If I can just keep awake and Jesus—if you'll pardon the expression—it's true what Constable Howard said, the dear man, we have got no cellar under the floor of our little hotel. They could crawl under the old house itself with a match! *He looks down through the floorboards.* There are ten defenseless horses out there in my driving shed, oh mother of God, my old mother snoring upstairs, God bless her, if I could get the horses up where she is and she herself where they are, poor darlings. Whose gleaming eyes are those? *Clock strikes two?* Is it Jim Donnelly hiding out from the constables? No. Is it them waiting out there under there, right beneath me with tinder, flint and matches? No, it's you—my faithful tavern Tabby—crouching for a rat. A rat! Up your pantaloon leg like a great judas iscariot. *He dances about as if a rat has got up his leg.* Past two o'clock. At dawn the stage coach will arrive and save the horses and the dawn will drive away the shadows and the eight Gallagher boys. Who's that galloping up to the tollgate now? My tavern's right by the tollgate to Heaven which is to be out of Biddulph altogether, altogether. *sings* Sure the barley grain shot forth his head *falls down, totally zonked; immediately little flashes of fire from percussion caps, firecrackers, start showing in the darkness at the edge of the playing area*

MEN Look at that, boys. *a flare up* The old grass himself's caught fire.

Shadows; flame. A horse whinnies. Horse hooves coming up the London road. As the light disappears, horsemen gallop by. We focus on the fire-lit interior of the Donnelly house. There is one candle at the window, sleeping forms on the floor, Mrs Donnelly mending a shirt. The constable with a lantern crosses the stage to knock on her door. Sleighbells. Immediately Mrs Donnelly lights another candle and places it in the window as a signal; waiting, on either side, are George Stub at his counter, and carpenters ready to start building a scaffold.

CONSTABLE Ah, Mrs Donnelly, I just seen the candle in the window and it reminded me to come in.

MRS DONNELLY A fine cold evening. Constable Hodgins. *Outside Donnelly comes up then retreats at sight of the signal candle.*

CONSTABLE I see you've got company coming. Do you mind if I just sit down and wait for him?

MRS DONNELLY Do I mind? I object, Constable Howard, but I don't mind.

CONSTABLE It's an awful cold night outside, Mrs Donnelly, to be watching in the woods or lying down behind a fence.

MRS DONNELLY My fire is at your service, Mr Howard, and you may warm as many sides of yourself as you have.

CONSTABLE Did you hear Andrew Keefe's stables got burnt down last night?

MRS DONNELLY Never.

CONSTABLE Yes and ten horses alive in them too. They woke up in time to put out the housefire.

MRS DONNELLY Housefire?

CONSTABLE That's what did happen, Mrs Donnelly, and there doesn't seem to be anything anybody can do about it. I know who set the fire. There's even a witness, but he's run away out of dread. Now how many heads do I count in all your beds and cradles? One two three four five six seven—the baby. James Junior, William, Patrick, John, Michael, Robert, Thomas and a baby? Eight children, Mrs Donnelly, and another on the way so soon? I thought there were just seven now.

Use the fence line stones for the sleeping children.

MRS DONNELLY You're observant, Mr Howard, but what you don't know is that one of those heads belongs to Sarah Farl's boy, Bill. She's getting married again and Billy's come to live with us for a while.

CONSTABLE *taking a candle and examining sleepers* I see. Well, well. Well, none of them have beards, I'll grant you that, although I suppose if one of them did you'd have a story as long. Oh you've no idea the stories I've been told: the giant goose that made a hole in the Haskett hay mow—it was a giant goose, of course, not your husband. And the child they had sleeping over there who always sleeps with its head under the bolster while nine others of them weigh down the top of it on either side. There again, I wasn't quick enough to realize it was your husband, Mrs Donnelly, the champion holder of breath in this township I can tell you...

MRS DONNELLY Mr Howard, what happens if my husband is taken?

CONSTABLE Oh he mustn't do that.

MRS DONNELLY And why not?

CONSTABLE I apologize, Mrs Donnelly, for a moment I thought you were referring to his giving himself up. No, no, he can be taken any time he wants to and it's going to be me that takes him.

MRS DONNELLY *patiently* And when you take him, sir, then what?

CONSTABLE Oh, Mrs Donnelly, I'll chain him and take him to Goderich Gaol. Just in time for the Spring Assizes, I hope.

MRS DONNELLY And then?

CONSTABLE He'll be tried for the murder of Patrick Farl. He'll either get off or he'll be sentenced.

MRS DONNELLY Is there not something else? Between being sentenced—and getting off?

CONSTABLE You mean a plea such as is oftimes made that the deed was done in self-defence or perhaps was an accident or—

MRS DONNELLY Yes.

CONSTABLE Mrs Donnelly. I was at the inquisition. Whatever your husband says happened at Mulowney's bee he should have trusted us enough to come out like a man and say so at the inquisition either at Stub's store or Paddy Flannagan's hotel. There were two days he could of come. Because what you're implying certainly was not what the witnesses testified to. In fact, my opinion was with the jury when they said that the deed had been committed with malice aforethought, that your husband wanted to do it, and he after all had an old grudge against the murdered man.

MRS DONNELLY That's not true. Don't say such things. Give me that candle! *She retrieves it in time to meet her husband with it at the door.* No. Who could we trust—not our landlords or our neighbours. We're alone. *She meets her husband coming in the door.* Here's the candle, Mr Donnelly, that should have warned you we had a British peace-making constable in our house. Something he's just told me, Jim, makes me wonder.

MR DONNELLY Howard? Constable Howard, I'm giving myself up.

MRS DONNELLY Is what you're doing right. Run for it.

CONSTABLE *grasping at his instruction book* Four hundred dollars! Lost!

MR DONNELLY I'm giving myself up for nothing and I want a warm by my own fire first.

CONSTABLE I wish I could have apprehended you properly, Donnelly. It seems by the book that if you give yourself up I don't get the reward.

MR DONNELLY Deliver me to the gaol, Mr Howard, I'll back you up there and they'll give you a pound or two for that surely.

MRS DONNELLY Whirlwind! What will happen to us, Mr Donnelly, do you know what's been said here tonight. Shall I wake the children, Jim?

MR DONNELLY One candle or two, Mrs Donnelly, I'd have come in you know. No, I'll see them again. *He bends down over the sleepers.* Oh God, he looks like his father! *Not knowing what he's doing after seeing the face of Farl again, Donnelly lunges up with a candle in the Farl gesture.* Handcuff me, Howard. No, don't you dare! Not yet till I've said farewell to my wife. *He takes Mrs Donnelly's hands in his.* Under the snow I was scraping away, the wheat in our fields looks green, Mrs Donnelly. The boys are getting old enough to cradle most of it; ask the Keefes and Feeneys to help, they're our friends. No one asked them for their opinion at the inquest either. Well I will now, and get a girl to help you with the binding of the wheat, Mrs Donnelly, don't try to do any of it by yourself. *He thrusts out his hands for the cuffs.* And if they decide, Mr Howard, to choke me off, there are seven men there under the blankets waiting to sprout up and show the world that I live.

In contrast to the paper snow used for the Brimmacombe murder, use milkweed down here.

Mrs Donnelly stands at the doorway listening to the bells of the sleigh as the constable takes her husband away. Reel whistling and sudden bright, fully-lit stage with all the company present. On stage right, Stub's store and he waiting at the counter for Mrs Donnelly's attack; to stage left, sticks are going to be used by a gallows builder. Mrs Donnelly down stage centre; Chorus in between her and Mr Donnelly, the effect is of crash! from snow bells to the reality of the verdict. Forming a circle around Donnelly and pointing at him

CHORUS Jury returned to Court with verdict Guilty. Sentenced to be taken to the gaol whence he came thence on the 17th of September to the place of execution there to be hanged by the neck until dead.

Stub with assistance starts building a scaffold. Mrs Donnelly surges over to Stub's store with a stick and begins to lay about her — lots of stones fall off counter as she makes her sweep. Barrels fall over.

MRS DONNELLY You lied to me, you grocer. You registry rat, George Stub, the lease eel and blackmouth deedpoll worm — you lied to me when you said my husband would get off if he turned himself in, and after you lied, sir, sir grocer, you rode into town and you bought our mortgage because if my husband hanged we'd lose the fifty acres, our last, and it would be yours for a while until they bought it from you; did the Fat Woman put you up to this?

Most of the actors kneel as if at church.

STUB *starting the scaffold-building sequence with sticks & boards*
8 days work of carpenters at $2 per day — $16.00

MRS DONNELLY Well sirs, you're wasting your time because he shall not, will not, hang. *Donnelly kids bring to centre stage a roll of paper which they unroll until it extends to the edges of the stage.* He will not be hanged either, do you hear that, inhabitants of Biddulph. There children, if we can fill that much paper with names and get it to the Governor General in time he will not be ... for you see he did not kill the man intentionally. It was an unlucky stroke given in liquor. If — thank you, Father Flynn, if you do not wish to sign this petition for my husband's life then remain kneeling.

She moves about as if visiting countless people. From time to time someone stands up, goes over to the roll of paper which is unwound until at the end of the scene it is completely extended again.

Yes, stand if you can see your way at all at all to helping a woman with seven boys and one more child on the way, thank you. Mr Grace, shure it's the least he could do after selling half of the farm out from under us in the first place. My Father in the heaven if this eighth child is an eighth boy I'll go hang myself from that elm.

It's got to be a girl, pray God send me a little girl. Thank you, Mrs Marksey, oh, oh, her husband is in the same gaol as Jim is, for burning down Andrew Keefe's stables. I better go easy on talk about gaol, if her husband doesn't get off it might cheer her up to see my husband get hanged.

It was an unlucky stroke given in liquor, you won't sign, I know why. You're a cousin of Farl's and you stand to gain by his tricking us out of half our farm. I still can't get used to our front field looking so narrow. Well, so you won't sign, good day to you, but privately in my own mind I'll curse you as I pull my shadow down the road in the sunlight: may the devil when you arrive in hell take your shinbone—and make it a flute and play nothing but the merriest jigs and reels upon it, but I'll keep that private—you've taken half our farm from us, but you shall not take half our family from us which is my husband. Now we've got—four hundred names. *There are still a few obstinate kneelers who will only disappear in the going-to-Goderich sequence; the paper is rolled up and given to Mrs Donnelly.*

And now I'll walk with these names to Goderich.

WILL When my mother heard that the Governor General was to be there for the celebration opening the railroad from Goderich to Brantford to Buffalo, she determined that she would meet him with the petitions we had helped and friends had helped her gather up.

The road from Biddulph to Goderich is represented by a series of short and long ladders held up firmly by the cast. Mrs Donnelly climbs over these ladders. We hear road sounds—barking of dogs, etc.—that accompany her journey.

MRS DONNELLY At Marystown the dogs barked at me

CHORUS And people who had signed wished her good luck.

Generally repeat this solo and choral response arrangement between Mrs Donnelly and the other actors.

MRS DONNELLY At Irishtown the grain wagons were all going south

CHORUS North she was going, north through their dust.

MRS DONNELLY There at St Peter's is he buried whom my husband killed

CHORUS His cold hands across reached the road and held back her feet.

MRS DONNELLY I dare not enter there to pray for his soul

CHORUS The chapel has no shadow. It is noon.

VOICE Last spring a man and a woman came to a sudden death... it is not known how, and were buried in their own field in Biddulph.

STUB Twelve hundred feet of pine lumber at $10 per M.

MRS DONNELLY Now I've reached the borders of Biddulph

VOICE Sarah Stratton, an old woman who was found dead... on the north boundary of Biddulph going to Exeter out of Biddulph.

MRS DONNELLY Well, she almost made it, but once past this tollgate and I am

CHORUS out of Biddulph! Past two tollgates, there are twelve still to

MRS DONNELLY Oak tree with your shadow Indian dark

CHORUS Lie and rest beneath my speaking saying leaves

MRS DONNELLY

The whip of that carter touched my cheek
I look like a beggar woman tramping the roads

CHORUS Clean white tower clouds walk in the sky

STUB Nine hundred feet of hemlock scantlings, $7 per M, $6.30

MRS DONNELLY Tollgate of the setting sun show me your latch

CHORUS Twilight rain on this roof from those clouds

MRS DONNELLY Falling down down as I sleep till the earth wheels

CHORUS Down to the dawn whose tollgate opens to all

MRS DONNELLY I'll pray for the dawn with these winter stars

CHORUS In the chill dark starting out before there were proper shadows

STUB Detlor & Sons for nails, hinges & bolts $2.90

CHORUS Francistown Rogersville Hensall Kippen
Brucefield Rattenbury's Clinton and turn

MRS DONNELLY I'm on the Huron Road now and I turn west to

CHORUS Holmesville where her member of parliament lived.

MRS DONNELLY Yes Mr Holmes. Hurrah for Holmes will be our cry from now on in. Our family's vote is Grit forever and I've seven sons who'll agree or else. Why sir, you've garnered almost as many names from this township as I have from Biddulph. My family's blessing on you and your family forever. And our eight votes, sir, someday. Except the one I'm carrying, God bless her.

STUB Nolan's account for Staples & Ring &c.

MRS DONNELLY The road's like a knife I cut through the bush with

CHORUS She climbed up the hill, the last tavern hill before

STUB Rope from W.E. Grace 24¢ Four long polls at $1 each

MRS DONNELLY From this hill I see the river. I see the blue lake

CHORUS The ship in the harbour flew a red and gold flag

STUB 20 cedar posts 1 piece of 5×6 maple scantling

MRS DONNELLY I'll have time to see the mayor of the town. I'll change my dress, comb my hair somewhere. Somewhere. I won't see Mr Donnelly till I've delivered the petitions. What's that hammering sound I hear? My own heart more than likely.

STUB One mask 12½¢ One white cap for prisoner 50¢.

CHORUS The evening of July 7, 1858.

The Governor General has already made his entry, walking slowly along the railing of his yacht. Unlike nearly all the others in the play perhaps he and his lady should be in period dress; they are out of the play, both in fact and effect. Perhaps marionettes. They look down at us—at them—their subjects. Distant salon music of the 1857 period. Lady Head enters.

LADY HEAD Edmund, won't you join us for the music?

SIR EDMUND Perhaps in half an hour, Mary. I'm held out here by some rather grim official business. It's the convict Donnelly's wife. She's just come aboard.

LADY HEAD How very very curious. May I stay to watch?

SIR EDMUND You find someone begging for her husband's life of interest, do you?

LADY HEAD I'm not just idly curious, Edmund. I wish to see her.

SIR EDMUND She is reported to have walked every step of the way from her township, Biddulph, which is forty miles away back there somewhere in the bush.

LADY HEAD How do we know this fact for sure?

SIR EDMUND Well, my dear, the mayor of this town told it to me at dinner tonight and also presented me on the spot with a petition for Donnelly's life from the citizens of Goderich.

LADY HEAD You were having much more interesting conversation than I was, my dear. You've no idea what I suffered through. I think living in such an out of the way place jellies the brain. The palm trees we had last time, Edmund, were so much more interesting than these pines.

SIR EDMUND You find it dull and I'm sorry for that, my dear. They and we have done all that's humanly possible to make it of interest; new railroad opens tomorrow—railway celebration, four hundred to dinner and a ball for thousands, fireworks. Mary, I do wish you wouldn't—

LADY HEAD Why?

SIR EDMUND These scenes with the condemned convicts' wives are, can be, extremely embarrassing. They usually kneel, try to grasp my knees and there are tears.

LADY HEAD What are the extenuating circumstances, Edmund? Was he guilty or innocent or is it just that he's her husband?

SIR EDMUND I don't think you can call him innocent. But my feelings are, from what the locals say, that he did not present his part of the story soon enough, or could not present it, since he eluded the constables for a year or two. Now he has almost got himself hanged.

An aide de camp approaches and whispers in his ear. Our eye takes in Mrs Donnelly at extreme stage left. Her dress is exactly right; it embodies will—and grows out of the dusty, road-fighting woman we have just seen, but is also miles apart from that. An obscure tapping sound. Walking across, she curtseys ever so slightly.

MRS DONNELLY Your Excellency, I have three petitions to present, praying that the life of my husband might be spared.

SIR EDMUND Mrs Donnelly? Pray be seated. As you might probably have learned, a decision as to royal clemency is made by my advisors after consultation with the judge who sentenced your husband.

MRS DONNELLY Nevertheless, sir, you might give to your advisors some impression of the petitioners' present view of the case. There are names among the hundreds who signed these addresses to your Excellency, names of men who could have prevented the whole tragedy except they were drunk and such was their hilarity that they liked nothing better than to watch two men who were even more drunk attempt to destroy each other, sicced on by their howls of encouragement. They were not men enough to admit to this—neither at the inquest nor at the trial where they heard their earlier lies read out to them. Faced with Donnelly's wife, however, they signed their names or made their marks to the truth at last. I shall bring the truth out of Biddulph yet and my husband alive back some day to his seven children and his farm. I wish you and your lady good-night, sir, and I beg you to consider what is written on scraps of paper my friends and *she gives him the petitions* myself have caught pity and truth in, name by name, and then pasted together—by my children—into the sincere prayers you hold in your hands. *As she leaves, neatly backing up and then turning, a ladder has been set up with Mr Donnelly behind it; she goes over to see him; at another ladder she will wait for the letter from the Executive Council—at her front door back in Biddulph.*

LADY HEAD What will she do now, Edmund?

SIR EDMUND *pause* She'll say goodbye to her husband at the gaol over there and then start walking back to their shanty back somewhere in the bush. The Executive Council meets a fortnight from tomorrow. God knows what the Attorney-General will decide; if I know Macdonald's mind he'll be appalled at the number of votes he might lose. *He unfolds the petitions.*

LADY HEAD Ah, this hand was learnt a long time ago from a priest who'd been trained abroad, wouldn't you say? I haven't seen an M like that since I was at school. Some of them put capital letters in the centre of their names. Oh, it's a Norman name—D'Arcy.

SIR EDMUND This is the third or fourth murder in that locality although in his favour I will say that this man at least gave himself up. Now she'll wait at her doorstep for a letter with our seal upon it.

LADY HEAD What do you think, Edmund?

SIR EDMUND What does it matter, my dear.

LADY HEAD It does matter, Edmund. *They walk along the railing back to the music.* I feel that I shall remember that woman for the rest of my life.

SIR EDMUND Oh, I believe her. But you asked me and what I think is this. Something in her presence seems to say—that she's not fated to save her husband from his sentence.

We now focus on Mrs Donnelly standing in front of her house in bright summer sunlight, the cicadas strumming away with the heat. A galloping horseman throws the letter with a red seal at her feet. One of her children picks it up for her; she throws it on the ground again. Humming sound of cicadas.

MRS DONNELLY I walked all the way to Goderich. I met him. I gave him the three petitions and now they've all turned into this letter and I won't open it. It's so hot and bright, the cicadas shrill shrill shrill away. Everything turns into a letter. That letter. It's like the handspike he saw on the ground and then he picked it up. I hate the fact that there's moments each like a bridge of dread and why does there have to be an earth that goes round and round. There. My hand feels the letter. How heavy the seal makes it. I'd like to seal my letters with that heavy a red wax. If it says no—we'll throw the farm, what's left of it, we'll throw it away and move into town, get John Grace to put us up again, take in washing, cook. *opens letter* If it says yes, your husband may live, I'll give one cry against my doorframe here and then—wait for him to come home, get going on the next petition to get his sentence shortened.

She reads the letter, gives a brief cry and turns to her family. Some of them reply from offstage or from the Chorus. The seven sons can be represented by two lines hung with shirts; one for now—the other for when they are grownup.

MRS DONNELLY Boys, how old are you now? *As they tell her their ages, in the background the Chorus (as if a legal clerk and assistant) go on about expenses. A train whistle. Very shadowily the trip Mr Donnelly takes to Kingston lies under the boys' recital of their ages.*

CHORUS	KIDS
James	17
William	13
John	12
Patrick	10
Michael	9
Robert	6
Thomas	5

WOMAN ONE Expenses taking convict James Donnelly to the Penitentiary. Cab from gaol to station at Goderich

WOMAN TWO Two shillings two sixpence

WOMAN ONE Paid railway fare from Goderich to Paris

WOMAN TWO For three

WOMAN ONE Railway fare from Toronto to Kingston for three

WOMAN TWO Cab from station to Penitentiary and back

WOMAN ONE Dinner for two at Kingston

WOMAN TWO Three shillings nine pence

WOMEN Expenses taking convict James Donnelly to the Penitentiary.

MRS DONNELLY Children, yesterday was July 28th and that day your father was sentenced to seven years in prison. How old will you be when your father comes back?

CHORUS	KIDS
James	24
William	20
John	19
Patrick	17
Michael	16

MRS DONNELLY Robert, you'll be thirteen and Thomas will be twelve when Mr Donnelly comes back to live with us again. Back from prison where he'll have been seven years of his life.

JENNIE *A girl comes running in.* My name is Jennie and I'm seven years old when my father gets out of prison.

ALL Seven years. *the line fence; the boys kick the stones of the line fence this way and that*

JAMES & JOHN Why is our father's farm so narrow? Because he was cheated by the farrow. Of the pig and the sow, the fat woman who now snores as the moon lights our labours.

WILL There are other ways of getting that fence down than that, James and John. As a matter of fact that's the poorest way I ever saw and you'll drive our mother mad with the law suit over it.

JAMES We thought awhile. *The church bell rings midnight and they put the fence up again.* So what's your better way, Will?

WILL I'll make the fence disappear by playing my fiddle at it. Someday. *The two brothers look at each other.* I'm practising up for it. You'll see, the fence will dance away away.

JAMES We believed him. And it almost happened.

The Christening Scene will already have started to merge in, but beginning to be established should be the Girl with the Sword, the Fat Lady with her turnips and grindstone.

ALL Six years

PRIEST *In white vestments, standing beside Mrs Donnelly with a baby in her arms, he gives her a candle.* Receive this burning light and see thou guard the grace of thy baptism without blame; keep the commandments of God, so that when the Lord shall come to call thee to the nuptials, thou mayest meet Him with all the saints in the heavenly courts, there to live for ever and ever.

ALL Amen.

PRIEST Jane Donnelly, vade in pace et Dominus sit tecum.

ALL Amen.

Jane, the small girl, simultaneously puts four small stones on the ground by the door step and plays house.

JENNIE

Here I'm sitting sewing
In my little housey
No one comes to see me
Except my little mousey

ALL Five years.

Will Donnelly limps to centre stage pursued by a mob of jeerers, led by the Fat Woman as a girl, with a cap on her head.

MOB

Cain killed Abel, Donnelly killed Farrell
Your old man killed Farrell, Will
Where's your father, they asked young Cripple
He's down at Kingston on the old treadmill

With tree branches Tom and John Donnelly appear. The mob runs jeering away, all save the Fat Girl, who trips. They beat her and tear her cap.

JAMES & JOHN Tell us your names.

GIRL Jim Donnelly and John Donnelly.

JAMES & JOHN If you'll repeat what you said to our brother Will just now we won't give you a licking. You were singing it, weren't you, well, let's just hear you sing it again.

GIRL I won't.

JAMES & JOHN You won't, eh?

GIRL I won't do a thing the sons of a murderer want.

JAMES & JOHN Then you'll have to take a licking from us then. *They beat her off.*

Reaching for his fiddle as if to heal wounds, Will plays far upstage on his side of the fence. His playing produces a girl from the enemy farm who dances, whirling a sword.

MAGGIE This may be the last time I can show you the sword, Will. Oh please stop playing so I can stop dancing. *He doesn't.*

WILL Maggie, why? *finally stopping*

MAGGIE My brother says I'm not to let you see it again or he'll tell my Aunt Theresa.

WILL In that case let's begin my last look. *She takes the fiddle and plays, while he practises sword play.* Does no one in your family that took half our land away from us be able, Maggie, to read the writing on this sword?

MAGGIE No, Grandmother says the man's not born yet can read that sword. Her father's father found it on the battlefield a hundred years ago. *The Fat Lady rolls grindstone out and darts her eyes about suspiciously.* Now it's your turn of the promise. *He plays and she dances.* Oh... oh I must run back home. Will, please don't play or they'll hear you. Play, play! Don't stop. I can't stop dancing. *She disappears, to reappear at the "front of the farm" by her aunt with her grindstone.*

FAT LADY When I needed it to chop up turnips for the pigs, where were you with that old sword, Maggie?

MAGGIE Playing, Aunt Theresa. Looking for the black hen's nest. *She dances whenever her aunt is not looking.*

FAT LADY Don't go too near the line fence we have to share with those squatters, Maggie. They'll try to pull you over and insult you. I can hear that damn cripple's fiddle playing back there. He'll make our red cow with the brass tip on one horn bear a freemarten, between him and his mother cursing us. Why this sword's too dull to cut even turnips with, whatever have you been doing with it, here turn the grindstone while I—*sharpens the sword*

MAGGIE You'll grind off the old writing that way, Aunt Theresa.

FAT LADY Dull as the dead it is. *grinds* What writing? *Will covers his face; then we watch the Fat Lady turn her big buttocks to the Donnelly front door and chop up turnips. Out of the Donnelly house steals a younger kid with a slingshot which begets a routine underlining the story of the Donnellys' seven years with father in prison told by the sweet priest we have previously heard on the subject of diocesan history. It is almost as if the boy might also ping the priest.*

PRIEST While the father was away in the Penitentiary and taking away with him, I might add, the useful and fruitful influence a father always has, e.g. there was no one to put the fear of God into the seven boys with a big or little stick, the wretched family managed to survive by the genuinely heroic efforts of Mrs Donnelly. Three times she gathered petitions for remission of her husband's sentence and sent them to the government.

VOICE With regard to this request for further clemency, "altogether premature."

PRIEST George Stub, who now held a mortgage on the Donnelly farm, sent a letter intimating that

STUB The time for the payment of a large sum overdue on this mortgage thereon has elapsed

MRS DONNELLY *emerging from the house with household chores* We sold the pigs and took out a second mortgage from a railway conductor. *overlap*

PRIEST Now it is rather interesting to relate that the family who had bought up the south half of the Donnelly farm in 1856 and very nearly chased the Donnellys off all of their property—this family decided to move away. The south half of the farm was up for sale—

MRS DONNELLY The children begged me to try to buy it back, but there was just enough money to send Will down to school in the town. No, we would wait, would have to wait for the years to go by before our farm would heal itself from being cut in half by that turnip chopper over there.

The stone finds its target and Fat Lady emits a howl. Mrs Donnelly takes a stick and pursues Robert Donnelly, but even under her arm he manages another direct hit. This should somehow lead to a routine with whistle accompaniment where both women pursue the scamp, with the Fat Lady almost crossing the fence. Then silence and

MRS DONNELLY Mrs Ryan, you have dropped your sword over the fence. *pause* Do not attempt to come over the fence or I shall charge you with trespass. Here—I shall throw the sword over the fence and I am shamed to see that glory used to chop turnips, but the fox has so long fouled the badger's den I shouldn't be surprised. And I shall punish my own child.

A magistrate's court is set up in Stub's store in Lucan. Fluidly, you should be able to establish this out of the line-fence chairs. Kneeling in rows, holding ladders, the courtroom audience react with loud heehaws and ladder motions.

CHORUS Four years.

STUB Remember, that in magistrate's court, Will Donnelly, you must speak the truth. Why—for what reason, did you lead these other boys of the neighbourhood to steal six fleeces of wool from the premises of Patrick Ryan, entering and breaking the curtilage.

WILL I can't tell you, Mr Stub.

STUB How much is the value of a fleece of wool, Will?

WILL Five dollars.

STUB So how much would six fleece bring you on the market down at London?

WILL Don't know, I think it would be thirty dollars.

STUB You think it would be thirty dollars; you know it would be thirty dollars. Where is your father, Will?

WILL I think he's in prison.

STUB You think he's in prison; my boy, you know he's in prison and your little gang will soon join him and he can break a few of your skulls together while he's at it. Johannah, what have you to say for your son's behaviour?

MRS DONNELLY Sir, there's a pair of special shoes this lad has wanted for some time that cost quite a penny. Have you any notion how quickly his shoes wear out?

STUB Then let him go barefoot, Johannah Donnelly.

MRS DONNELLY And have him the barefoot hobbledehoy of the school, I suppose.

STUB Take him out of the school. Since you can't quite afford it with your fifty acres you maybe shouldn't be trying. Between you and your high notions and your crippled son you've corrupted half the youth in the settlement. Shirts from clotheslines and stamps from the post office is how it started; next fleeces of wool and next

WILL Maybe it was we wanted to buy the horse.

STUB And all six of you were to take turns riding it, or were you to climb up on it all at once? What horse?

WILL The one the King of the Indians had when they were camping over by the river. He said we could have his gray horse for thirty dollars.

STUB The king of the Indians? You mean an Indian Chief, I presume. Has anyone seen Indians camping over by the river lately? Let alone a King of them? *pause* Will, did he wear a crown?

WILL They'd come up along the river for the flax picking and he was the King of them.

STUB Will, this is like the story you told about the old sword that disappeared for a while on your road. When it was found again it was seen to be nothing but a rusty turnip knife. Will Donnelly not only—is always into a new one each day, a new strange story. Look at him. Just as he stands is he not a strange story?

MRS DONNELLY *puncturing* No stranger than your own story, Mr Stub. That you should be a Justice of the Peace in 1864 when in 1848 in October of that year you led a mob to burn down the Africans' barns, to steal their land, not steal their shirts or their fleeces, but their very existence. *laughter* But that was some time ago, and with the profit from that bold adventure you've supported the Party that gave you a commission of the peace, aye and your arsonist brother a place on the Grand Jury. Yes, Donnelly is a strange story, sir, but you law-abiding high-flyer, never as strange as—could never compete with yours.

STUB Silence, Johannah Donnelly. I'll send you both down, mother and son. Down to the Quarter Sessions. Too are charged you!

ALL The Queen against Johannah Donnelly.

MRS DONNELLY Let us hear the charge against me then. How many fleeces of wool did Judith Donnelly get away with?

STUB Can no one here think of what she should be charged with?

FAT LADY I can. I can think of what to charge her with. I'm willing to swear out an information at this very moment that I saw on the Friday following the Thursday the fleeces were reported to be missing, I saw this woman out in her back yard washing something white. And it looked like fleeces to me, Mr Stub.

ALL The Queen against Johannah Donnelly. Receiving stolen goods.

MRS DONNELLY You'd even gore your own ox to goad me, wouldn't you. Because your son is charged as well as mine, don't forget, and I've read somewhere there's a lovely penalty for perjury and malicious arrest, but perhaps you'd like to take back that charge. *pause* Anything goes, I see, if you can plunge your horn into me, into us—up to the very last wrinkle. *A small girl comes with a note for Mrs Donnelly which she reads while keeping an eye on the bailiff who, carrying a staff, conducts Will to behind a ladder. To read the note, Mrs Donnelly puts on glasses.*

ALL Three years.

MRS DONNELLY My dear girl, have you not heard the trouble we're in. You'll have to tell your mother I cannot come to help her for I'm waiting to hear how my son's trial goes. And my own trial promises to be next. *pause* And Farl's wife will be there at this raising bee. Her marrying again does not make her any less the widow of the man my husband killed. I can't bear her looking at me. *pause, a bell at a prison*

We now focus on Will as a prisoner, his body behind a ladder.

CHORUS The Queen against William Donnelly et aliter.

VOICE Indictment withdrawn. No bill. Insufficient evidence.

MRS DONNELLY I'll go, sweetheart. I'll take your mother this bread and some meat. I'll walk back with you, darling. *We now lose sight of Mrs Donnelly as the cast expands into the crowd of people at Gallagher's Bee.*

CHORUS The Raising Bee at Gallagher's on the Cedar Swamp Line.

The crowd is spaced out over the stage held by something that is happening just offstage left. Tom Cassleigh is dealing out whiskey to men as they finish washing their faces and hands in a horsetrough. There's a towel they dry themselves with but one of the men reaches for the apron of a woman. A small tense scream. Some of the men are deeply drunk and occasionally stagger or fall over. As someone rolls a wagon wheel down stage left and leans it up over a chair, a man throws some water at another, flicking it out of a dipper.

MAN TWO Six eggs to you Rody, and half a dozen of them rotten. *These two men square off for a fight, but Cassleigh, who is as powerful among these people as Stub is in the village, walks between them and says:*

CASSLEIGH Why waste your time on each other, Rody and Dan, when there's more fun to be had over here. Donegan! *To a man sitting on the edge of the stage rather out of it all.* After all, would you like a drop now from my jug—Mr Donegan?

DONEGAN No, I would not, Cassleigh. I said you and your gang stole my oak tree and, until we settle that, I'll not drink from your jug. If you want to know I'm going home.

CASSLEIGH D'ye hear him, men? He's going home. *Suddenly we and Donegan are faced by a gang of men with sticks, one of them turning his handspike into a torch. Not all join Cassleigh's mob. Some hang back; the women bunch in fear—save for the Fat Lady who calmly gathers some wood.* Donegan, we stole your oak tree, eh? Say that to our faces, eh? Now you're afraid to, darling, aren't you. *A barrel is rolled over and filled with sharp objects.*

DONEGAN *Backing up off stage as the men push him over.* I only want fair play about my oak tree. It's sorry I am I mentioned it. What d'you want with me at all? *Whatever does happen to Donegan? perhaps we should be dimly aware that he is being put into the barrel. We see nothing nor hear anything of the usual cruelty paraphernalia—just silence; the men and women on stage come over gingerly to take a look, then register—shame, disgust, fascination, even joining in.*

MEN What about your oak tree now, Donegan!

Just as one does join the offstage mob, Mrs Donnelly enters stage right with girl. Opposition—she—the non-joiner as against the tormentors—in the darkness of the cellar or underneath a wagon.

MRS GALLAGHER Oh, Mrs Donnelly. I'm sorry I asked you to come. Some of the men have too much drink into them and they're tormenting the life out of Donegan who asked about—why would he mention it when they're so—asked about his oak tree he says Tom Cassleigh stole on him.

MRS DONNELLY Complaining to that man about your oak tree is a mistake surely. He'd brain you with it.

SARAH FARL What is to be done, Judith Donnelly.

MRS DONNELLY What's to be done—are they not letting him go yet?

SARAH FARL They're saying they'll clip off his ears.

MRS DONNELLY Are there no men to stop this?

SARAH FARL They're afraid of Cassleigh. Or they like watching.

MRS DONNELLY Where's Mrs Cassleigh?

SARAH FARL Not here, Mrs Donnelly. But in the same churchyard as my Patrick lies buried.

MRS DONNELLY Sarah Farl. I cannot help calling you that although I know that your name is now Sarah Flannery. And I once a very long time ago knew you as Sarah Donegan.

SARAH FARL Judith Donnelly who were once Judith Magee. You alone of anyone here can save my brother. Tell them to stop.

MRS DONNELLY *kneeling* Sarah Flannery that was Sarah Farl. Very well then. *covering her face* Have you forgiven me and mine then for what we did to your man? And for what my husband is now in prison for?

SARAH FARL *pause* You won't let them go on, will you?

MRS DONNELLY *getting up* Yes, Sarah Farl. Sarah Donegan that was, that I used to see running up Keeper's Hill in her bare feet. I will save your brother. *She pauses at the lip of the stage. As she begins her speech to the tormentors below, slowly Stub and his counter fade in at stage right. The priest will soon begin to mount a centre-back pulpit which is in effect the roof of the Donnelly house.* Leave that man alone. What in heaven's name and the name of hell do you think you're about with him. Have you, Mr Cassleigh, tortured him enough? Put that knife back where it belongs, Mr Cassleigh, if you still know what pockets are for or do you carry the knife permanently stuck in your hand like a thorn. *Cassleigh comes towards her with his knife, but her glance forces him to weave out from the wheel, through it, and around the barnyard.* Get back, you savage. Have you not killed enough when you got your friend to tap the Englishman over the head at our doorstep on our road. Tom, let me see the knife. *He– click!– gives her the knife.* Give Mr Donegan back his clothes . . . raise him up out of that mud. Dung! There's fields of grain to garner with bread for you all and you'd rather be thorns to each other. There's tables of food for you to eat and you won't come and sit down at them. Well, you won't sit down at them. Get back to work, you fools. You tribe!

For a moment she stands isolated: Stub on one side, Cassleigh on the other. She has won and Donegan is rescued. She disappears to help him. As the priest begins the people all enter centre area and kneel. Slowly everyone kneels but it would be hard to tell when we saw Mrs Donnelly kneeling. Candles.

PRIEST When I turned this poor man in his bed last evening the flesh actually fell from his bones. I looked to heaven, my friends of Biddulph, my friends of St Patrick's parish, and I was, and I still am, afraid that the hand of God will fall on Biddulph some day and fall with great weight. I want all those who tormented and burnt and cut this man to come in the presence of all the congregation and ask God's pardon.

A pause during which one man rises. Before he rises there is silence filled with the buzzing of a fly against a window.

GALLAGHER Father Crinnon, I come forward in the presence of all the congregation and ask God's pardon. I stood by while the crime was done. Nor did I even offer to help the woman who risked her life to save the man. I ask God to pardon me—and to pardon me too for ever being in such company.

PRIEST *coming down from pulpit* Domine exaudi vocem meam.

CHORUS Si iniquitates observaveris, Domine, Domine quis sustinebit. *candles*

PRIEST For Thine arrows stick fast in me. And Thou hast laid Thy hand heavily upon me.

They move to upstage where they face us as the audience of the Medicine Show. Their candles are its footlights. The Donnelly house lies between us and the stage of the show. Stub becomes the Showman counting his take; beside focusing on him we look too at the front gate of the Donnelly house where Tom and Jim Feeney prepare their scene.

CHORUS There is no health in my flesh because of Thy wrath. There is no peace in my bones because of my sins.

TOM Two years. *He is sharpening a jackknife on a stone.* My name is Tom Donnelly and my best friend was a boy who lived up the road called Jim Feeney.

JIM What're you doing with the knife, Tom?

TOM See, I can cut my name on my arm. T-O-M.

JIM What about your last name.

TOM Haven't got any more arm. Your turn, Jim.

JIM Ouch! How'd you get it so sharp?

TOM Whetted it for half a day on the doorstep. I. Now for your M.

JIM Uh

TOM Don't you want me to finish it?

JIM No! You know I can't stand pain, Tom. *Screams as Tom grabs his arm and finishes it anyhow.*

TOM Now—cross your arm with mine. Your blood, my blood, mixed in brotherhood. *train whistle*

Their arms crossed, the boys freeze. We focus on the Showman counting his take while the last scene of the Medicine Show Donnelly play is winding up. This last scene is played on ladders held up by the footlight holders.

SHOWMAN Shamrock Liniment?

SON Must have sold 40 bottles.

SHOWMAN So how many tins of the East India Tiger Fat?

SON 55

SHOWMAN So... $252.35 cents off these yokels tonight that came to see our little penniless dreadful—"The Black Donnellys". Or the Biddulph Horror.

SON Paw, we sure scared it out of them tonight.

SHOWMAN Yeah. Which part do you think, my boy, scares them the most?

SON The part where they draw lots to see who'll kill the girl?

SHOWMAN That's worth 16 bottles of Shamrock Liniment right there, isn't it? *He takes out his watch.* Oh it's the Jim Feeney weeps over his betrayal of Tom Donnelly for five hundred bucks and he never even got the money scene. Listen to him whine.

FALSE JIM Pat, you have always used me white.

FALSE PAT What's on your mind, Jim Feeney?

FALSE JIM Pat Donnelly, you are as square a man as ever I met. Pat, I can't sleep nights for thinking what I done to Tom. I didn't know they was going to murder them. I thought it was just to scare them or at the worst shake him up a little.

SHOWMAN Christy Dominy, that's my cue. *He rushes out to be ready.*

FALSE PAT Jim, what was the one thing you ever done that you're sorry for?

FALSE JIM I sold Tom Donnelly, Tom Donnelly, the best friend I ever had.

SHOWMAN *on a shorter ladder held up by his son* Showing, folks, that there were those that loved the Donnellys as well as loathed them. Will it ever be known who killed them that dark night of February 4, 1880? One thing is known—after the Donnellys left

Biddulph at last there was peace. No more fires, no more mysterious outrages and who today would guess that in that tranquil countryside such dire events had once took place. In the words of the Old Song we close. *He sings with banjo, fiddle.*

Oh all young folks take warning
Never live a life of hate,
Of wickedness or violence, lest
You share the Donnellys' fate.

Their murdered bodies lie today,
A mile from Lucan town
But the memories of the awful feud
Time never will live down. *applause, train whistle, scream*

We focus again on the boys with crossed arms.

TOM Now—cross your arm with mine, Jim Feeney. Your blood, my blood, mixed in brotherhood. *train whistle*

MRS DONNELLY *coming out of the house* What is this unearthly silence out here, boys? John or Mike, before you go out to the fields again, hold the lamp for me while I hang out your shirts. The moonlight doesn't reach over the wash house yet on this side of the house. But it will. Rising pretty full moon you are. Why are you two boys hiding your arms, eh? Jim Feeney and Tom Donnelly, the two scamps. What month is this we're in, Tom?

TOM July, mother.

MRS DONNELLY And Mike, what's the date yesterday?

MIKE 28th

MR DONNELLY So it is the twenty-ninth of July. There's your seven shirts all hanging on the line for you to put on for mass tomorrow if father comes back. So you'll look like seven gentlemen instead of the seven devils I've raised.

TOM They let father out yesterday.

MRS DONNELLY I was wondering if any of you'd remember that he was sentenced on July 28th, seven years ago. He could be here tonight.

MIKE Not if he's walking, mother. *train whistle*

MRS DONNELLY Do you see your father tramping the roads with a bundle on his back? No, he'll take the cars. And the stage. Oh, he'll come walking up the road from the Chapel where he'll get off the London Road. Now I'll wait for him here by the gate with this lamp. Bring sheaves with you when you've finished the field.

Your father will want to see what his farm's been doing, right away. I'll stand out here with my lamp. You will come tonight. I know you will. I'll hold this lamp until either its oil runs dry or you're home. Moon, you hold your lamp, stars; I hold mine. *night sounds* I stand. I'll stand here years after tonight —a seal in the air—long after my house and my gate and my curtilage have become dust. A lamp hanging in the air, held by a ghost lady.

In the halflight, Mrs. Donnelly's ghost comes up behind her and eventually takes the lamp from her; they stand back to back, move away from each other but they never face each other; in effect, we are looking at another deep down dead leaf self of Mrs. Donnelly.

GHOST Mention me, Judith, and I float up from the culvert where I'll hide to frighten travellers years from now. A ghost lady with a lamp, no—a lamp floating in mid-air up and down by the fence by the road.

MRS DONNELLY Who is that behind me?

GHOST It's no good to turn around because you cannot see me or even hear me, but only sense me with the drumming eye of your heart.

MRS DONNELLY Yes, I can hear you. My heart can hear you. What will—

GHOST You'll die unconfessed, Judith Donnelly. And wander these roads for a certain while. Dead leaf. Float light.

MRS DONNELLY What have I got ready for him to come back to? Were there—

GHOST There were ladders with certain rungs, Judith, you could have avoided, you know.

MRS DONNELLY Seven years I've waited for my husband to return.

GHOST Your first mistake was to stay here at all.

MRS DONNELLY And give up my husband's farm that we've fought for?

GHOST Well, its ground loves you. But why did you have to talk back to that Orangeman Stub?

MRS DONNELLY I should have been weak and let him call my son a thieving cripple?

GHOST Oh yes, and lived.

MRS DONNELLY When she asked me to save her brother at the bee—

GHOST You should have said, save your brother yourself, and you should have let Donegan then be cut to ribbons by Cassleigh.

MRS DONNELLY Will Cassleigh never forget that then?

GHOST During the day, but not at night.

MRS DONNELLY Why should we be afraid. Look at all the neighbours who signed their names for my husband's life.

GHOST Stub and Cassleigh can change that with

MRS DONNELLY How!

GHOST With their tongues and their words. Did you see that boy who's such a friend of Tom's?

MRS DONNELLY Yes, Jim Feeney. My sons have many such loyal friends.

GHOST *laughing* From where I stand tonight wandering through, crossing times and places as I please—I saw some cheap Medicine Show put on a play in which that very Jim Feeney grown up to be a weak young wastrel sold your son Tom for five hundred dollars. And he had Tom's name written on his arm.

MRS DONNELLY Oh, if only we could get out of the pound we're locked in—it's like a house with twisty windows—what is it out there coming down the road?

GHOST It still may not happen. Ah, I can see him before you do. The darkness and the shadows changing into a traveller. Your husband. Coming back to you as one day his ghost will come back to me—with a ticket that confirms us across the river and finally out of Biddulph.

MRS DONNELLY Sleep voice within me. If I wait long enough my husband will come from where he has journeyed.

GHOST *As Mrs Donnelly walks away from her to meet Mr. Donnelly down in the audience corridor; when the Donnellys come up to the clothesline scene, the ghost has vanished.* Yes, sleep here if you can. Mrs Shea held her child in the rain barrel while a mob of 400 set fire to their house. She held and held until past the borders of life. I hold this. Past life. Past death!

All but the lamp fades; then we are back in 1865 *again; the line of seven shirts, the harvest moon, the woman with the lamp, crickets singing loudly, then fading as someone walks through them; Donnelly walks up to his wife and takes the lamp from her.*

MRS DONNELLY Boys, line up to see if your father can say your names still. *We see sheaves through the shirts, and the seven boys partly through them, although as the naming goes on the shadows of the seven Donnellys grow huge and by themselves towering over the theatre.*

MR DONNELLY James Will John Patrick Michael Robert Thomas. *to the shirts; train whistle far away; Mrs Donnelly brings out the sleeping Jennie in her arms* Jennie?

MRS DONNELLY She's still asleep.

MR DONNELLY Judith Donnelly, mother of Jane Donnelly.

MRS DONNELLY James Donnelly, senior, father of Jane Donnelly and these... seven.

MR DONNELLY Mrs Donnelly, I was thinking what fair seed we have sown and I have come back at last to harvest. *train whistle*

ALL

Then they sold me to the brewer
And he brewed me on the pan
softly
But when I got into the jug
I was the strongest man.

VOICE End of Act Two

Sticks & Stones

Act Three

JENNIE *as a grown-up to tell us the rest of the story* When I woke up the next morning I was to see my father for the very first time.

Behind her narration the entire company mime groupings that go through the story backwards and forwards; they make the Roman Line; they do the ladder journey format; they suddenly kneel, cross themselves... people caught in the Roman Line.

No, I did not know it at the time but in those few months and years after my father returned from seven years in prison, we—the entire Donnelly family—mother, father, seven sons and one daughter—were up for confirmation in a church called the Roman Line. No, it was a bigger church than that for it involved Protestants too. We were going to be tested for confirmation in a chuch called—Biddulph. Most of the people liked us at that time. That doesn't matter though. Those with power did not. Our confirmation came up and although we had known our catechism well, we failed.

CHORUS *tossing sticks and stones in patterned throwing and catching* Which are the sacraments that can be received only once?

JENNIE Your mother, your father, your brothers.

CHORUS Why can they be received only once?

JENNIE Just a minute, your lordship. I'm not ready for that one yet, but there's also the rungs of the ladder they've climbed which we can't see down down down, and there's also the other people and what they think.

CHORUS So what lot is this, pa?

JENNIE It was my father's farm. Half of its fields were lost to his enemies.

CHORUS What about the Mescoes & the Washingtons?

JENNIE Better to be black all over than just to have black feet.

CHORUS Who settled the Roman Line, Church Line, Chapel Line? *Form line.*

JENNIE Who owns it now, you mean?

CHORUS

Barry	Trehy
Feeney	Cassleigh
Cahill	Cassleigh
McCann	Marksey
Donnelly	Mulowney
Egan	Marksey
Quinn	

JENNIE Now that's not right. The Quinns were burnt out in '66, and they left. That was how you knew that you hadn't passed the catechism. A burning barn is a good strong hint with your house left over.

CHORUS Who bought up the Quinn place?

JENNIE Guess.

CHORUS Cassleigh.

CHORUS What have I done to you, man?

JENNIE Nothing, for a while. All was quiet. No bad names were even used. Everything seemed to be all right.

CHORUS Do you desire any one thing other than fiddle, sword and horse?

JENNIE Yes, to get back the other half of my father's farm. But when it came up for sale again our friend was afraid to sell it to us. The Fat Lady's family offered him so much money—where did they get all the money so suddenly? We had the Fat Lady for a neighbour again.

CHORUS Which of you robbers is buying my farm out from under me?

JENNIE There's fifty acres you'll never get and across the road the Mulowney brothers who'd never married offered to sell my father either one of their twenty-five-acre lots.

CHORUS Where's the grogboss?

JENNIE He couldn't buy both of them. One of the lots had blood on it, blood he had spilled. Meanwhile we all went to mass together and several New Years and Lents went by.

CHORUS Which is the last of all the occupations?

JENNIE To be the fenceviewers who had to decide our tile-and-ditch dispute with the Fat Lady's husband and nephews. There was a small creek ran through their farm, at the back, and our farm and then across into the next farm. But our back field kept flooding. *The chorus hold up a line of tile that more or less fits together.* They were applying the flood'em-out-test by plugging our tile with straw and rags. *Furious activity of plugging and unplugging. Lanterns—watchings, reel whistlings, a blue gauze sheet for the water. The Donnellys decide to use bigger tile and a line of this meets the line of smaller tile.* After we put in some bigger tile that would be impossible to plug up so easily, their backfield got flooded and they sued.

CHORUS We, the Fenceviewers of the Township of Biddulph in the County of Middlesex, have been nominated to view and arbitrate between William

JENNIE We won the case and the fenceviewers made the Fat Lady put in the same kind of tile we had at a dollar a rod. But it was a dangerous victory. *A bell rings.* Time to put a stone in one of the fenceviewer's threshing machines, and that is why, as they all had things happen to them of more than just mischief, I call fenceviewing the last of all the occupations.

CHORUS What are the extenuating circumstances, Edmund?

JENNIE We couldn't be flooded out, so something else had to be tried. Rumours were spread at market, mill, tavern and church that we were selling up and leaving the neighbourhood. Then a true report was also spread that we were fixing up our log house and adding a back kitchen. We had been seen talking to a house-framer.

CHORUS Is there nobody here can think what she should be charged with?

JENNIE Charged I was to sweep out the school, because there was to be a wedding dance there that night and it was potato picking time, in the fall of '67 and all our harvest was up at the barn or in stacks closeby. Ah, everyone was coming to that dance because we would be there and the bishop in his flame red robes would appear to say whether we could join the church of Biddulph. The bride has asked you to play, Will. That's been a wish he's had since boyhood.

The dance involves all the actors and extras if possible, maybe not; go through several reels, particularly those involving Mr and Mrs Donnelly dancing down Roman Line formations. Let audience just soak in the watching them all dance—something black about it, something funny. Then the back of the stage goes red, or the windows of the hall go red; there is growing confusion and then voices saying:

CHORUS Your barn's on fire, Donnelly.

A burning-barn model is carried down the line of dancers. We watch the Donnellys looking down at this till it is almost out. William breaks his fiddle, picks up a horseshoe.

JENNIE And what happened when my father and my brothers went to our well?

CHORUS They found the pump broken.

JENNIE But there was a flowing spring, so there was still water to be had, but what did it say chalked on a board over the spring?

CHORUS Over Donnelly's Spring it is written in chalk

MRS DONNELLY No Water for Blackfeet. *This should be chalked on the floor of the stage. The chorus chant this around Jennie and other Donnellys in circles, then as suddenly kneel with their backs to Jennie. Pause. Scene with Stub and Mr Donnelly set up.*

STUB Good morning, Jim. Bad news about your barn last night. I hear you're leaving us.

MR DONNELLY Why would I do that, Mr Stub, when I've just bought some land across the road and need your notary stamp so they tell me, on this piece of paper?

STUB The Mulowney property.

CARPENTER Are you giving up on the idea of making your house larger, Mr Donnelly, or do you still want me to

MR DONNELLY I'm not giving up anything, Mr Thompson. Come over for tea this evening and we'll have a talk. I've got a house and a barn for you to work at. And you can start right now by being witness for my signature, where is it, Mr. Stub, that I make my mark? *He puts on his spectacles.*

STUB Hold on a minute, Jim—before you sign. There was a man just in here swearing out an information against your eldest son—James Donnelly Jr.

MR DONNELLY Ah, they're still disputing my son's farm over there.

STUB So you say, but this man says your boys are squatting on property that is his.

MR DONNELLY My son has to live somewhere, Mr Stub, and although the land is a bit swampy he went ahead and made a heavy investment in that property a full year before your informant was heard of.

STUB My God, Donnelly, is it to start all over again? There'll be a fight and each one of your boys'll have seven sons—you shouldn't be buying land in this township, Jim, you should be selling it.

MR DONNELLY The way you talk I'm doing the right thing. Seven times seven is forty-nine they told me once, and we'll need all the property we can get to house the overflow. Why selling my land here would be just what those who burnt down my barn—want.

STUB Here's where you make your mark, Jim. *pause* There isn't enough land in this township for seven Donnellys, Jim.

As Mr. Donnelly is holding the pen, the company makes a big sound with sticks on the floor—the sound of his pen scratching.

JENNIE My father walked out of the store and down the roads of Biddulph.

CHORUS But first he paused and flung back—

MR DONNELLY Gallagher has eight boys. Do you want to know, Mr Stub, why we never hear you complaining of hordes of Gallaghers bursting this township at the seams? Because the Gallaghers vote Tory the way you do now. And I guess it's only Grits who mustn't multiply *pause* like myself. Andy Keefe, wherever are you rolling that barrel to?

KEEFE Up the road apiece.

MR DONNELLY You heard about my barn?

KEEFE I saw the glow in the sky.

MR DONNELLY Andy. What's in the barrel?

KEEFE I'm shamed to admit it, Jim, but it's buttermilk.

MR DONNELLY Why be ashamed. Until they burnt it down you were running a beautiful cheese factory down there on the ruins of your tavern.

KEEFE This is the one thing, Jim Donnelly, that's left behind from that beautiful cheese factory, the third occupation I tried since I came to this settlement of Cain. It alone did not catch fire.

MR DONNELLY Well then, Andy, why are you rolling it along the road here and so far from home? Are you going to see somebody with it or

KEEFE I've got a ticket on the five o'clock train tonight, tickets for my mother and myself, tickets to Michigan and I'm just rolling this first down the road and down their lane and if they're not home I'm leaving it with a note saying—You forgot to burn this.

MR DONNELLY And if they're home, Andy?

KEEFE I've a pretty speech prepared, a speech of thanks prepared for leaving a Blackfoot at the very least a barrel of buttermilk from his cheese factory. *sound* There's Tom Cassleigh galloping after us. I think I'll roll my barrel down this sideroad so you can talk and keep him by you for it's his house I'm delivering this to, Jim.

Cassleigh drives up in a wagon and stops to address Mr Donnelly. This wagon can be mimed with two actors supporting Cassleigh in a ladder, and one actor as horse.

CASSLEIGH Is it Jim Donnelly whose barn was burnt up last evening?

JENNIE What did my father reply?

MR DONNELLY Tom Cassleigh, it is that Donnelly whose barn was burned up last night when he and his family were away at the wedding.

CASSLEIGH We're at the crossroads, Jim, and there's empty roads for miles with nothing on them, no one coming towards us; let's have a talk, Jim.

MR DONNELLY *examining* Tom you've got yourself a new wagon. Sure get down from it and we'll have a talk.

CASSLEIGH New position in the world, Jim, new wagon.

MR DONNELLY *lifting up horses' hooves* New position?

CASSLEIGH Haven't you heard? I'm now the first Catholic Justice of the Peace in this township.

MR DONNELLY Sure, Tom, the bench needs someone of your experience to tell us how it is from all the sides. Why, Tom, there's one new shoe on this horse—it's clean from the forge.

CASSLEIGH What of that?

MR DONNELLY Well, as you know, that horse lost a shoe last night. By the light from our blazing granary my sons found it for you. *Holding up the horseshoe, Donnelly uses it as bait to lure Cassleigh down from his perch, play soccer with it, kick it under the wagon, etc.*

CASSLEIGH Donnelly, give that to me. Yes, we want you out of the township. Last month at haying time we offered you good money for your miserable fifty acres, so see what happened, you Blackfoot face of a dog, you went into town to buy even more land today.

Perhaps Donnelly has got the horseshoe on the end of Cassleigh's whip and dangles it up on the wagon making Cassleigh jump.

Do we have to make the offer again?

MR DONNELLY Oh make the offer again, Tom, and see what we say.

CASSLEIGH We say? Who's on your side?

MR DONNELLY A great many people with good hearts into them.

CASSLEIGH We can change that. For one thing the next drainage dispute won't go your way, with me on the bench.

MR DONNELLY But Tom, maybe we'll take your offer. Tell me what it is. We're at the crossroads, there's no one coming towards us for miles, let us talk.

CASSLEIGH *panting* Would you believe it. We're willing to buy you out at the same price we offered at haying time.

MR DONNELLY And when the Donnellys are gone the whole line will be yours, won't it? No one else to stand up to you or stand up to Mr Stub. There's a thing I said in Ireland once that perhaps you heard.

CASSLEIGH We let you go then, Donnelly, but fathers swore sons to follow you and show you up for the Blackfoot be-by-yourself you were that night.

MR DONNELLY I said something that night and I'll say it again.

CASSLEIGH Donnelly, there's one more turn. *pause* Come and join us again, Jim. We can use your seven sons. Don't count on your Protestant friends. It could have been Stub who burned you out. They use you, Jim, don't you see? Already your sons are blamed for things they do to us. And when we do things to them we're spreading the word it's you.

MR DONNELLY *throwing the horseshoe under the wagon and visibly affected by this* You damn weasel, sneaking in and out behind the wheels of your cart. Yes, let me out of Biddulph.

CASSLEIGH *silky* We'll let you out of Biddulph, Jim. Follow your other Blackfoot friend to Michigan if you like.

MR DONNELLY *pause* No, this is a new country we live in, it's not back in the old country we're living. Mrs Donnelly and myself are free to do as we please. No one has to be afraid of secret societies, secret people; we're not in Ireland, do you hear, Tom Cassleigh.

Donnelly is now after Cassleigh.

CASSLEIGH In the daytime, Jim. But at night—confess, you dream your dream you are back under Keeper's Hill and the Whitefeet knock on your door to ask you some questions.

MR DONNELLY No.

CASSLEIGH This is your last chance then. Get out. You killed one of us and you must pay in exile or kind.

JENNIE But in crawling under the wagon after the horseshoe my father had thrown there, Mr. Cassleigh in reaching for it—jammed his shoulder in the spokes of his wagon wheel—his horses moved a bit and he was pinned.

MR DONNELLY Aye, I killed, shure I killed—fighting for my name and my family and my land in hot blood. On this very road down at the tracks you killed—by cold proxy. Having myself seven sons and a girl I ask you what children have you? What have you got between your legs, Cassleigh—a knife? And you're afraid of us. *searching around for a stick* You're so afraid of not having that horseshoe you've got yourself stuck beneath your own wagon, haven't you. My wife, Tom, is the only person in this settlement who ever stood up to you. She stopped you from cutting up Donegan and until she's afraid and wants to leave I'm not either. Now—I'll beat your horses with this stick and they'll gallop off with your face down in the gravel. *Once he finds the stick, some gesture with it parallels the stick action in the scene with Farl.*

CASSLEIGH Donnelly!

The horses shift, but Cassleigh is still trapped.

MR DONNELLY Hush. Not so loud or they'll bolt. There, there, my beauties. Why you caught your arm trying to reach for the horseshoe; here I'll put it a bit closer. I'll jam it right into your mouth, Cassleigh. Bite onto it, there. *He frees him and pushes him up onto his wagon.* Did you think, Cassleigh, my boy, that after being away from my land for seven years I was going to run away from it because you faction of sneaks said so? Look at this road. *scooping up gravel* This part of the road your grand new cart rolls on I was the first pathmaster of. I built this road before you were ever heard of or the Fat Woman and her husband who got half our farm away from us. Before Stub drove out the Africans and you killed the Englishman, I helped make this road with Andy Keefe who you've finally chased out, to your shame. Well, Tom, there's some horse dung; I didn't put that in my road, but have it anyhow. You drove out Donegan, but you'll never get Donnelly's oak tree nor drive out his wife. Hold tight to you seat; here, take the reins, because I'm going to larrup your horses one great larrup to show their master who's the master of this road. *whack* You ask me to kneel, do you? And swear? *He throws stones after the retreating wagon.* Donnellys don't kneel.

CHORUS Where is your father, Will?

JENNIE A dozen years after this a mob led by Tom Cassleigh, and by this time he had turned nearly everyone against us, at night, this mob broke into my father's house, clubbed them to death and then burnt the house down over my mother and father's heads. *She is looking directly through ladder rungs at Cassleigh.*

CHORUS Boys, how old are you now?

JENNIE Two of us were old enough to see what had happened. Patrick left when he married, so did I. Old enough, coward enough, I mean. We could see that we could never join that Church that the bishop had finally come to with fire for mitre and a torch for a crook and had not just slapped us all lightly on either cheek as token for the sufferings we must endure as followers of Jesus, no—the old ruffian had knocked us on the floor, to the floor and kicked us with his hooved boot and punched us with his thistle mitts and said: get the hell out, you bugger Donnellys. No water for you, but we've fire.

CHORUS Why was I created lame?

JENNIE Let me think about the answer to that one, Will, is it

CHORUS Why was I a Donnelly?

Distribute this speech among the women; some men join in later.

JENNIE Because from the courts of Heaven when you're there you will see that however the ladders and sticks and stones caught you and bruised you and smashed you, and the bakers and brewers forced you to work for them for nothing, from the eye of God in which you will someday walk you will see *use ladders held up and moved back and forth by the cast* that once, long before you were born, *sometimes together, sometimes solo* you chose to be a Donnelly and laughed at what it would mean, the proud woman put to milking cows, the genius trotting around with a stallion, the old sword rusted into a turnip knife. You laughed and lay down with your fate like a bride, even the miserable fire of it. So that I am proud to be a Donnelly against all the contempt of the world. I am proud that my mother confirmed my brother in the forest with the fiddle, long before the bishop and the friar could get hold of him, and I wish now I had shared my mother's fate beside her. *solo* But oh, still would it have been different. I loved my mother and I nearly saved her even three days before they burnt her with their coal oil.

Because you were tall; you were different/and you weren't afraid, that is why they burnt you first with their tongues/then with their kerosene.

train whistle

And there were other times I tried and there was this dream about the time I tried and was to try. And the dream I am going to show you repeats itself to me like a creed I have learned I cannot tell when.

Barking of a dog. Mr and Mrs Donnelly appear very neatly dressed as for a journey, or like figures in a legend.

I dream that I've come up to visit the farm, my mother and father are all alone, the boys are all away and I persuade them to leave with me. Before something happens. Good. Because if they leave, then the boys can leave; but if they stay then the boys have to fight for their parents and their work all the time. There's a train we have tickets for and—it stops at the crossing near Andy Keefe's tavern. We have lots of time, except—

MR DONNELLY Jennie, we can't leave. The little dog you sent us for a present. Where is he? *whistles* The devil a dog is he, he doesn't seem to want to come with us.

JENNIE We spent five minutes catching the dog. *train whistle* And we start walking down the road, when my mother looks back.

Raise the clothesline of shirts here.

MRS DONNELLY Jennie, the boys' shirts are all left out on the line. I was sure we took them in and it's going to rain. *barking—*

Mrs Donnelly folds up the clothesline.

JENNIE So we take in the shirts, but the little dog I gave them—

MRS DONNELLY No, no, Jennie. There's lots of time. The train will wait. Now you watch, Mr Donnelly. He'll come to me. He likes a piece of bread. Now there. Hold onto him this time, Jim. *The shirts appear on the line again.*

JENNIE I knew it to be a dream even in the dream because there was still time to catch the train but—there they were on the line again. Mother, come anyhow. We'll wait at the station for the next train.

MR DONNELLY *helping his wife take in the shirts* Your mother's bringing her sons into the house out of the rain. Will our daughter not come in as well?

JENNIE *kneeling* Mother—father—you've changed your minds about leaving then?

MRS DONNELLY About leaving—oh yes, Jennie.

MR DONNELLY We're not to buy the farm in Michigan after all, Jennie. Wait till next year and this wheat the boys have sown is harvested.

MRS DONNELLY Jennie, your father and I will never leave Biddulph.

The parents stand watching Jennie. Singing the "Barley Corn Ballad", the cast make a pile of sticks and a pile of stones on the stage and leave them.

The

St Nicholas Hotel

Wm Donnelly Prop.

THE ST NICHOLAS HOTEL, WM DONNELLY, PROP.: The Donnellys, Part II is written by James Reaney and was first performed at the Tarragon Theatre on November 16, 1974 with the following cast:

Ken Anderson
Nancy Beatty
Jay Bowen
Tom Carew
Peter Elliott
David Ferry
Jerry Franken
Rick Gorrie
Miriam Greene
Michael Hogan
Patricia Ludwick
Don MacQuarrie
Keith McNair
Gord Stobbe
Suzanne Turnbull

Directed by Keith Turnbull

Designed by Rosalyn Mina

The original playing time was:

Act One—48 minutes
Act Two—59 minutes
Act Three—49 minutes

The story of this play concerns a race, a race between the Donnelly boys and their enemies. The road the race takes place on has tollgates with signs on them saying: NO DONNELLYS ARE TO... run a stage line, marry my daughter, & c., & c.. 'Helped' by their brothers, William & Michael Donnelly smash through most of the tollgates, but their victories only drive their enemies to build stronger & stronger barriers until, at last, Michael is suddenly & brutally murdered.

It is a tale of barrooms, wheels, horses, nuns, tops, convent yards, derailed trains, homeless boys, tavern brawls, refinements, squalors, wedding cakes, drunkards—and ghosts. In a certain hotel deserted for thirty years there is a stain on the floor no ordinary scrubbing brush can ever wash away.

JAMES REANEY

MOTHER ...but we're outdistancing him I see, here we are shut up in a box with four wheels and the window blinds down for the heat...

The St Nicholas Hotel Wm Donnelly Prop.

Act One

The barroom of the City Hotel, London; later on it will be the barroom of the Royal Hotel in Exeter, the St Nicholas Hotel (Wm Donnelly, prop.) in Appin and Slaght's Hotel in Waterford. The barman seems always there; his somewhat skullish face and presence will remind us later on before we go to sleep that—this is the man who eventually killed Mike Donnelly. Behind the bar is a picture of Wm Donnelly's black stallion, Lord Byron. Passengers to the stages to the north slowly fill the benches at the sides of the room we too are waiting in; we see actors spinning tops (each one seems to have one) and hear them singing songs from the play. Like a cloud shadow the stage picture is slowly invaded now by the story of a road; the actors stop being actors and become fighters for the ownership of that road, a map of which goes all around the walls of the theatre from Crediton to Exeter to Clandeboye down to Lucan to Elginfield to London to St Thomas to Waterford, and advancing towards us comes the

STAGEDRIVER (NED BROOKS) *belching* Are there any passengers for Masonville, St John's, Bobtown, Ryan's Corners, Lucan, Flanagan's Corners, Mooretown, Exeter? Now loading at the front door please.

MIKE DONNELLY Are there any more ladies and gentlemen for Calamity Corners as tis sometimes called, St John's, Birr—my old friend Ned here calls it Bobtown, the more elegant name is Birr. Elginfield known to some as Ryan's Corners, Lucan that classic spot if it's not all burnt down, Clandeboye, Mooretown, Exeter **and** Crediton. If Ned here hasn't sawn it to pieces the coach is waiting for you at the front door and it pleases you.

STAGEDRIVER What does it matter if it's Bobtown or Birr; elegance be damned, Mike Donnelly, it's my team will get you there faster.

LADY *coming back in* Which stage is yours then? Louisa, there are no less than four stages out there all with different names. Sir wh–

STAGEDRIVER The Favourite Line
Hawkshaw's Stage
Good Horses, Comfortable Stages & Fast Time. Leaves the City Hotel for all points north at two o'clock, p.m.

William & Mike Donnelly pass out announcement cards.

ANCIENT STAGEDRIVER *entering & flourishing a ragged whip* Come on everybody, Ho! for the North Uriah Jennings here, fifty years on the road, *coughing*

YET ANOTHER STAGEDRIVER Anybody here want a lift up north. You'll have to share the accommodation a little with

LADY TWO Martha, he's got six young pigs, two geese and a sack of flour in there already.

CHORUS *reading cards*
Notice
Exeter, Lucan & London Daily Stage: Change of Time.

WILL Leaves City Hotel at 2 p.m. and arrives Maclean's Hotel, Lucan at half past four

MIKE twenty minutes ahead of all other stages.

Both halves begin together, but the first half pauses so the names are spoken after the second half has completed its speech:

HALF CHORUS	HALF CHORUS
drivers	calling all places along the route for passengers

William and Michael Donnelly

Into the bar comes a hard-driving Irishman who has as much force as the Donnellys but all as hard as grindstone

FINNEGAN Just a minute there, Donnelly–whoa!! You boys aren't going to Lucan today.

WILL *with whip* It's Patrick Finnegan says we won't get to Lucan?

FINNEGAN Ah, yes, Will, because *to audience* good evening—don't you know my brother John Finnegan and myself, Pat, have bought out your boss and all his horses and wagons, so it's the Finnegan Stage now. Come along now, these passengers are mine, the road is mine and the wheels. Give your whip to my driver, Will. Mr. Brooks, here's—he's driving for me, Will. I don't need you Donnelly boys. *tries to take whip*

MIKE Give that whip back to my brother. *grabbing it* No one ever lent us a whip.

WILL No, my father bought me that whip with the very first money I ever earned, on St Nicholas day—five years ago and that's how long we've been driving our stage.

FINNEGAN There you go, Will, it was never your stage. It belonged to Hugh McPhee and now it belongs to Pat Finnegan. We leave at two p.m. sharp, ladies and gentlemen, passengers reach Lucan safely to connect with east and west trains to St Marys and Sarnia.

MIKE Do you want to know, Mr. Pat Finnegan, how Will and Mike Donnelly will still beat you to Lucan today by a good half hour?

FINNEGAN It's my brother and myself here run a store and tavern up the road north of here—why the place is called after our father Finnegan's Corners, for God's sake, there were three hundred buggies at his funeral. Sure our father built the Proof Line Road these fellows say is theirs. So step up into my stage wagon and see whose road it is. Mike Donnelly, we'll run yous off it. Are there anymore passengers— *exit*

MIKE Look, we're starting our own line with our own equipment. Mr. Jennings, how much do you want for your vehicle that's been fifty years on the road. Will, just take a look at his beasts.

WILL We'll have to get new horses, fast ones, where we can get—

CHORUS William Donnelly, Groom.

The actors "melt" into a scene at the London races. They are held back from the track by a long rope. The barman jumps up on the bar and interprets the race through a megaphone. We only hear the drumming of invisible hooves and see on human faces the effect of the race.

MIKE	BARTENDER
The horses for our stage line were bred from the winner of	The second day's meeting of The London Turf Club on the Newmarket race course attracted a large crowd yester-

this race. We had the rights to a mare called Irish Girl whose mother you may recall was Billet Doux grandmother to Sir Walter Scott. So, Will, is it let this race decide who'll sire the foal that is the nighhorse of our team on—what'll we call it.

Get a pool of extra silence around the naming of the line

WILL
The Opposition Stage

day afternoon. The weather was delightful and the track in good condition, except that it was a trifle dusty.

CHORUS
over & under Words blown away by the wind, dust & words in the stream of the time we all lie dreaming in

CHORUS
dreaming of horses and wagons going up the hill

This speech and the ones below go on simultaneously with Will's "Opposition Stage" coming in just after the Chorus's "dreaming in". The Bartender should blur his voice under and over the other levels so that we get the effect of a real racetrack where wind & distance play tricks with announcements; also it is a remembered racetrack where Mike Donnelly not only saw the horse they needed but also the first omen of his own death.

BARTENDER Dash of 1½ miles. Entries. Sleepy Jim, bay stallion & his colours are blue & yellow owned by Messrs Bookless & Thomas, Guelph. Florence Nightingale, gray mare. Scarlet & white.

CHORUS Down the hill

BARTENDER Lord Byron, full brother to Clear Grit out of Fleetwood the Second. He thus comes of good stock & will be heard of further.

CHORUS Long white road

BARTENDER Black & red, and *an actor runs around as Lord Byron —sometimes disappearing from view, then reappearing and followed avidly by all of the spectators' eyes* they're off! Although the delay in starting caused a good deal of impatience this, ladies and gentlemens, is an ex—citing dash. From the first it lies between Sleepy Jim, Nigger Baby & Lord Byron and, ladies & gents, as they first pass the string they are well abreast. On the turn, however, they're breaking up & now it's an open question.

It's an open question, ladies & knights, which is going to win. It's Sleepy Jim, no it's Lord Byron—past the string slightly ahead of Finnegan who flashed up from behind with Nigger Baby third. Lord Byron ran, ladies & gentlemen, without his regular *gasp from the crowd who see the jockey's death before the barman does* trainer & his victory here today is therefore a greater tribute to his speed. Sorry. Sorry to report. There seems to have been an accident there to Lord Byron's jockey among the oak trees there at the edge of the grove. A low branch.

CHORUS Words blown away by the wind, dust & words in the stream of

BARTENDER Time. Two minutes forty-nine & a half seconds.

Two human runners in singlets appear—one of them is Detective McCrimmon whom Finnegan will one day hire to pursue the Donnellys

BARTENDER Next ladies & gentlemen, it is calculated to have a foot race in addition, 100 yards, for a shake-purse. BANG!

The runners sweep toward us and then—whistles! and the actors all turn into a herd of horses in a Biddulph pasture; the Donnellys with their father have come to take out a team for evening training. Umbrella, fiddle.

MIKE Our father and another old man helped us to train the horses. Ploughboy! Pilot!

MIKE & CHORUS Farmer. Indian.

MIKE You see our horses came running to their names!

MIKE & CHORUS Manilla. Ginger.

A team comes up for training, umbrella thrown at them, horses shy, then calm. Slowly, all the horses grow used to umbrella & fiddle.

MR DONNELLY Throw the frightening old floppy thing at him again, Mike. And again. There my beauty. Again. There. Whisper to you. The fiddle, Will. *excruciating notes* There my beauty, my dove.

We return from the horse pasture to the tavern; crowd is a crowd once more.

MIKE Our brother Patrick had been apprenticed to a Carriage Works in town here. As a blacksmith. He helped turn the rusty old vehicle we bought from Jennings into a pretty smart, smooth road bird with new wheels for wings.

anvil in distance

FINNEGAN Are there any more passengers for London? Sure you'll want to see Mr Barnum's Circus that's in town today and we've put on an extra stage just to accommodate the crowd.

WILL & MIKE On the sides of our stage what did we have painted?

CHORUS *with varying strength and texture*

The Opposition Stage.
Between London & Crediton
through Exeter daily at 4 a.m.
First Rate Accommodation Prices Moderate
Proprietor, William Donnelly,
Driver, Michael Donnelly.
William Donnelly, Gentlemen.

LADY Prices moderate, Mr. Donnelly? How much is a ticket to Lucan on your conveyance?

WILL Seventy cents, m'am.

TWO GIRLS Mr Finnegan, does your stage go into Crediton?

FINNEGAN Shure, and it can be induced to.

TWO GIRLS Are you entirely sure because your advertisement notes your destination as Exeter which is just four mile short of where Uncle Dan Philip lives.

FINNEGAN Girls, I'll get you there if I have to take yous on my back. *to lady*—Sixty cents.

A routine where she wavers between Finnegan & Donnelly, running back & forth.

WILL Fifty

FINNEGAN Forty it is.

WILL & MIKE Thirty it is.

FINNEGAN Donnelly! Twenty, Madam.

WILL Sure that's nothing at all. We'll take you for a kiss and a penny. Michael, take the fare.

Held on Mike's arms and another's as in a cart, after being kissed she says

LADY I prefer the Opposition Stage. A smooth ride with fast, evenly matched horses. Polite & skillful drivers. One hardly knows where the time has gone when—the diligence stops, the driver jumps down, *but cows are faintly mooing, as if we had reached her farm, and the actors giggling under her effusiveness have crept around to confront her as embarrassing cows* with firm hand takes yours and helps you across to your very gate.

CHORUS Her father's cows have come to meet her. *laughter*

FINNEGAN Allaboard for the circus excursion. *horn which he or his driver blows* Here comes Finnegan. Here comes Finnegan. *Will Donnelly walks behind the bar and lights a candle as we slide into the next scene. Most of the tavern crowd depart. We hear them getting into the stage & driving off. More horn blasts & "Here comes Finnegan". "The Favourite Stage". Behind Will Donnelly there is a picture of a black horse. His wife Norah brings in a tray of glasses and sets them behind the bar. The light changes. Fiddle. Wind.*

CHORUS *a drifting voice* Yes, Bill Donnelly ran the St Nicholas Hotel down here at Appin. Was still running it when he died in the nineties. My father bought me some ice cream there in 1924.

And now we are at the St Nicholas Hotel, years after what we have just been watching

NORAH Well, so our visitor will not stay the night, is that

WILL He'll come back. I put something in his cutter

NORAH It's too stormy a night for anyone to come out save the odd traveller like this reverend gentleman. But perhaps he's right, he should push on to Glencoe now rather than in the morning.

WILL No, He's going to stay here tonight. You'll see.

NORAH Are you that lonely, Will?

WILL Well, if he does not come back maybe we should call up the children and have a game of dominoes. *pause* Norah, you know the sort of travellers we get at the St Nicholas Hotel —grain-buyers and sewing machine agents, but—and neighbours into the bar here, but—it's seldom anyone comes down this road from the past, from up there. *The candle wavers.*

NORAH Hsst! That blast came from Biddulph for sure. Sure there's water from there flows by here, in the river doesn't there. But the reverend gentleman did not seem Biddulphian to me, Will.

WILL We'll find out. I've met him somewhere in the seventies when Mike and me drove stage.

NORAH So that's why you've lit the candle. I'd forgotten, forgive me, tonight's

WILL Tonight's the night they murdered Mike, Norah. In a bar not unlike this one

Enter Minister with a block of ice in his hands.

NORAH Sir, you've come back to us out of the storm?

DONALDSON Who put this block of ice to my feet in my cutter?

WILL I did, now I'll ask my son to put up your horse *through a door* Jack, we've a customer after all.

DONALDSON I had to come back to find out why—

WILL To keep your feet warm, you might as well stay with us, sir. What time is your appointment tomorrow in Glencoe?

DONALDSON Sabbath School starts at nine. But how would that keep me warm?

WILL By bringing you back to my St Nicholas Hotel instead of you driving seven miles on through a blizzard. It's warmer here than that.

He takes the ice block and puts it in a pail; all through the evening we watch it slowly melt till it is used by the scrubwomen at the end of the play to wipe Mike Donnelly's blood off the floor.

DONALDSON Now, sir, I've met you somewhere before. The name of the hotel you are running is the St Nicholas Hotel, proprietor is–

WILL My name is William Donnelly. *pause* Perhaps you'll want to hitch up your cutter again.

DONALDSON Now why would you say that, Mr Donnelly?

WILL Aren't you afraid of me?

DONALDSON No. Quite the contrary. I remember you and your brother when you ran the stage between London and Lucan, excuse me **one** of the stages. The Opposition Stage.

NORAH That must be a good many years ago, sir. Twenty years?

DONALDSON More than that. I started visiting the Presbyterian Church in Lucan on appointments which I would receive, oh let me see now—the fall of 1875. I preferred your stage although people at the church warned me not to patronize your line. *to us* Once I happened to come down to Lucan from Parkhill by train—hence to Irishtown by your rival's stage—The Finnegan Line. The Finnegan Line. I asked the driver how the new railway had affected the stage route between London and Lucan. What has become of the Donnellys?

STAGEDRIVER *belching* Ugh, the Donnellys've been run off the line at last.

DONALDSON And what do they do now then?

STAGEDRIVER Yes, what don't they do, sir. They're a bad lot and we're bound to get rid of them.

DONALDSON Yes, Mr Donnelly. A small glass of wine would not go amiss. Thank you. Then I said *to him* It's strange that young men so good looking and so polite as I've always found the Donnelly boys to be, should be so much run down and set on by all parties, Romanists, Protestants and Secretists, when they are so very polite and strive so hard to live down all this opposition, by attention to business and kind treatment of all who favour them. He replied:

STAGEDRIVER You do not know them, sir. They just put on appearances to deceive strangers. I once thrashed Mike and I will thrash him again.

DONALDSON *pause* Which son is Mike?

STAGEDRIVER The second from the youngest. No sir, the people are bound to get rid of that family some way or another and that too before too long.

DONALDSON We had reached the railway station and I told him what I thought as a teacher of the Gospel. I said: "You surely do not mean what you say, or you would not speak so to a stranger: there's room enough for the Donnellys and their opponents also in the world. Why, man, competition is the life of trade; we are all the better of the opposition lines."

STAGEDRIVER *laughing* You're too good yourself, sir, to understand what this family is like. **We** are bound to snuff out that family and we shall do it, so that it shall never be known how it was done.

DONALDSON He turned on his heel and left. So, yes, I was never afraid of the Donnellys. William Donnelly. Mike Donnelly.

WILL About when would that conversation be?

DONALDSON In January of 1879. As early as that

WILL As early as that then we were marked out for slaughter.

DONALDSON Mike, what happened to Michael Donnelly?

WILL Oh they got him first at the end of that year—just before Christmas, December the 9th, 1879.

DONALDSON This is the 12th Anniversary of his death then? *pause* I find it very pleasant to be sitting by such a warm fire after travelling through such a storm this afternoon. *They listen to the gale outside for a few moments.* You have settled here, Mr Donnelly, in this peaceful place after a stormy journey far worse. Far worse.

WILL Yes, I keep the inn here, I travel about in the spring with my stallion—True Grit out of Lord Byron and this may astonish you, but people are saying that I am the best constable this village ever had.

NORAH Sir, I am going upstairs with a warm brick for your bed. I promise you no more ice blocks. How soon do you wish to retire?

DONALDSON I may never drive this way again. Midnight. Until then Mrs Donnelly, I should like your husband to explain what lay behind the bloody statement of that young man at the railway station. Why did they all hate you so much?

NORAH Oh sir, that would take till the dawn itself. *passing out of the room*

WILL I'll tell you why the stage drivers for the other lines hated us so much. *He takes a scissors from Norah's sewing basket.* They blamed us for cutting the tongues out of their horses. Like this. *laughing & illustrating!* But at first it was something not quite so Sodom & Gomorrah we were blamed for.

Screams & curses off stage; some monumental collapse of Mr Finnegan's stage. Yes, a wheel has come off, for into the barroom it rolls. Passengers enter, shaken & muttering.

FINNEGAN Who in the mother of Hell's name loosened the bolts and cut the nuts off my wheels. Oh funny it is, Cripple, and one of my wheels skated right into your hands, and funny it is, Mike. Well it wouldn't be so funny if I'd been going down Mother Brown's Hill and they'd come off; we'd been all killed. *pause* Ladies & gentlemen, be patient for the twenty-minute delay there'll be while we fix up the wheels. You see what they done, don't go in his stage, you see what they done to me. Oh, Alec *to bartender* give me anything you got, oh

MIKE Now, are there any more passengers for St. John's, Birr, Elginfield, Lucan, Finnegan's Corners, Mooretown, Exeter, and even Crediton.

He has been outside for a quarter of this; we hear his voice again outside and nearly the whole chorus eventually decide to follow the hypnotic elegance. Left now are only a maidservant (Maggie) and the Fat Lady.

MIKE Now leaving the City Hotel—the Opposition Stage.

MAGGIE Cousin Patrick, do me a pleasant thing and allow me to take the Opposition Stage out of town. They'll be put out with me I'm late to serve dinner.

In a necessary manoeuvre we can't see, the Donnelly Stage goes around the hotel, so that it circles the barroom and Maggie follows it inside in a circular, birdlike, trapped motion.

FINNEGAN Your father says, Maggie, you're to have no truck with the Donnellys, shun them and if you get on with them I'll drag you off of—I'll tell your father, miss.

MAGGIE No need to, Patrick Finnegan, I'll do that myself *pause wavering* Some day. Well how long do I have to wait then, for the sake of heaven?

FINNEGAN How do I know, the blacksmith made no—but I swear I'll get them, for it's only them would do a trick like that, loosen my wheels *runs outside* I'll snuff them...

FAT LADY Maggie Donovan I'd wait a week, a year not to have to take that Blackguard's Donnelly wagon. I'd walk up to Biddulph on my bare knees rather than use their coach.

MAGGIE Would you now.

FAT LADY Why girl, it's them and their mother cheated us out of half the farm that should've been ours. Don't you know how their old woman put a spell on my cows so they bear freemartens and my daughter is barren. Have you no ears?

FINNEGAN The wheels are back on, Maggie. We'll catch up to them. At Holy Corners. Why yes, why won't we. He's got the weight of all my passengers—

MAGGIE And you've got the weight of only one of his—Here comes Finnegan! Tootletee too!

FINNEGAN Onto the stage, girl. Don't you dare make mock of me.

MAGGIE I won't go. *Fat Lady & Finnegan chase her all over the barroom until he picks her up in his arms and carries her out.*

FINNEGAN Well, you will. You will even if I have to hitch you to the wagon and drag you to Lucan. *horn* The stage for Lucan, the favourite line. Here comes Finnegan, Aroint thee, ye jades, I'm after you, Donnelly.

Whip sounds &c. but also Maggie laughing. In the fading light the bartender with his skullish face listens & thinks.

BARTENDER *He comes towards us and actors with tollgates mime the flow of the road against him.* Finnegan's stage and Donnelly's stage goes north on the road that goes north from here through crossroads and tollgates and Lucan until the road is outside the parsonage of the English priest.

The barroom clock strikes six. A **decisive** *lady at the top of her youth, Miss Maguire enters & rings a servant bell. She has managed the parsonage for her father ever since her mother's death ten years ago.*

MAGGIE You rang, m'am.

MISS MAGUIRE That chamberpot needs emptying. Yes, I did ring and I have been ringing to no avail until now why?

MAGGIE Oh, Miss Maguire, the wheels fell off my cousin Patrick's stage.

MISS MAGUIRE Very nice that must have been, was anybody hurt, were you?

MAGGIE Not enough to mention, m'am.

MISS MAGUIRE Your being so late puts me in half a mind to say you cannot go to vespers, but I suppose the priest would denounce me from the pulpit if I did so, could you finish up this room and be at the door till Mr Stub calls.

MAGGIE Yes, m'am.

MISS MAGUIRE And did you leave the silk thread in your basket?

MAGGIE Oh thank you, Miss Maguire, I was so afraid you'd keep me in for being late, just dump the basket out and you'll find the thread, never mind my things.

She goes out with the chamberpot; Miss Maguire looks into the basket. Off stage we hear: "Good evening, Mr Stub. The upstairs drawing room, if you please sir." The Reverend Maguire enters first; an old, snowy vicar.

MR MAGUIRE Daughter?

MISS MAGUIRE Father? Mr Stub is coming to see me tonight.

MR MAGUIRE Then I shall drop in later, Mercilla I've no intention of ruining your tête à tête with the foremost merchant of Main Street.

MISS MAGUIRE Are you composing your sermon? I shall tell him that is why you are absent. I suppose you are wondering what I am doing in the maidservant's basket.

MR MAGUIRE Did she give you permission to rumple it out like that?

MISS MAGUIRE Oh yes. You're always worrying about the servants, father.

MR MAGUIRE We are servants too, you know, Mercilla. *He fades away.*

MAGGIE *still with chamberpot* Mr Stub to see you, ma'am.

GEORGE STUB *with nosegay for Mercilla* Good evening, Mercilla.

MISS MAGUIRE Thank you, Mr. Stub. I'd ask Maggie here to put these in some water in a vase, but I'm terrified what she might do. So. Do please be seated, Father is busy in his study with next Sunday's sermon, I'm finding the silk thread for the banner you're having me mend and so—what else?

GEORGE I've bought the land for a house on what the villagers call Quality Hill.

MISS MAGUIRE Is it going to be what size of a house, George Stub?

GEORGE I want you to decide how big it should be, Mercilla.

MISS MAGUIRE Because I'm to be the mistress of it, is that it?

GEORGE *sweating* Yes.

MISS MAGUIRE And you're not married to someone else already?

GEORGE I've been alone in my bed for a year & a half now, Mercilla.

MISS MAGUIRE What a way you have of putting things. Why I've been alone in my bed ever since I was born. Well, seeing it's your second marriage and I'm older too than is usual, I feel that I ought to put some things in your way.

GEORGE In my way?

MISS MAGUIRE Yes, because I needn't get married. So—make it worth my while.

GEORGE I've already mentioned the house I'm building.

MISS MAGUIRE Glad you did because I'd not come to live above an old hardware store. Now, here are the rules. After all I'm mending your silly old Masonic banner for you, you do some promising for me.

GEORGE Mercilla.

MISS MAGUIRE Who are you anyway?

GEORGE I've been a self made man. You know what a great thing I've made of the store, and I'm—

MISS MAGUIRE One of the rules I might make tonight is that I expect the man I marry to be somebody, really somebody, like a member of parliament. What about that George?

GEORGE It'll never come to pass. I'm far better behind the scenes. I get too excited in public.

MISS MAGUIRE Didn't I hear you say once that you'd been promised a senatorship if you could get a Conservative candidate in in this riding?

GEORGE Yes.

MISS MAGUIRE Then that's the rules. It's some day to be Senator Stub, or else. I have depths of meanness, George. Don't ruffle them.

GEORGE If I promise to obey the rules, I want things to be clearer.

MISS MAGUIRE You mean when? I'll think it over tonight after you'll be gone.

GEORGE I'd like something on—all this.

MISS MAGUIRE Something on account. Here take my hand.

GEORGE No.

MISS MAGUIRE Oh, my mouth. Here, stop me from talking so much. *Her father enters.*

MISS MAGUIRE Remember sir, I am no widow. You may be a hot blooded widower, but my father has kept me in his parsonage, a chaste spinster, for many more years than Jacob served Laban for both Leah and Rachel. And I haven't minded that a bit.

GEORGE Good evening, Doctor Maguire. It is a pleasure to see you looking so well.

DR MAGUIRE Mr George Stub. How many faces of the poor did you grind in the main street of Lucan today?

GEORGE Business is business, Doctor Maguire I have to foreclose and get my money back sometimes twice in a month.

MISS MAGUIRE Look what treasures I'm finding in the girl's basket. What are these strange lumps of metal, George, and here's a locket. *a small bell rings* Father, Maggie said I could "dump the basket out."

DR MAGUIRE I don't think she meant you to open her locket.

MISS MAGUIRE *tempted and walking about the room* It's the one she's always wearing and she's had the catch fixed by a jeweller in town, why not here in Lucan, ah—George, open it for me.

GEORGE These are the nuts off the axles of a wagon. Her father must have given her a list of things to bring him home on the farm out there. And this—I hate to tell tales on your servant girl, Doctor Maguire, but this is a picture of William Donnelly, William Donnelly Cripple.

DR MAGUIRE Is there no other name you can call him then?

GEORGE No, sir. I'll never call him anything else but that. He and his gang of cutthroats are one of the reasons that this riding often does not return a Conservative Candidate.

MISS MAGUIRE But George, he's devilishly handsome.

DR MAGUIRE Mr George Stub, if I may venture an opinion in the face of your prejudice, I think he has a very sharp intelligent face. So that is Maggie's secret. Do you know I was asked to officiate at his brother Patrick's wedding not so long ago.

GEORGE You would have met the whole monstrous family then.

DR MAGUIRE Monstrous, not at all. They were a very handsome, unusual family with a—as if there was something there they weren't telling you. I disagree with you totally, Mr Stub and here's the text for my sermon. Four wheels! *picking up the nuts* Now as I behold the living creatures, behold one wheel upon the earth by the living creatures, with his four faces. The appearance of the wheels and their work was like unto the colour of a beryl....

GEORGE Mercilla, I must leave. Please show me down.

MISS MAGUIRE Follow me, Mr Stub. Father, George Stub is leaving, oh it is no use when he starts quoting scripture, no use at all. *They leave. As he goes on quoting from the Bible (Ezekiel I) he juggles the four nuts:*

DR MAGUIRE And they four had one likeness; and their appearance & their work was as it were upon a wheel in the middle of a wheel. When they went, they went upon their four sides; and they turned not when they went.

Maggie enters with a cup of tea. She collects the nuts, the locket, and begins to work at the banner with the coloured thread.

MAGGIE Miss Maguire suggests, sir, that you take a drink of this camomile tea to calm your nerves. I have lit the lamp in your bedroom and changed your pillow case.

DR MAGUIRE Ah, I have frightened him away. The Bible is a great help in getting me rid of people I don't like.

MAGGIE Mr Stub is no angel of mercy, sir, but your daughter has to have some sort of life. Surely you don't expect her to be cooped up here in the parsonage by the river on this lonely stretch of the road all her livelong days.

DR MAGUIRE I know what I know. He's the worst of a whole set of flinty hearted shopkeepers, just because my daughter comes from what he knows as an old family he wants her to be the lady in his new big house. You mark my words he'll call it Castle Stub–

Mercilla enters and calmly slides into her father's flow

MISS MAGUIRE George Stub is not going to call his new place Castle Stub, father. He's going to call it after me–Castle Mercilla, that is, if I marry him. Take heart, father, I've put so many obstacles in his way.

DR MAGUIRE The best obstacle is a firm "No". You've no idea what his set, the five families that consider themselves the aristocracy of the village look like from the pulpit. I once dreamt their pale marble faces turned into sheep and I walked around with my crook– *on his way to bed* –until this exquisite pain around my ankles made me look down. There was George Stub, the biggest ram of them all, gnawing away at my leg. Blood.

MISS MAGUIRE *also retiring* Good night, father. Maggie, clear up the teacups. Goodnight. I shan't get up for breakfast, nervous exhaustion, nervous *repeat this last phrase ad libato*

CHORUS *singing*

Oh St Patrick was a gentleman
Who came of decent people
He built a church in Dublin town
And on it put a steeple...
No wonder that those Irish Lads
Should be so gay and frisky
For sure St Pat he taught them that
As well as making whisky...

Maggie clears the chairs of the previous scene, but leaves the Masonic banner Mercilla has been mending in the centre of the floor; as members of the chorus light candles and kneel by their chairs we are changing from Maggie as a servant with a cap to Maggie remembering a world of power and love that might have been hers forever.

MAGGIE As I go to my bed over the kitchen of the parsonage I think I see in the moonlight on the floor–a letter, an envelope coming up through the floor, but it is my sleepy brain remembering what many people would regard as a–the strange thing that happened to me in the church tonight at vespers. *The Vespers service in the background. There are other kneelers.* Will Donnelly crawls under the floor of the church, the old wooden frame church, and he as I kneel is pushing the letter up to me through the cracks in the floor. My father and brother are so against me seeing him that it is only by letter or accident we can meet.

WILL *lying down* I sent her my picture which she had cut out to be placed in a locket.

MAGGIE And I in turn pushed a letter down through the crack in the floor. *A letter comes down from above into William's hand.* I address you with these few lines hoping they will find you in good health as they leave me enjoying the same blessing at present. I thank you for your picture. Until my next birthday you will understand why I cannot wear it in public. Dear William, I was a long time about getting this picture for you. You can keep it now in hopes you think as much of me as I do of you.

WILL In my next letter which she burnt to save it from their attention I proposed marriage and on April the 30th, 1873 my girl replied

MAGGIE I now wish to inform you that I have made up my mind to accept your kind offer, as there is no person in this world I sincerely love but you. This my first & only secret, so I hope you will let no person know about it. But I cannot mention any certain time yet.

They start rolling on the floor towards each other; this ends up with their standing back to back or kneeling back to back or with the banner veil between them. The rolling might be right over each other, but never so that their bodies coincide.

WILL In our dreams we did this & wore the lockets although she was afraid to wear hers in the daylight.

MAGGIE At night I am your wife; in the daytime I drudge for a woman who does not know whether she wants to be married or no. But although my hair is bound up for you and you alone to let down, Will, make no mistake, there was always something between us that summer—a fence, a veil, a muzzle on him, a wall about me, a floor between us. But I cannot mention any certain time yet. You can acquaint my parents about it any time you wish after the first of November next.

WILL *Fiddle; since his letters are lost, we hear him play chords & enharmonics instead.*

MAGGIE Do not think that I would say you are soft for writing so often, for there is nothing would give me greater pleasure than to hear from you, but no matter now. I think soft turns is very scarce about you.

WILL *Fiddle*

MAGGIE No, Will. Those who told you that I said I could never marry a lame boy are liars. If you have ever heard anything of the kind after me and it has given you pain, ask youself if I have ever wanted that for you. If it does not suit you to wait so long, let me know about it, and I will make it all right.

WILL You'll never know, Maggie, how much it's not like me to talk to a woman about that. Because my foot's deformed they think he's not a man. They'd laugh if they knew I write you a letter every day. But, Maggie, they'll come at you about the foot and what can you tell them? Why that he's not a cripple when he's on horseback, nor is he a thing soft when he has a pistol in his hand which makes all men equally tall; *fiddle* nor am I a Cripple when I'm driving or writing or riding I'm—our stage is a bird with wheels for wings and I'm free.

And the scene changes to early morning in Lucan with the two rival stages getting ready for the daily race to London. The convention for the stage wagons should involve at least one wheel each and a solid block of actors "inside" the coach; other actors are the sides of the road and move against the coaches to give the illusion of a journey; a sleepy tollgate man with his gate is the first of a series of such gates which will keep stopping the stages as they gallop down to London. The drivers hitch up horses and check wheels and parcels; passengers.

CHORUS The Opposition Stage

NED BROOKS The Finnegan Stage. My name is Ed Brooks from Exeter. First carefully checking the wheels of my stage with a wrench I climb up determined to beat Donnelly this day, to beat him in the race to London even if it kills me. *A red haired boy makes his first appearance; Tom Ryan.*

MIKE Tom Ryan, you can't come with us today. You should be at home in your father's house. Why you've been sleeping all night in Pilot's manger lad, are you stage struck?

TOM Mike Donnelly, ask your brother if I can go with yous again today. My old man won't let any of us come near the place right now and I watched the stable for you all night. Mike?

WILL Mike, where's the bridle for the off-horse—Ploughboy. Tom Ryan, they sneaked that away on you when you were sleeping—sure you can come, but go up the street and get us a new bridle. Knock on the shutters till they open up. You don't want him along, do you Mike, is that it?

MIKE It's his father I'm thinking of. "The Donnellys've stolen my only son away from me, work him to death on their stage line."

WILL Pilot's shoe is loose, Manilla then. I'll let you drive her then, see if you can control her, my arms were out of their sockets the last time she's such a puller. *horn* *Tom runs up with the new bridle.*

MIKE Ah, but we're having a race today I see so maybe I won't hold him in. *The Finnegan horn blows.* Here comes Finnegan. Put those packages with me, Will. Haw, Ploughboy. Easy does it, Manilla, there girl, there...

CHORUS

Out from the yard of Levitt's Hotel
The Main Street of Lucan all quiet and still
Down the road between Goderich & London

The Tollgate keeper reaches up a cup on a stick; we hear seven pennies.

WILL

Down with that tollgate, Let us out of Lucan
Thank you, Mr. Kelly.

MIKE

Yes we hope to surpass him
We'll win your wager,

CHORUS

a spark in each window,
people getting up

TOM Mike Donnelly, I think the coach is a boat.

MIKE Tom Ryan, it has wheels. Sit into the seat and you can feel the road coming up against our wheels. It's no boat you truant. Where's the sails?

TOM I've heard Will call it a boat once and I see the sea all around us. Somehow I feel like jumping off into the water.

MIKE Did you hear that, Will? On the way back we're putting you in a trunk for safety's sake and our own peace of mind. Where'd you buy the bridle, Tom?

TOM At Mr Stub's store.

MIKE Well, Will, do we turn back?

WILL For a penny I would. That was a foolish thing to do, Tom. Don't you know who our enemies are yet? We'll take it off at Birr, the blacksmith will have one there and, Tom, tonight you must take it back to Mr Stub and tell him it was a mistake.

TOM Why was it a mistake?

MIKE Because we never buy anything from Mr Stub and as you charged the bridle that means he'll be after us for a debt.

CHORUS

So early in the morning, shadows aren't yet and stars still out.
The big elm, St Patrick's, the taverns at Elginfield.

MIKE Open up Mr. Scandrett, Let us out of Biddulph.

This chorus has several "tracks" and ribbons of sound and imagery rippling through it; there's an old doggerel song about the road; there's also a quiet voice naming the concession roads whose numbers get smaller as we get closer to London.

CHORUS

concession 16

Proof Line Road straight down to London
Down the hill, whizzing down, down into the hollow
Rain in our faces, up the hill.

two stages converge on one passenger

FINNEGAN COACH That's our passenger

DONNELLY COACH No, she's ours.

WOMAN But I'm a Finnegan customer

MIKE Too late now, ma'm, and we can't stop for we're in competition and—whree whurrah!! we're ahead of you now, Finnegan!

CHORUS

concession 15

Proof Line Road straight down to London!
Sun's up. Travellers to where we come from
Gallop up to meet us. Up the hill down the hill
The four tavern corners. Holy Corners! *sing*
The taverns they lined each side of the way.
As thick as the milestones in Ireland today.
And then the farmers all thought it was fine
If they once got as far as the London Proof Line.

concession 14

Up to then any man that went for a load

concession 13

Generally spent two days on the road;

concession 12

And I hear that Sam Berryhill says to this day

That some took three—when he kept the Bluejay!

concession 11

MIKE Gate, Mr Walden, why so slow. Wait a minute, how'd he get through the check gate so fast

WILL If he gets a pass, we get a pass. That's not fair.

CHORUS

concession 8

Montgomery House, there, the bar goes east and west!

concession 6

Monaghan's, Talbot's—both bakes bread and brews beer.

concession 5

Up the hill, cross the creek, down the hill to the

concession 4

River valley: McMartin's and the last tollgate

TOM Let us into London, Mr Murrow

CHORUS

& over the river

concession 2

Past the mill, tree branch shadow, up Mount Hope
The Convent of the Sacred Heart

DONNELLY COACH

concession 1

We're turning out to pass him, he's going faster,
watch yourself, Brooks, your front wheel, He's fallen
down on his head. Horses run away. On his head. The front
wheel came off.
At one end of our journey, we'll stop for a while
Watch your step, sir. Take my hand, m'am.
At the City Hotel. No, the Dead House for him.

In the conventions worked out for this accident, Brooks should be held upside down so that his words come from an overturned face. Chorus might try some upside down speech too.

MIKE Oh for God's sake, Will, he's dying. Don't try to talk, Ned we'll put you in our stage and take you to a physician. *pause* He wants to talk to you, Will.

BROOKS I got the other one to come over just when life comes to the edge-place where you can see for ever and ever because you're neither alive nor are you dead. I said, Bill Donnelly, you done this to me and my wife and little ones will curse you and I'll tell you how your brother Mike's going to die. Fair play, neighbour.

They'll never finish scrubbing up his blood. My God, neighbour, I'm gone. They'll never finish scrubbing up his blood.

His body is carried away and laid on the bar.

WILL What did he tell you, Will.

WILL Nothing. Nothing that matters, Mike.

MIKE Look at them looking at us. They all think we killed him.

WILL Yes, Mike. Now how did we kill him? He tightened his wheel at Lucan, but still we managed. Maybe at Swartz's Hotel, or maybe at the Montgomery House at the eighth concession?

MIKE Will. I don't want to drive stage anymore.

WILL Why?

MIKE Odd how there is always something happening when we're by. *pause* So how did his wheel come off then?

WILL Get your head up, my brother. My brother what does it matter whether we killed him or Fortune did. We might just as well have, for they blame us anyhow. Get your head up and we'll turn and face them.

MIKE The boy, did you get him to do it?

WILL *irony* Oh Yes! And Mike. I also got our father to train our horses so well that when Brooks' passenger that was riding beside him fell directly in front of us you were able to stop those horses on a penny, or he'd been cut to pieces instead of standing over there gawping at the Donnelly brothers whose same father failed to train one of his sons still to hold up his head though all the world is thinking you should crawl.

Mike's face clears; he holds up his head and they turn to face a crowd that is growling at them.

CHORUS We the undersigned jurymen summoned upon the inquest held upon the body of Edward Brooks do hereby agree that deceased came to his death from injuries received by being thrown from the Exeter Stage which was caused by the forewheel of said stage coming off and that the deceased came by his death accidentally

This scene dissolves into a bakeshop where a baker poudly shows off a wedding cake to an apprentice.

BAKER Isn't that the lovely object now?

APPRENTICE Who ordered this cake, Pa?

BAKER Why it's for John Finnegan owns the store up at Irishtown, he sent down for it as there is some farmer getting his daughter married in the vicinity. Now what did you find out about delivery?

APPRENTICE Went to the Western Hotel. They say that there'll be no Finnegan Stage today, the driver fell off this morning and got himself killed. So they said to send it with the Donnelly Line – it's the best anyhow for moving a cake and they leave the City Hotel at 2 o'clock.

BAKER By golly, we'll start packing it right away then. Get me some straw. You know I sort of hate to see it get wrapped up in a mere brown paper box.

A city bell rings twelve; a street fiddler plays "Buffalo Gals"; distant sounds. A penny in his cup. The chorus illustrate the shadows changing of the buildings near the City Hotel.

CHORUS

Shadows of the buildings and the trees along the white road
Disappear at noon.
Sun, you golden stage, make our shadows
Passengers again to night, now longer and longer in the stream
We all lie dreaming in

BAKER What can I do for you, sir.

MCKELLAR I'm the new stage driver for Finnegan's stage and I've come to collect the cake his brother ordered here.

BAKER Well, golly, now, we were led to believe that The Finnegan Stage wasn't running today. But we found a way to send the cake.

MCKELLAR What way?

BAKER The Opposition Stage. They're real good at carrying cakes. I've had good reports from customers whereas you people seem to sit on them or – it's too late. They'll have left town by now. With the cake.

MCKELLAR Look you old gossoon, do you not know there's a war on between them and us? I'll catch up to them and I'll get that cake back. *The baker and his boy run out of the shop after the stage-driver in protest.*

Already simply set up; Maggie's father washing feet in the coal scuttle containing the block of ice; his sister & Maggie. Plus another aunt waiting to take Maggie away.

FAT LADY Ever since you came home, Maggie, from service at the English priest's you're so slow in doing things. You was two hours I swear looking for these eggs. Take this switch and keep the flies off your father while I finish packing your trunk.

MAGGIE Pack my trunk, is it. Where am I going then?

AUNT THERESA Maggie, you're welcome to come back with me to Limerick and stay as long as you like where that fellow won't be bothering you.

MAGGIE What fellow won't be bothering me?

FATHER Cripple. Whoever was playing that fiddle under your window last night till all hours, whoever wrote me a lawyer's letter asking for your hand, who came to my door and took me by the beard to tell me how old you are.

MAGGIE And how old am I? Am I not of age All Souls' Day, father?

FATHER I don't know, maybe you'd better call Father Brennan to look it up, in the baptismal register, have you? *pause* But All Souls' Day doesn't change the spots on Cripple, he's a Donnelly and no girl of mine's of age who's thinking of marrying that Cripple. I'd rather see you going to your grave.

MAGGIE Father, if only you'd speak a little faster. Faster! What have you got against Will Donnelly, tell me now, father, you've never told me. Is it the father killing the man at the bee?

FATHER Keep switching the flies off of me, will you? It's evidence not fit for the ears of either a young girl or an old one. He's been the mastermind of a gang in this neighbourhood and fleeces of wool, post offices, derailing a train have been some of that gang's amusements for the last four years until now high and mighty he starts his own stage line.

FAT LADY Brother, this girl'll never understand I'm afraid and it's a secret place we'll have to put such a girl. Her brother is getting married to the proper sort, but no she has to cross battle lines. Have you no gratitude for your upbringing, girl?

MAGGIE All the money I've ever earned as a servant girl you've received, father. I emptied chamberpots so you could buy two new cows. Yes, look at what my brother's marrying. All Mary Egan talks about is cows. Will Donnelly's the only young man around here with brains in his head who didn't go into the priesthood, and no girl is to take a look at him, is it?

AUNT THERESA A fine priest that lame devil would have made.

FATHER Theresa, see if Martin's got the cart hitched up. Maggie, you're right. Will is a clever boy. Clever at getting the forewheel of a stage to roll off so the driver gets killed. Yes. But he is a Donnelly and they are to be left alone. They don't dig with the right foot. They always are digging with the wrong foot. Since Cripple's threatening to come and kidnap her—yes Maggie—Theresa, Tell Martin to drive over to Finnegan's Corners, but when it gets dark to turn & take her down to Gallagher's. That's right by the Donnellys and they'll never think of looking there.

MAGGIE I'll run to him now. Will! Will! Come and rescue me, take me away.

She is pursued; there is a struggle and we see her next taken away tied in a net. We are now moving closer to Finnegan's store at Irishtown; first to a tollgate house where a bag of pennies is poured out for counting. The counting of the money into a tin box goes under the dialogue like the road itself.

MOTHER Come, children, help your father count the take at the tollgate today. The shadows are getting so long they're joining together anymore travellers up or down the road, Sam?

The privy cleaner or cessman comes towards us; he is whistling "Buffalo Gals."

TOLLMAN Just foot travellers. There's that old fellow makes a living cleaning out privies. Good night there, you look dusty.

CESSMAN Oh I doesn't mind the dust, thank thee, Mr. Scandrett.

CHILD He always whistles the same tune doesn't he.

MOTHER Heading north down into Biddulph. What was all that racket today with the second stage that went through.

The tollgate scene begins to move forward and dissolve.

TOLLMAN They were chasing the Donnelly Stage. The Donnellys got away on them with something. A cake. A wedding cake.

We are in Finnegan's store up at Finnegan's Corners.

FINNEGAN No Donnellys are allowed on Finnegan premises ever again no, neither his store nor his tavern nor his very privy.

MIKE Even so, Mr. Finnegan, an express parcel from the Forest City Confectionery on Horton Street. Where shall I set it down?

FINNEGAN I said get out, Mike Donnelly.

MIKE Now, now, Mr Finnegan, I do believe it is a cake. I'll just set it down on the floor here and that will be Cash on Delivery two dollars, twenty-seven and a half cents.

FINNEGAN Don't you dare tell me it had to be by your line that cake come, when I've got my own stage line, now get that bloody parcel out of here.

MIKE Well, it is a puzzle but the upshot of it was that our Opposition Stage was preferred. Twenty-seven and a half cents plus two dollars. Careful, Finnegan, it's a cake.

FINNEGAN Is it now, well it's a *he kicks it around the shop.*

MIKE I see how it is, Mr Finnegan. We have to pay for the cake, do we. You should know all about that, you're the bailiff of the Division Court up here, and another thing before I say Goodnight—don't take any more passengers to Crediton. We bought the rights there, you have not got them. Good evening, Mr Finnegan.

Finnegan backs him out of the store with a gun. Bill & Mary Donovan come forward behind the dissolving Finnegan with a quilt which is their wedding bed.

BILL Come to bed, Mary. I'm told it's our wedding night.

MARY Well, you're the boss now, but it did just cross my mind.

BILL What crossed your mind?

Maggie's father is quietly washing his feet in the tub William Donnelly put the ice block in.

MARY Did you never hear of the custom of leaving the bride alone for three nights.

BILL Yes, I have, now why don't you get into the bed?

MARY It did just cross my mind that—they'll come looking here for Maggie.

BILL *yawning* Who'll come looking—

MARY Bill Donnelly and his gang.

BILL Well, they won't find her. She was in the cellar during the wedding, but she's crying in the garret at Gallagher's now. Father keeps moving her, and Will Donnelly keeps just missing her. You should of seen the letter he wrote Pa.

WILL Dear friend, my sole business last night (yes, I was in the crowd myself) was to have satisfaction for some of your mean low talk to your daughter that never deserved it. I want you to understand, dear sir, that I will have my revenge. You or your son will be prepared to receive me and my Adventurers before long again, and if old friend I want it impressed on your mind that if the business must be done on the way to church I can get any amount of men to do it so you may just as well stop getting yourself into trouble first or last.

MARY Sending his gang of scoundrels into your father's house and pretending it was a tavern and them constables searching for a horse-thief when all the time it's Maggie they want.

BILL So come on then.

MARY Is she never to be married off then, or what is to be done with her?

BILL She'll either marry one of the Gallagher boys who's soft on her by next Saturday, or then it's Lent and it's too late to get married so I think Father plans to let the sisters take care of her. If I were her—

MARY *getting into bed* Good, then this nonsense will be over. Galloping around the countryside trying to kidnap your lovely sister because he loves her. She doesn't really love that Cripple, does she?

BILL Mary, she does love him, and I don't blame her for it. I do blame her for not making a run for it, but I suppose she can't.

MARY Oh a woman can never do that. The man would never marry her then. How can you say she could really love him?

BILL Mary, she does. If ever I saw love. Not like us. Your mother and my father put us together like a pair of cattle.

Shivaree serenaders gather in the shadows.

MARY Speaking of cows, Bill Donovan, what sort is your cows?

BILL Don't you like my cows?

MARY I never saw such miserable calves as them two you had in the yard today. Maybe it's late they were

BILL Cows, Mary, always cows.

MARY That's how the Egans and the Trehys got where they are now. Cows

BILL And where might that be now?

MARY Why I think one of them's in bed with a young bull, or is that not what you think you are sir?

BILL Ah, Mary

MARY Take it back then that your sister really loves Will Donnelly, that cripple and devil.

BILL She never loves him, I was wrong, it's a lie.

MARY That's better now— *knocking* Hark! there's somebody going to shivaree us.

VOICES Shivaree!

MARY Get them to go away. Give them some whisky, Mother of God, it is the Donnellys, Bill.

MIKE Tell us where Maggie is and we'll go away.

BILL *at window* Boys, she's not here now and if she were she'd say to leave her alone.

MIKE Oh no you don't. We got a letter here from Maggie. She says she's being held against her will and to come and get her.

BILL Mary, shall I tell them she's at Gallaghers' and get them off our backs? *she runs and stops his mouth at the window.*

MARY You tell them where your sister's hidden & I'll withhold bed privileges. I'll ask for my dower third of the farm back and my red cow with the white ear back.

BILL She's not here you blackguards. Off with you, Bill Donnelly.

Silence. Husband & wife return to bed. Then a blast of sound. Choose from buzzsaw sounds, guns firing, drums, horns, fiddles, maskers, circle of dancers around a bonfire, maskers entering bridal chamber and lifting up Mary.

MASKER We found Maggie, Bill. She was under her brother's bed all the time. Is this her, Bill? Quick, for God's sakes, we can hardly lift her off the floor.

WILL'S VOICE No, that's not Maggie, that's too fat for Maggie. That's probably Mary.

Bill & Mary crouch as the sounds melt into the newspaper's account.

MARY Mother of God, there goes the chimney.

CHORUS

RURAL ROUGHS ON RAMPAGE

ATTEMPTED ABDUCTION IN BIDDULPH

MAGGIE *in lay sister's working costume, with attendant nun*

I wasn't there of course. He was too much in love to unravel their cunning, and so—we lost sight of each other.

CHORUS

THE BIDDULPH KU KLUX DISGRACEFUL CONDUCT OF LOVE-SICK SWAIN

Newspaper boy, "extra, read all about it," bulletin readers in front of newspaper office, &c.

CHORUS HOW HE WENT ABOUT IT AND HOW HE FAILED TO SUCCEED

MAGGIE And a needless enemy was my brother who before had been our ally as much as he dared, but after the serenade

BILL Except to say hello I don't speak to that man. Speak to Will Donnelly—no, and Mary and me have the very next farm to the Donnelly place now, no, William Donnelly, no. No.

CHORUS THE MIDDLE AGES REVIVED LOVE'S LABOUR LOST EVIDENTLY

WILL *with whip* Read that cheap newspaper heading again.

CHORUS THE MIDDLE AGES REVIVED

WILL That's enough, thank you. Middle Ages Revived by whom? Me or them?. We were hauled up in court, but I got off I suppose because Maggie had asked us to take her away. My God, I was never to see her again. And I'm not in the least sorry I tried to steal her away if that's what you call a life for a woman. *to Maggie's father who is in bare feet at the tub* And I'm not in the least sorry for any thing that happens from now on in that happens to those who try the same trick on me as you pulled on that girl that was once my sweetheart. I'll switch the flies off you you old fool.

He has taken Maggie's father up & and is about to whip him, but then throws him down & chases him out of the theatre or attacks his feet with a toy whip & spins him out of the room.

HALF CHORUS Question. The Convent of the Sacred Heart *sung; "incense" music as before.*

At Mount Hope on Richmond Street, why does the Opposition Stage always slow down?

HALF CHORUS Answer. Oh I can answer that. When Will Donnelly is the driver

MAGGIE He senses that I am drudging here in the kitchen of the sisters' house. And when he is not the driver he has told the others to slow down at the chestnut tree because he knows that I wait each day for the sound. In the morning, in the evening—down the hill, past the mill and over Brough's Bridge until you can't hear the wheels or the hooves anymore. You hear the other stage. You hear your own heart. I scrub the stones of the convent yard as close to the gate as I can, but it is no use—the gate is locked. Someday, in the middle of the night, there will come such a knocking at that gate and it will be smashed open, and the nuns will run hither and thither screeching because my husband has come for me and in my wedding dress I will enter his coach to drive up his road forever. I love William Donnelly.

As Maggie lies dead before them, the Mother Superior confers with the sisters as to where Maggie should be buried

NUN Mother Superior Finnegan, Maggie Donovan is dead. What shall we do with her? *they kneel*

MOTHER What were the last words she said, Sister Feeny?

NUN Her last words were

MAGGIE & NUN I love William Donnelly.

MOTHER Sister Feeny, where do you think she should be buried.

NUN *pause, then crisply & swiftly* By William Donnelly's grave up in Biddulph.

MOTHER Sister Gallagher?

NUN In the convent yard where the rest of us lie.

MOTHER Sister Egan?

NUN In the convent yard, Mother Superior, but close by the gate.

MOTHER And that is where Maggie Donovan lies buried.

MAGGIE I love William Donnelly.

William Donnelly sings a verse of "Buffalo Gals".

I asked her if she'd be my wife
Be my wife, be my wife
She'd make me happy all my life
If she stood by my side

CHORUS End of Act One.

The St Nicholas Hotel Wm Donnelly Prop.

Act Two

Actors spin tops, dance, recite poems, until this recitation of poems slowly fades into Tom Ryan standing up on the bar and letting us see the story from a new angle.

TOM RYAN And I'll recite you a poem I learnt once at school while we're waiting for the two o'clock stage to Lucan which I may have the honour of driving, young though I am, since the Donnelly boys have to put in a appearance in court.

Waiting for Pa

Three little forms in the twilight gray
Scanning the shadows across the way:
Six little eyes, four black, two blue,
Brimful of love and happiness too,
Watching for Pa

Soon joyous shouts from the window-seat
And eager patter of childish feet
Gay musical chimes ring through the hall
A manly voice responds to the call
"Welcome papa!"

The actor playing Ned Ryan, Tom's father, now proceeds to growl drunkenly.

TOM RYAN Well ladies and gentlemen, my home life wasn't like that quite, and since I'm said to be one of the reasons for the Donnelly Tragedy, you don't understand me unless you understand what waiting for my Pa was like. Tom Ryan is my name, this is my Pa, here's my Ma and a couple of my sisters. What are we doing? We are all waiting one cold winter morning for Pa—to get his rump off a chest that contains bread, cheese, tea and other necessaries of life which he refuses to let us have

Tom Ryan starts to saw a rail.

NED RYAN They might cook it and poison me.

TOM RYAN It's a cold day outside, but there's no fire in the stove because—

NED You're ruining me with all this wasting of my substance, Stop the sawing, Tom stop sawing that rail! or I'll take this ax to you.

MRS RYAN It isn't enough to be starving but we must freeze to death as well.

NED Tell your son to stop sawing that rail and to clear out of here. *starting to give chase*

TOM Oh I admit I was pert and I should have stopped sawing, but I couldn't sit there and see my sisters and my mother shivering much longer.

NED Get out of the house you bastard brat, talking back to your pa.

TOM Don't hit me Pa. I was only. I will go and I will never come back, and I stepped out onto the road and looked in the snow for somebody to take me in: Who will take in the barefoot Ryan Boy?

The actors set up the Roman Line gamut of Part One as the road he will run up and down.

Barry?	Trehy?	
Feeny?	O'Halloran?	*He is rejected by*
Cahill?	Cassleigh?	*everyone in various*
McCann?	Flynn?	*ways: backs turned,*
Egan?	Marksy?	*clubs, kicks &c.*
Quinn?	Farl?	
Gallagher?	Duffy?	
Clancy?	Donovan?	

Bell and jug sound for the tavern and the church; then Mrs Donnelly comes towards the rejected boy and accepts him

MRS DONNELLY Donnelly. *We see her at the end of a corridor of people. We renew her acquaintance now.*

CHORUS Yes, the Donnellys took him in.

James Donnelly, the Younger, sitting invalid in a chair by the stove should also register here. His mother has just finished giving him medicine.

MRS DONNELLY Tom Ryan, climb up on the stove there and stop your shivering till I get these dry feet on you; here's a pair of Tom's pants to put on those you got on are drenched, what devil has your father got into that he drives you out barefoot in this weather or was there a reason, Tom?

TOM I was only sawing a rail, Mrs Donnelly, to get a fire on so we would be warm.

MRS DONNELLY Get behind the stove now and hide in the woodbox, your father I can see in the lid of my tea kettle coming in our gate. Can you not get the key to the pantry away from him while he's asleep?

TOM He sleeps with it tied round his leg, Mrs Donnelly.

MRS DONNELLY Well there are four of you and one of him, he's no giant, give him a clout and get the key some fine day Good day to you, Ned Ryan?

TOM But he's always got the ax.

NED Good morning, Mrs Donnelly, Have you seen my madcap, scapegrace harum scarum son, Tom about?

MRS DONNELLY No madcap, scapegrace, harum scarum son of yours has run in here, Ned Ryan.

NED Then I just heard your stove say something about an ax.

MRS DONNELLY My stove talks a lot to itself, Ned Ryan, what with the kettle getting up steam and the wood crackling inside and the wind in the chimney. Do you not see my stove has a name? She's called Princess and she just saw the ax you're holding in your hand. I'd have said something myself at the strangeness of a father with an ax in his hand.

He backs up and slides off; Mrs Donnelly returns to sewing. Tom gets up on top of the stove (bar) and continues.

TOM Pretty soon, he'd drag me back home again and say he'd try to be decent to us, but it didn't last and as I grew older if I could I helped the Donnelly boys with their stage, and if I couldn't I stayed home and caused trouble. Like—I set fire to the barn once with him—Pa—in it, he barely got out in time and he thought it was lightning, and I pissed in his whisky after drinking half of it, oh my God was he mad at me. *violin screech—a poltergeist bottle flies through the air, disappears and we hear it smash.* Yes, I can make things like that happen if I don't abuse myself for a month. It's like having a fit and I can will it that I'm going to have a fit. One day I asked my mother if it was true I had been born. And she said

MOTHER Yes, Tom Ryan, you were born.

He starts to pack a carpet bag.

NED And where might you be going, great high and mighty one with your clothes barely covering your thin little parsnip of a rump and your hair like a snipe's nest on fire, oh little runt of mine.

TOM My mother here tells me it's St Bridget's Eve and tomorrow I'm old enough so I'm leaving forever.

MRS RYAN Oh son, where will you stay?

TOM *pause* Donnellys.

MRS RYAN Could you not pick a better place than that den of everything wicked.

TOM If you want to know mother, there's love there.

NED Your poor father over here, Tom. Will you not give him a look, will you shame him before all our neighbours?

TOM I'm not going to hang around here anymore and hear you say mean low things to my mother.

MRS RYAN Would you live with people whose sons tried to carry a poor girl off, Tom?

TOM Yes, because she wanted to be carried off from a house that was worse than this.

MRS RYAN Could you not get a job in the town building the new lunatic hospital they're putting up?

Tom starts his speech now and walks into the George Stub scene.

NED It's into the lunatic hospital he should be going. *growls*

TOM But of course the first thing I did to the Donnellys was to bring them trouble in the shape of the bridle I bought for them on tick at Mr Stub's store.

STUB Tom Ryan, lad, just ask your boss William Donnelly, gentleman, when in the name of Heaven is he going to pay for the bridle you tapped on my shutters for last summer?

TOM Mr Stub, it was a mistake, and we brought it back.

STUB I know that, lad, but I didn't accept the return, it's used and I want my money.

TOM We paid for the use.

STUB Not by agreement, that's not the way I do business but I tell you, lad, I'm suing William Donnelly, gentleman, in Division Court next Tuesday so be warned.

TOM Aw, sue away. We'll never pay you for it, you old skinflint. But he kept summoning Mr Donnelly, sending summonses and we just wiped our ass with them. I used to ride up and down on the stage, they gave me a cap to wear. There was another lad hung around the Donnellys a lot—Will Farl. Some of the people were shocked that he got on with the Donnellys so well.

The two boys crouch by the Donnelly stove; Mrs Donnelly is sewing while James Donnelly Jr sleeps in a rocking chair.

WILL FARL Why aren't you sitting still, Tom does your shirt itch you?

TOM Old man beat me last night, my back's all welted up.

MRS DONNELLY Tom Ryan and Will Farl, what were we talking about just now—yes, you say that you'll help my sons against their enemies, what kind of help do my sons need against what kind of enemies?

TOM Oh—help.

MRS DONNELLY Wouldn't it be wise to consult us first before you go helping. *train whistle* What is the latest sample of your helping my sons, please tell their mother.

WILL FARL We've just put a log across the railway down at Granton.

MRS DONNELLY Now, just how does that help Will & Mike?

TOM Why don't you know George Stub, your Will's arch enemy is coming back from the fair at St Marys tonight. Most women would have screamed here, but

MRS DONNELLY Is he coming back from the fair at St Marys now, why Tom and Will Farl, my husband, Mr Donnelly's at the fair too. You wouldn't want him to be train-wrecked, would you?

TOM There's lots of time, we'll take the logs off, Mrs Donnelly. See the welts, Will Farl?

WILL FARL You know I remember my father whaling me like that. And people ask me why I like to stay at the Donnellys' so much.

TOM *train whistle* We'd better get a move on, Will Farl there's the train. So why is it you like to stay at the Donnellys' so much then?

WILL FARL They killed my father. *They run off; train whistle*

Mrs Donnelly turns to her patient and says:

MRS DONNELLY Were you listening, James Donnelly the Younger, or are you still asleep from the medicine the doctor gave you.

JAMES JR Oh mother, I'm still asleep from the medicine the doctor gave me.

MRS DONNELLY Good, because it's time you had another dose of it.

JAMES Mother, I won't take it. *pause* I won't take it unless

MRS DONNELLY Unless what, high and mighty

JAMES Where's the saw? Let me hold it in my hand here. And I'll *she gets the saw. Gives him medicine. Sleepily he continues* I'll pull his beard out.

An actor sitting on the side benches with his fingers drumming on wood suggests the rain pouring down outside.

MRS DONNELLY Hsst. There's a whirlwind outside and the sky is dark. Your father's late home from the fair. Maybe he'll bring you something James though you're a trifle big and old for a bauble and did you pull his beard out in this big fight you had with him.

JAMES Ah, *in his sleep* it fell out of him. By God, I'll knock your brains out, there's no constable in Lucan able to take me.

MRS DONNELLY When I get you on your feet, my son, it's off to the priest and you're taking the pledge. It's either the water wagon or smash and when the smash comes your father and I won't be able to help you one little bit.

JAMES Where's Will and where's Mike?

MRS DONNELLY Where else would they be, but driving their stage up and down in this rain.

JAMES Where's John and Bob and Tom?

MRS DONNELLY Out plowing. Tom went up to the blacksmith's.

JAMES Why isn't Pat home helping us fight Finnegan?

MRS DONNELLY Why isn't he? Have you asked him sure enough and get him into trouble. Is that why you came back from Michigan to get us all into trouble?

JAMES No. No. I came to help Will and Mike smash Finnegan. Where's father?

MRS DONNELLY He's just coming into the yard this very minute and if you're not quiet and good I'll tell him on you. Mr. Donnelly I'm surprised to see you home from the fair at all.

MR DONNELLY I am myself. There was a log across the rails. How'd you know about that? *pause* How's our first one?

MRS DONNELLY Mr Donnelly, Doctor Quarry says—and he knows this himself for he was told—that even if we get him to stop the drink he's got only two more years to live.

MR DONNELLY It's his lungs. And they're bad. How is he now then?

JAMES Never felt better in my life. I'm going into Lucan.

MR & MRS DONNELLY No, you're not. *They hold him down till he falls asleep.*

MRS DONNELLY And what's that you've brought us home from the fair to give to a little one perhaps some time. *He gives her a top and she spins it. There is a whipstick that comes with it which she uses.* I wonder how much longer they can all keep going, Jim?

MR DONNELLY Stub was on the train.

MRS DONNELLY And I knew that too. The things I've heard this afternoon, Mr Donnelly, and I was at no fair.

MR DONNELLY Jim, says Stub, Jim—

STUB *train whistle* Jim, thought I saw you back here coming back to see what in hell's holding up this train. Jim—if you and your boys get me Ward Three next election *pause* and you alone can do it—I don't care how, tell them not to vote or vote for my man who's going to be an Irish Catholic, Jim, yes—if you can promise me that Finnegan will stop running his stage wagons tomorrow.

MRS DONNELLY Yes, and my husband said—

MR DONNELLY Nothing. We're promised long ago to Mr Scatcherd.

MRS DONNELLY And you are so promised

MR DONNELLY And yet

MRS DONNELLY *whipping the top* Yes. It would be nice to stop, but we can't oh no we must keep on spinning and spinning, Mr Donnelly, because if we stop spinning we'll fall down and over and we hit them and they hit us and we—one day—our whip-arm's broke off. Go back to him and say yes!

MR DONNELLY Never!

TOM Mother and father, wake Jim up will you? There's a fight up town and Will and Mike can't get the stage past Levitt's.

MRS DONNELLY Your brother's not fit to go out anymore, Tom.

Hush...

JAMES No, mother. The medicine worked, I'm well. Father ...Get my horse Tom.

MR & MRS DONNELLY Get back in that chair. *He escapes them.*

JAMES You heard what Tom said. Every man's needed, my brother's in a fight!

MR DONNELLY Take your coat, Jim. At least put something on your back.

MRS DONNELLY Take your hat, it's rain—he took the saw.

MR DONNELLY Come back here, Tom and Jim. What's he got the saw for? *Exit*

FINNEGAN Now I can explain the saw. Exactly a year ago, Thursday, September the 20th, 1874, someone took my stage wagon after dark and sawed it to hundreds of small pieces. I built a new stage. 1875. Today, Friday, September 20th—someone took that new stage out of my stable, dragged it up the road a piece and sawed it into even more pieces. There are to be no stages on the road, but Donnelly stages, are there? The Donnelly tribe is getting to be a terror to the neighbourhood.

John Macdonald approaches the bartender and buys a stage ticket. His mother and sister, Norah, approach for the same reason.

MACDONALD A ticket, one way to Lucan please.

BARTENDER Which line will you go on...

NORAH Two tickets the same to Lucan please, for myself, sir, and my mother here. The Donnelly Line.

MACDONALD Not the Donnelly Line for your brother, Norah, nor for your son, mother, but the Finnegan Line, please.

NORAH Please yourself, brother John, if you want your bones shaken to a jelly by Mr Finnegan's drivers. We'll be in Lucan before you.

MACDONALD I want the two of you to get your money back and come on the same coach as your brother and son is going on. The wagon you're going on carries away more than my mother and my sister, for it bears away sister's reputation and any love for her son my old mother has ever had.

MOTHER Will you lower your voice in a public place, my son John Macdonald. Why you've palled around with Donnellys ever since you can remember, what have you suddenly determined against them?

MACDONALD Mother, you know and I know what Norah's up to with their Cripple now he's lost the Thompson girl.

MOTHER Don't you dare call him a cripple, or there's people here standing'll see me haul off and give you the clout you so long for. Let Norah decide the man she'll marry, one thing, it can't be you, you get such rages into yourself about your sisters, it's the land you're worried about isn't it, that father likes William Donnelly a lot, not just that Norah does, is that not so?

MACDONALD Your husband and my father make me wonder sometimes if I am his wife's husband's son.

As the quarrelling Macdonalds leave the barroom, the other actors form two coaches indicating that we have dissolved into the street outside the City Hotel, but just before this happens Mrs Macdonald raises her arms and says:

MOTHER No wonder he likes Will Donnelly. At least Will Donnelly can talk straight when it comes to naming his relatives. I've even heard him call his mother his mother and his father his father, but with you John, your mother, why your mother is liable to be your grandfather's daughter and your sister, she's not your sister, she's your unborn grandchild's great aunt. *And out the Macdonalds go to immediately return as if we then saw them step out of the hotel and go to their respective coaches. We are getting ready for a decisive journey up the road, this time to some startling new developments.*

MACDONALD Mother, I'm sorry, but this wouldn't happen if Donnelly would just leave us and Norah alone.

They shout at each other through the windows of the stages, then the Finnegan horn, the tollgate and penny convention, the slight up and down movement of the two stages' passengers indicate that they're off!

NORAH Brother, who's been at you? I'll tell you I'm proud he's in love with me, can you not remember the love you once felt for himself when you were always over there...

MOTHER Mrs Donnelly had more to do with bringing you up than I did, now look at you. Sure, Father's given you one hundred acres already, he's not made of gold, leave him alone about his property.

MACDONALD When I get home, Norah, I'm going to dig up all the potatoes in the front field you've been planting and I'll cut down the orchard mark my words if I see you talking to him when we get to Lucan, it's lucky it is there's no Cripple driving today I supse I'd see you both up on the driver's seat with him. There go the Cripple lovers, folks, my mother and my sister.

NORAH Oh, mother, give me the parcels, which one is the iron we bought I'll crack him one on his skull.

MOTHER Pay no heed to him, darling, I just hope and pray he doesn't get up his courage at the taverns and try to drag us off at a tollgate, but we're outdistancing him I see, here we are shut up in a box with four wheels and the window blinds down for the heat and you can hear the drivers cursing each other through the roof. You have to pretend not to hear.

NORAH A ride to Lucan is a sentimental education I can tell you. You'd hear Finnegan's driver say— *trumpet* hold your ears. I guess only men would understand why they'd have to get down and fight about that, once a Donnelly said, "And your father wasn't married either, McKellar". To which came the reply: *trumpet* to which Mike Donnelly said:

NORAH & MIKE "You'll not drive the stage another morning with your life, McKellar".

MOTHER I don't mind hearing a good bout of swearing if they're really good at it, but it does slow up the journey which is somewhat more important, and that last remark by my future son-in-law.

NORAH I think it was Mike said that, Mother

MOTHER Well, whoever it was, that would lead to both stagedrivers putting in an appearance at a local Justice of the Peace along the road called Squire Ferguson.

WILL Squire Ferguson, I wish to lay a complaint against Peter McKellar re perjury in the information he laid against me and Mike last July the third, 1875.

SQUIRE Mr Donnelly, I don't think you can do that.

WILL Oh yes you can. Victoria, 1859, Chapter 1, subsection 6. Give me your manual, sir, and I'll show

NORAH When Finnegan's witnesses would try to go down to the courthouse, Will Donnelly would get them arrested somehow at Birr for disorderly conduct. I bought him a couple of old law books for a Christmas box, and it was what we called the game of information and complaint or Legal Amusements. And if two of the Donnelly boys got arrested why their mother had had the foresight to have seven sons, so it would be Tom or Bob or John would drive if they'd snared my Will or Mike into their clutches.

MOTHER And they'd be at it again.

A brief horn and fiddle contest. Finnegan's horn taunts are returned with interest by Donnelly fiddle sounds.

MAN ON FINNEGAN STAGE I used to ride both lines and turn about and you could see what was going to happen, sooner or later... oh, there were happy times too I observed in my going back and forth. I can remember the whole Donnelly family going down the road on their way to Bothwell to get Jennie married off. Or the day Mike all dressed up went down to London to get married to Ellen Haines, her father kept the City Hotel there. Mike didn't show up for a week after that, too tired, still abed at two in the afternoon his brothers said, stagedrivers make good husbands, all that jouncing up and down, God knows, but sooner or later...

NORAH Yes stagedrivers do make good husbands. I was so proud of the way William drove and acted to his customers and I knew then that my life with him was like this journey. Through it all we would eventually come to the St Nicholas Hotel here off the road and out of the storm. My old mother's fallen asleep. Where does she dream she is?

LADY ON OTHER STAGE Asleep!! Not me, I keep thinking when the wheels will they come off, when will the wheels come off, oh mother, when will the wheels come have those Donnellys loosened the wheels?

CHORUS fur hats in winter, straw hats in summer.

MAN our collar limp, our hat crushed, our watch stopped, our brain dizzy with vertigo, the elastic band of our wig snapped, our false teeth displaced in their setting, curses not loud but deep,

MIKE Gee Ploughboy Gee Pilot

CHORUS were carriers of passengers upon a stage or covered wagon from the City of London to the Village of Lucan

FINNEGAN Hrup hrup there you slow beasts, don't try to beat me at the bridge, Donnelly, there's not room for the both of us.

MIKE There's two sides to a road, Finnegan

CHORUS the defendant, William Donnelly, did not safely & securely carried upon the said on the said

MIKE Oil your wheels, Finnegan.

The "coaches" are getting closer to each other & are blurring in outline just as things do before they collide.

FINNEGAN Your half of the road's the ditch, Donnelly. *horn & fiddle*

CHORUS

August the 31st, 1875
maliciously ran races with other stage coaches

MAN I think that Finnegan kept as close as he could to the Hotel side to keep Donnelly from getting to the Hotel before him.

MIKE The ladies wanted a drink of water at the hotel. He made a quick turn as quick a turn as ever I seen. I had ten passengers three in the driver's seat besides myself seven inside *using the whole team of actors, suggest the collison*

CHORUS plaintiff was thereby wounded & injured in consequence on the said road and suffered great pain and expense in and about the cure of her wounds and injuries. And the plaintiffs—Mrs Louisa Lindsay & Miss Jennie Lindsay—claim five hundred dollars *groaning* damages.

MIKE What did you do that for, Finnegan? *whip*

FINNEGAN *whip* Mike Donnelly, I'd do it again like as not until and again till I've run you off this road. *The two stagedrivers confront each other among a pile of coach fragments and accident victims slowly re-assembling themselves; but the scene is darkening, a bell rings, Mike Donnelly's face grows red from some fire he is looking at.* I said to myself under my breath why in God's name is Mike Donnelly's face turning so red. *turning around* He's thinking he's looking at my stables going up in flames with five horses alive in them. *running out into a blazing stable door as the tollgate between Birr & Elginfield is set up with the money pouring out for counting of the day's take* Mother of God help me save my poor beasts from Donnelly's fire.

TOLLGATER Guess that's all for today, let's count her up, sunset's hanging on there quite a while. Good night to you, sir. You're our last traveller for the day.

TRAVELLER That's not the sunset by the way.

As this scene develops there should be well-spaced red glares that build till the Donnelly Boys in a photograph scene are surrounded by Hell with a mob of farmers in front of them with sharp hayrakes.

SOLO *sings* Patrick Finnegan's stables burning

CHORUS Dies irae dies illa *ecclesiastical*

SOLO Solvet Finnegan in favilla

WIFE Sam and me's been seeing quite a few red glows in the sky north of here lately every night.

TRAVELLER Oh it's them Donnellys, another barn they've set fire to if it's a friend of Finnegan, burned down Pat Finnegan's stable last week with six horses in it burnt up alive.

TOLLGATER That's one step up from loosening wheels and having you up in court for insult and battery, isn't it.

TRAVELLER A considerable step indeed. I guess you see the Donnelly boys every day?

TOLLGATER Twice a day regular as clockwork—their coach, Finnegan's coach down to town; except one day last week both the stages were awful late and then part of the Finnegan wagon limped by, and then two thirds of the Donnelly conveyance and then the rest of the Finnegan and then the hindwheels of the it was a Armageddon of a road catastrophe I can tell you.

WIFE That night we saw our first red glow. *Three or more farmers come up to listen with hayrakes, big wooden spikes on them: lanterns*

TOLLGATER And I can tell you ladies and gentlemen, when the other Finnegan stable got burnt up in Clandeboye why there was people said—what next?

WIFE	SOLO
What next, indeed, Sam. The Maclean's Hotel where Finnegan ties up his stage, someone got into their kitchen and broke every dish and cup and teapot and soup tureen Mrs Maclean had to her name.	William Donnelly's stables burn too CHORUS Tuba Finnegan spargens sonum Per sepulchram regionum Coget Biddulph ante thronum

CHORUS
Oh them Donnellys

FARMER ONE Is it all the members of the family the mother and the father?

TOLLGATER There's some say as that they called the oldest of the boys back from where he'd been hiding out in Michigan—James Donnelly the Younger—and he drinks you see, and they just sort of let him loose at night

FARMER TWO There's others say after the outrage at Walker's Hotel where they cut the tongues out of the stage horses there...

ALL Cut the tongues out of the horses!

FARMER TWO God yes, have you not heard—Finnegan went to hitch up on Monday morning and his horses were all—hacked open, dying or dead, and they had to be shot; the farrier said—put them out of their misery and there was a whole bunch in the village said—lynch Tom Donnelly or Will or Mike or Jim, yes, Jim he's the one and it's Bob who sets the fires and it's Will who plans it all. *Will & Mike drive up to the gate*

TOLLGATER Toll there, travellers. Oh—it's you

WILL Good evening, Mr Scandrett. Mrs Scandrett. *pause* I said Mr Scandrett—Good evening. *pause* Mr Scandrett, there's a lady passenger felt under the weather at Swartz's Hotel coming up from London today and she asked us if we could come and pick her up down there later in the evening.

WIFE Sam, don't let them through, Sam. They're lying. They're out for night mischief.

FARMERS Sam, we'll help you keep the firebugs out of our township. Nobody's going to cut our horses' throats.

MIKE
Gate, Mr Scandrett.

A suspended moment in which we look at the Donnelly boys held back at the gate. They look at us still as a photograph. Who are they? What are they?

SOLO *sung*
Donnelly's new stage
sawn to pieces

CHORUS Confutatis maledictis

SOLO Sawn to pieces Watson's horses

CHORUS Flammis acribus addictis

The penny slides into the Tollgater's cup, a Donnelly penny

WIFE I saw blood on his sleeve I could swear. I was going to be sick then—

ANOTHER TRAVELLER *from our side of the gate* Good night, Scandrett. Whoa. Guess we don't need to go any farther, Lila. There's Will and Mike waiting for you and I'm glad you feel more like completing your journey than you did at three o'clock there. *The gate finally comes down to let Mrs Shoebottom through.* Good night, Bill, Mike. *He turns around and goes back towards us.*

LADY Thank you, Will Donnelly. Thank you, Mike. You're kind gentlemen both of you to put yourselves out so for an old woman like me. *They depart with her.*

WIFE But when their hands came down to help her up into their buggy the blood on their sleeves was gone.

Bar noise & scene. Mike going through with trunk

MIKE I heard what you said, sir. If you ever say again that my brother Tom robbed Ned Ryan of eighty dollars I'll kill you. *Exit*

Voice of man who enters as Mike leaves with trunk

SOLO VOICE The Donnellys are coming, they're walking over from Levitt's.

A knocking, then a door-rending;
Lock up your doors, close the bar; hide everybody.
Jim, Tom & Bob enter to face a lone bartender, Frank

FRANK No Donnelly gets a drink at this bar; I'll not serve you, James.

JAMES I see. And it's a good bar you used to have too, Frank Walker.

FRANK Used to have!

JAMES Because you'll get a scorching inside of six weeks as it's laid out for you now, but I don't intend to have anything to do with it.

FRANK What'll it be, Jim Donnelly, what'll it be?

JIM Three gingerbeers for us lads here and a big bowl of porridge.

FRANK Don't you mean three bowls?

JAMES No, it's not for us. One big bowl of porridge and hustle it.

Constable Berryhill enters swaggering with his warrants in pocket

BERRYHILL *with beard* I can lick any man in this tavern, I can lick any man in Biddulph. *He backs away from Jim Donnelly* Jim Donnelly I've got twelve warrants for your arrest.

Out of range we hear a scream from Berryhill & he returns in the power of James Donnelly, Jr

MIKE He had followed my brothers to Walker's Hotel.

BERRYHILL They tore half my beard out.

JAMES Oh—the beard fell out of him

MIKE By the time I got there my brothers and their pals were throwing stones at him.

BERRYHILL Several of the stones weighed five pounds each.

MIKE That's a lie. Frank, how much does that one weigh?

FRANK Got a bit afraid when I saw the stones flying through the air. *Weighs a stone in a balanced scale on bar:* It's three pounds? *Mike smiles*

WILL My brother Mike then hauled James and the others off and parted them.

BERRYHILL But left me with them and you know what they made me do, that James Donnelly the Younger took the warrants out of my pocket and *they tear up the warrants, sprinkle them over the porridge and feed it to Berryhill*

FRANK You're probably going to hit me, Jim, for asking you this, but why?

JAMES I'm only feeding him the ones we didn't do, Frank. This one here – I'll eat myself, yes I did beat that grocer up and I couldn't stand the way he whined and whoever is doing all those terrible things on these warrants will stop doing them. Frank, when the powers that be let my brothers have half of the road again. I started eating the paper and then it tasted bitter, I took it out of my mouth and saw Dr Quarry's signature why it was my death certificate and it was getting time to take the saw back to my mother and father.

Facing us a change comes over him: he dissolves from the bully into someone coughing blood on his sleeve and crawling toward us, towards his mother who waits for him.

MRS DONNELLY

Yes, my oldest son came home and after the doctor came it was time for the priest to come, but he did not come and we waited and he did not come so that it was I who had to lie down beside this grown man and lead him backwards and forwards through a life he had forgotten the deeds and maps to. As he whispered in my ear, yes, what do you want me to say, I could see life for him again some time. But for the first time I saw my own death. Just before he died I told him what I was to tell another son of mine not many years after.

Ritual walking confession, his back to us, she with her face as his life pours out. They are walking through his brutal life under some of the next scene, then he parts from her forever. The chorus divide into those watching the news bulletin board where several are chalking up headlines, and others reading newspapers.

CHORUS

Nominations for North Middlesex

One of the Donnellys is Dead!
hilarious reaction

SOLO

Solvet Jacobus in favilla

CHORUS

Another diabolical outrage—a horse disembowelled with a scythe. Flammis acribus addictus
Fiendish outrage—a tree across the London, Huron & Bruce railway this morning. The trestles of the Grand Trunk Railway bridge at Lucan Crossing sawn through by some fiend in human form. There is work for some clever detective in Lucan.
Voca me cum benedictus,
Dies irae, dies illa
Dona eis requiem.
The Detective. Our serial for the month of December. A Detective's Diary, or

Mrs Donnelly's arm cannot keep her oldest son here anymore; she lets it drop to her side and walks across the chorus gossipers.

MCCRIMMON *disguised as an old beggarwoman* How I brought the Donnelly Gang to heel. Gentlemen, are all the blinds down and the doors to Mr Stub's store room locked? Yes? Then I will resume my civilian garb. *flinging off his disguise* Mr Finnegan, I have been for some time engaged in ferreting out at your behest the perpetrators of certain crimes which have been committed in Lucan & its vicinity. Today is—I make this interim report to you on Thursday, February the 24th, 1876. Sunday—5th of December, 1875—we met here as you recall in camera.

FINNEGAN First of all, let me introduce you to Mr George Stub at the back of whose store we are hiding. Mr Stub, this is the private detective the town council gave permission to bring in. He's been here incognito already for about a month and I sure hope to hell he's going to tell us what we can do to prevent all our business affairs going bust. Gentlemen, Hugh McCrimmon.

CHORUS A giant in size, he was gentle as a child. Shy as a woman, his heart was bold as a lion's Modest as a maiden.... And in first place in the five mile dash! Hugh McCrimmon!

MCCRIMMON Yes. For my athletic prowess in weight-lifting and footrunning alone I have won over a thousand gold medals both here and in Uncle Sam's dominions. You may remember how I asked you each to tell me your story and to tell me **all** of the story. Because there is a great detective up in the sky *all glance up* who does know and He'll make it known if you don't so I want all of the truth. My notes. This family—seven of them have done all these terrible things and they've been charged, but the constables can't arrest them. Too bad the one died and got away on us. You say no witnesses will dare to testify for fear of reprisal, in short they're running this town with a reign of terror, you want to run it and I'm here to help you. Chapter One, sirs, is to

STUB I'm having Will Donnelly arrested today if you must know—he's owed me a bill at the store in there for a bridle for over a year now and I'm having him arrested for debt.

MCCRIMMON An arrest for a minor debt? Rather small potatoes, don't you think?

STUB He won't pay, his bowels hate me so much he won't pay that debt even though today is his wedding day, he won't pay it to keep out of jail.

CHORUS May the God of Israel join you together and may He be with you, who was merciful to two only children: and now, O lord, make them bless Thee more fully. Alleluia, alleluia.

PRIEST William Donnelly, wilt thou take Norah Macdonald here present for thy lawful wife according to the rite of our holy Mother the Chuch?

WILL I will

PRIEST Norah Macdonald, wilt thou take William Donnelly here present for thy lawful husband, according to the rite of our holy Mother the Church?

NORAH I will *they hold right hands*

PRIEST Ego conjungo vos in matrimonium, in nomine Patris, et Filii et Spiritus Sancti, Amen

He sprinkles them with water. Then he blesses the ring, gold & silver coins.

Bailiffs appear at the back of the church with staves

PRIEST Let us pray. Bless O Lord, this ring which we bless in Thy

Name, that she who shall wear it, keeping true faith unto her husband may abide in Thy peace and will, and ever live in mutual charity. Through Christ our Lord, Amen.

He sprinkles the ring with holy water in the form of a cross. The Bridegroom receives from the priest the ring and places it on the fourth finger of his bride.

WILL With this ring I thee wed, and I plight unto thee my troth. *silent Lord's prayer*

BAILIFF Are you just about through. Because which one of you is William Donnelly; we've come with writ against him for debt.

PRIEST Look, O Lord, we beseech Thee, upon these Thy servants, and graciously assist Thine own institutions, whereby Thou hast ordained the propagation of mankind, that they who are joined together by Thy authority may be preserved by Thy help. Through Christ our Lord. Amen. Mr & Mrs William Donnelly, who are these men?

WILL Father Flannery, they are bailiffs for a debt I refuse to pay to a man you know well, mother and father, who used the ignorance of a child six months ago to snare me now on my wedding day. How many days?

BAILLIFFS It says here—ten days in the jug, Bill.

WILL Norah. Meet me at Tom Ryder's wedding dance which is to be in ten days time at Fitzhenry's Tavern. Promise? We'll recommence there and no, mother and father, don't offer to pay, as a man I've decided not to. If George Stub wants me in jail he can have what he wants. And when I want him to lose this election that's coming up then I can have what I want. Got my fiddle there? I'll give you a tune as the bailiffs here march me off. Attention! March! *He goes off playing "Boney over the Alps". They listen to it dying away and then follow.*

NORAH Mrs Donnelly, you gave Will that fiddle didn't you.

MRS DONNELLY Are you thinking if I hadn't you might have your husband in your arms at this very moment, Norah, instead of his doing such a proud fool thing?

NORAH No. I've never been so happy in my life to have married such a man.

MCCRIMMON Chapter One. January the twenty second, I wrote to my sweetheart. Chapter Two. I visit the outlaw's nest—in disguise.

Our attention focuses on John washing himself at the Donnelly farmhouse. Mike drives into the yard.

MIKE What are we going to do, Jack? There's a detective on the way out here.

JOHN He's already here. The boys brought him home with them.

MIKE Do they know who he is?

JOHN They think he's a pal, he stood up for them in some dispute at the Dublin House and slapped a man down. You should see him, he's all muscle. Should we tell them?

MIKE No. It'd be too much for their minds to bear. Is he disguised?

Mrs Donnelly enters, kisses Michael, and shows him a baby shawl she has knit.

JOHN *whispering* He's got an eye patch.

McCrimmon enters & slouches around. Bob & Tom stand behind him.

MRS DONNELLY Nellie was just showing me the baby, Mike, what shoulders he has already on him, and this is what I've knitted for Jenny's child and your father and me's off to the christening in St Thomas. Bob and Tom are you not going to say goodbye to your mother and father? *They come over to kiss her; she singles out the lounging pirate for a glance.*

MCCRIMMON *vulgar voice* Well, look at who it is. This must be your mother, boys. Old Johannah Donnelly herself. *He is hoping to provoke something.*

MRS DONNELLY I always thought that gentlemen stood up when a lady came into the room.

MCCRIMMON I'm no gentleman, and this is no room. *laugh*

MRS DONNELLY The yard of any house I live in, sir, has a very high blue ceiling called a sky, and I call it a room particularly if I say so and I step out into it. *he shambles & bows*

MCCRIMMON Mrs Donnelly, I'm enchanted to meet you, met your two youngest ones while strolling through the village, and I gather you do not mind if they entertain a stranger at your high ceilinged residence. *glances up*

MRS DONNELLY Strangers are always welcome here and I'm only sorry my husband and myself won't be here this weekend since we're going to St Thomas to visit my daughter and granddaughter there. Tom and Bob, why don't you take your friend to help father catch the driving horse. It seems to me I caught a glimpse of you earlier on looking at one of my son's shirts on the clothesline. *She comes over to him with a shirt & claps her hands together in front of his face.* Well, if you're that interested in our laundry and linen out here, you can mend the big tear in that one yourself which was no doubt got in the sort of place my boys would meet you.

TOM Mother, he stuck up for us. You and Will always do this to our friends.

MRS DONNELLY Do what, this is the first one I ever caught pawing over my clothesline. Off to help with the horse now. *They exit.* Mike and John, who is that Man? Of all the orphans and has beens and poor lost souls you've brought home for me to take the edge of hunger off them, this is the only one I cannot seem to stand. How in Heaven's name can Tom and Bob not see that he's a rascal.

JOHN Mother, you don't know what a dreadful comment this is on your character.

MRS DONNELLY How so, is he really a good man? *The boys laughing as she leaves.*

MCCRIMMON And with that she swept out. I took notes on all they said and done, but she breaks any pencil I have around me to describe. But I put them through their paces, and they never caught on. For instance, *vulgar voice again* Bob. Which would you rather see—it burn, or put it out and have it cool in your pocket—a nice green dollar bill? *He sets fire to a dollar bill & floats it, Bob watches in fascination and fails the test utterly, squiggling as it burns and obviously "interested" in fire.*

TOM You know, Jake, you're not the only clever person around here and this is all among friends now. *He sticks a lead pipe in his trousers & drops a penny from his nose into the pipe.* Mike?

MIKE I haven't the skill, Tom, but I bet your new friend can't do it either

McCrimmon takes the pipe & sticks it in his trousers.

MCCRIMMON Bender's the name, Mike, Jake Bender

JOHN Ladies are present, Mr Bender. *After making sure they're not, McCrimmon balances the penny; Tom pours a dipper of cold water down the pipe. He roars & chases after them.*

JOHN *With head to ground.* What a runner he is, Mike. You can hear him pounding the earth like a giant. Where is he now?

MIKE Where the creek runs through. He's caught up to them. He's bringing them back, one under each arm. Look at the front of his pants!

McCrimmon entering & modestly turning his back to us; Stub, Finnegan et al resuming the backroom positions. The wedding party music strikes up.

MCCRIMMON Yes, I was the first man to bring the Donnelly gang to heel. She got a pair of pants I had to leave out there, but I got all the sons save Mike into the jails and prisons they belonged in. Thursday February the 24th, 1876, Gentlemen, my constables are ready, I hear the dance about to start over at Fitzhenry's Hotel over there and we'll soon see some more wildcat action.

STUB Well, I hope so, the room we used to meet in got burnt down. What kind of a case have you made out against them?

MCCRIMMON *going over to barrel* They've got about thirty friends. I'm going to select the weakest and dance him on a rope till he tells us what he knows about the Donnellys' activities, starting right here with this redhaired lad in the barrel. It's Tom Ryan the little sneaking spy is it. Chapter Three!

He closes the barrel & they roll Tom off as the wedding sweeps in. A fiddler jumps out over the bar; someone collects money in a hat to pay him; the bar in full flow, someone ladling out punch, girls sitting on boys' knees:

BOY What will you dance?

GIRL Your will is my pleasure, Dan.

FIDDLER What'll you have?

BOY Barney, put your wrist in it or Kitty here'll leave us both out of sight in no time. Whoo! Success! Clear the floor. Well done, Barney. That's the go.

The dance: Polka, Schottische, Reel if time. Play Will's march "Boney over the Alps" when he & John enter, Norah, Mr & Mrs Tom Ryder—the new bride & groom whose party this is.

CONSTABLE(S) *with staves* John Donnelly, we've come to arrest you for assualt & battery of Joseph Berryhill. Read the warrant if you like. Come along, now, John.

JOHN But it's dated a month ago, why have you waited till now when I'm at the dance?

CONSTABLE Come along with us to the lock-up.

WILL Come back here, John. Don't be dragged away by that fellow.

CONSTABLE Come back here, Jack Donnelly.

WILL Stay here, John. You're staying with me at this dance. I'm just out of jail and my brother's not going there and I'm not going back. Bob, where's Tom and Will Farl?

VOICE Give it to him. Will

CONSTABLE Hey you! Bring that man back here, he's my prisoner *grabbing*

JOHN What's this about, Bawden? When you arrested me before I went with you like a man.

CONSTABLE Yes, when you had to *pulls at John, crowd pulls the other way*

VOICES *chanting* We won't let John go ever from this party oh

WILL Let him go, you son of a bitch. You couldn't have tried this at a more infuriating time I'll blow your heart out of you or any other man that'll try, just try to take him or any other of the family. *Melee, shots. All out save the hanging scene.*

MCCRIMMON Chapter Four! Tom Ryan, the militia are rounding up your friends and herding them into the lock-up so there's no one to gallop by and see you hanging up in this tree, so just tell us the answers please like a good lad.

Constables enter with John & put him behind a ladder

CONSTABLE The Queen versus John Donnelly. Assault and resisting arrest.

CHORUS Three months in the Central Prison

STUB Three months! It should have been three years!

MCCRIMMON I can't get this youngster to talk. Tom Ryan, I want you to tell all you know about those Donnellys. You're such a friend of the Donnellys, you're into all their plans

TOM Hang me, hang me and get it over with, I won't tell.

MCCRIMMON You won't tell. No? Pull him up *pause* Now will you tell on the Donnellys?

CONSTABLES The Queen versus Tom Donnelly. Misdemeanour.

CHORUS Nine months in the Central Prison. The Queen versus Bob Donnelly

Again the two are brought in & placed behind ladders with clanking sounds

CONSTABLES Shooting with intent, two years in the penitentiary

MCCRIMMON Do you know anything about the burning & cutting up of those stage wagons? Do you know anything about the meat that's been stolen?

TOM Listen, mister, if you'd let me see who you are I'd tell you everything. *McCrimmon motions to have his eyebandage removed* Ready? *pause* I done them things. I stole the meat because I was hungry, I broke the dishes in the hotel, The Donnelly boys themselves would like to know who does half the things—*he is pulled up*

MCCRIMMON The young liar. If he wants to go to prison with those he loves so let him go.

CHORUS The Queen versus William Donnelly.

Ryan comes to his ladder cell about the same time as Will.

CONSTABLES Shooting with intent. Nine months in the county jail.

MCCRIMMON Gentlemen, I'm ashamed of the brevity of their sentences, but we could not break the boy. I wish you'd warned me that he was subject to fits. Chapter Five!

TOM Will, I'm so proud to be in jail with you. I love the jail.

WILL Oh God, Tom Ryan. I hate the jail. Did Norah send anything along with you when you left Lucan now?

TOM A bar of soap. Here. *throws* Has it got a saw in it, Will, you're eating it?

WILL I know I am, Tom, and it's going to make me terribly ill.

MCCRIMMON But despite all that, gentlemen, I have rid your township of the vermin for some time and you Finnegan are again the King of the Road and you Squire Stub—can look forward to an election campaign where your candidate will meet only fair opposition, not the shears, clippers and torch he very well might have. Gentlemen, my pay. *Just as they give him a bag—*

VOICE *Lady reading newspaper* Well it says here that William Donnelly is very sick of a low fever in the jail and is not expected to live much longer—his wife is petitioning the Attorney General to let him off his sentence.

MCCRIMMON Chapter Six! Thank you. Thursday, August 22nd. Today I proposed to my beloved and was accepted. She will marry a man who has just been appointed Chief of Police for Belleville.

He exits into the audience with the quilt that is Mike & Nellie's bed held behind him.

CHORUS Like a flower, Eunice found herself and her pink frilly dress swept into the powerful arms of the brave Detective, winner of many athletic events.

Mike & Nellie in bed.

NELLIE Always seem to wake up before Mike. Listen for the children. Take a look at the newspaper. Think. The village has been quiet since they're all gone off to jail. Didn't get Mike though. In his dreams he's finally got off the stage, you can tell from his breathing. When he first wakes up there's a minute before he tenses up for the day on the road which goes by our window and in that moment you can tell him things that might get him too excited later on, apt to rush off and hit somebody. But there's something I've got to tell him before it's too late. When we first met at the dance–I broke off my engagement with a lad called Sid Skinner because I fell so in love with Mike. Sid and me'd been courting for a year, but I could not help it, Mike was the man for me, but Sid's been coming to my mother's house on Horton Street lately, tipsy from his work at the hotel and saying he's going to kill, you, Mike. Wake up, Mike, so I can put this to you. I've never told you but the man who tends bar at the City Hotel used to be in love with me. Mike?

MIKE What time is it? Five o'clock by the light. Nellie?

NELLIE Mike.

MIKE Do you want to spend the rest of your life here in this house on Main Street of Lucan? Don't be afraid to tell me.

NELLIE You know how happy I've been with you, Mike, wherever you are and whatever happens.

MIKE I don't mean that, I know that, but have you ever thought you'd like to live another place?

NELLIE Yes, oh God yes, Mike. *Finnegan's stage horn* Mike, there's Finnegan's stage–it's later than I thought, you'll be late for work.

MIKE Nellie, I don't know why I've been ashamed to tell you, but yesterday was the last day I'll ever drive the Opposition Stage. They've won. Without my brothers beside me I can't go on. So I've got a job as a brakeman on the Canada Southern and we'll leave today for St Thomas. Do you feel ashamed of me?

NELLIE God no, Mike. There was something else I wanted to tell you, but its all right now we're moving so far away, what's the matter.

Stage passes with horn and shout.

MIKE *shaking fist out window* I'll drive over your grave yet, McKellar. Oh God, I loved driving that road. *pause* Nellie, there's smoke coming out of our kitchen window downstairs, they've set fire to our house, quick get the babies, Mother of God save us from Finnegan's Fire.

A red glare we have seen before. Viewpoint: roll on floor with baby dolls; scream from wife.

CHORUS

The Election of 1878
Then shout John A. forever boys,
That is the heading cry;
Every election we will win,
The time is drawing nigh,
The scheming Grits may bag their heads
That is if they've a mind,
Or go and dig up taters
With their shirts hung out behind

STUB Gentlemen of Ward Three, it gives me great pleasure to see the Conservative Meeting at the Donnelly Schoolhouse so crowded tonight. As I see some of our Grit friends here I trust and hope that you will give our speaker a fair hearing. May I give a particularly warm welcome to Mr William Donnelly whom the Grit government of our fair province has seen fit to release from his chamber at the Queen's boarding house where he was reportedly deathly ill. Although looking quite recovered from his fever, I would ask as a special favour that he not overtax himself or it might bring on another—attack. As you all know the Conservative Candidate for this riding is an Irish Catholic nominated by his Irish Protestant brothers. Gentlemen, I have been requested to perform a very pleasing duty this evening and it is to introduce to you the next member for the riding of North Middlesex—Mr Timothy Corcoran. *applause*

CORCORAN *manipulates a puppet version of himself* Gintlemen farmers of Biddulph, yees are ruined by Mr McKinsey and his free trade. Ivery market in the country is filled with Yankee horses, cattle and hogs. Yees are losing fifteen cints on ivery bushell of barley ye sell, and yees can't get over half price for yees pays and oats, bekase millions uv bushels uv Yankee corn comes into the country not paying a cint of duty. You farmers have to pay tin cints more for yare tay and two cints more for yare sugar—Mr Chairman, I see a hand up at the back of the room.

MRS DONNELLY *who has been following the speech in a newspaper and has been reading along with the speaker for a bit says:* This is the same speech as he gave in Ailsa Craig a week ago. It's all printed down here in the Advertiser

STUB Don't heed that hand, on and louder, Tim

CORCORAN —two cints more for yare sugar, yes, Will Donnelly what did you want to ask?

WILL If, Mr Corcoran, you were elected to parliament next Tuesday and say in a year's time—say your party got in, Macdonald's party—and again there was a scandal about money and there came up a vote of confidence in the government how, Mr Corcoran, would you vote?

CORCORAN I don't know. When the time comes, Bill, I'd know by that time because I'd have studied it up you see.

WILL Although you are a Catholic the Orange Lodge supports your candidacy, Mr Corcoran. What is your vote likely to be when their Grand Master tries to ram a bill through Parliament for the incorporation of the Orange Lodge?

CORCORAN Oh, Will Donnelly, never fear I'd never vote for such a thing.

WILL But Mr Corcoran, you would have to as a member of the Conservative Party.

CORCORAN Yes, I suppose I would. Mr Stub—

VOICE It's Mr Stub should be telling us instead of Tim

VOICE Sure, it's well known George Stub here gets a senatorship if Tim gets in

VOICE Sure, send him to parliament by voting for Tim. I say three cheers for the Grit Candidate Mr Colin Scatcherd who has one face under one hat. Hip Hip Hurrah.

In the cheers, objects fly at the speakers who withdraw. The newsclerk chalks up results on the bulletin board; a feeling of tension, torches, election night fever, close arithmetic.

CLERK Mr Scatcherd . . . the North Middlesex Riding has been won by the Grit Candidate in a tight race. Mr Scatcherd has won the seat by seven votes. *Cheers for Scatcherd led by Will Donnelly*

STUB *in the drawing room* Seven votes. We lost by seven votes. We were supposed to win by four hundred! Where's my wife Bridget?

BRIDGET *parlourmaid* Master Stub, your wife has gone back to live with your father in law. She said to tell you it might look like a Senator's house, but she read about the election results in the paper and you had not kept her promise to her.

STUB She's nervous and overwrought with the baby coming on. Bridget, what's your family's theory about why we lost. Is it not just the Donnellys?

BRIDGET Sir, my brother says, sir, it is the Donnellys. Without them and we'd have a Catholic gentleman in parliament this evening and maybe in Sir John A's cabinet, but no—it's the Donnellys don't want that.

STUB Could I speak to your brother some time, Bridget. How long has it been since he's back from the States?

BRIDGET Please, sir, not very long. He just arrived on the Finnegan Stage from town a good hour ago and sure I'm giving him a bit of supper in your kitchen.

STUB Tell him to come in here. *pause* What's your name?

CARROLL *wiping mouth* I told him what my name was.

STUB James Carroll. Did you leave here for the States because you were in any kind of trouble, Jim?

CARROLL No, sir. My father married again and I could not get along with my stepmother, after he died, she got his land away from us and I've come back to see about that and—

STUB Your mother was a Farl, was she not, Jim?

CARROLL How'd you know that?

STUB Donnellys killed her brother, didn't they?

CARROLL Yes. What this man was asking me to do was what my mother on her deathbed made me promise to do. To kill the Donnellys. But at first no one had the courage, no one except my poor dead mother, to say that. At first it was drive them out of the township, they were all out of prison more or less and all back on top of us so I was made a constable in Lucan and my aim was to find one victim of the Donnellys brave enough to stick to his story and fight it out in the courts and keep after them again and again until we had these Donnellys behind bars or out of the township or—out!

NED RYAN *falling flat* I've been robbed! Tom Donnelly robbed me of, he and Jim Feeney, robbed me of 85 dollars!

CARROLL When did the robbery take place, Mr Ryan?

NED Wednesday night, whatever night that was. About a year ago.

WILL Mr Ryan, what did you have to drink at Walker's Hotel?

NED Well, I do not get drunk often. I treated Tom and Jim to some whiskey, but I myself had some sherry wine and some ginger wine.

WILL Is it true you were come into town that day for a spree, that you had been at the following hotels first: the Dublin House, the Queen's, the Royal, Fitzhenry's, the Western, Levitts—

NED Never at Levitt's, never darken his door, haven't got to Fitzhenry's, still haven't got there!

WILL Is it true that you have several times lately entered my father's house and my own house in search of your son who has run away from you?

NED My son! Waiting for his pa to come home with some food for the table and the Donnellys have stolen all his money away from him and I'm at home waiting for my son and he does not come to his pa and you want to know why—because the Donnellys've stolen him away from his dear pa and ma like the fairies used to steal little children away when you weren't watching.

WILL Is it not true also that although you say that my brother choked you when you fell down, the inmates of the house who took you in could find no marks on your throat?

SQUIRE I dismiss this case, Ned Ryan. I think one of the constables summed it all up when he said that you were so drunk that night you couldn't have known your mouth from your arsehole.

CARROLL Your honour, may I as a friend of Ned Ryan's here and as a—may I say that I am not satisfied with the way my friend's case has been handled. We will bring it up before another magistrate

WILL Your honour, in view of Mr Carroll's statements, I would like the fact that the charges against my brother, Thomas Donnelly, have been dismissed, I would like a certificate made out to that effect.

CARROLL Yes, and I could make you out a certificate about the way justice has been administered in this village so that his family and their ruffian friends can bully and terrify a township of three thousand inhabitants. You Donnellys say you're persecuted; ask the horses and cattle and the barns and the stables and the women and the men here like Ned Ryan who's lost his boy to you who is being persecuted. Is there anybody in this room who'll stick up for this gang of mad Donnelly dogs—look at his foot!—whom some of you think of as being so wonderful. And I hear one or two of yous thinking of renting my father's farm from my stepmother and there's some of you stopping at the Donnellys' for a drink of water at their well. There's a whole lot of you still doing that and if we hear of any such, or of any man or woman offering Mrs Donnelly a ride in their cart on the way to mass or *He menaces the whole theatre; we are afraid of him*

WILL *lightly and suddenly entering* Now is that you, Jim Carroll, sitting on that horse of yours, under the tree talking to yourself about us give me that whip of yours there before you hurt yourself with it and come out of the shadow so we can get a look at you. Yes, you won. You smeared our name for all time so that when children are naughty their mothers still say to them

WILL & CHORUS be quiet, or the Black Donnellys will get you.

WILL Isn't that what most of you in this room think of us as being? Because of him my mother was turned into a witch who rode around burning down sheds and barns, because of him ... but there's one thing, Jim, that some people coming after will remark on. And that is—the difference between our handwritings. There is my signature. There is his. Choose. You can't destroy the way my handwriting looks, just as you can never change the blot that appears in every one of your autographs and the cloud and the smudge and the clot and the fume of your jealousy. There! the living must obey the dead! Dance the handwriting that comes out of your arm. Show us what you're like. Very well, I'll dance mine.

First Will, (fiddle) then Carroll, (trumpet), dance; the latter falls down in a fit. Placards displaying their signatures are held up for us to see.

WILL Oh now Jim, I didn't mean you were to fall down in one of those fits you have now and again. Is it your heart sometimes, is it your mind sometimes, is it your great big feet sometimes, Jim, is it that you couldn't stand the way the Donnellys dressed, the way they looked right through you, the way my mother looked down at you. So you clubbed her to kneel at your feet, but you forget that our eyes don't kneel at your feet, but you forget that our eyes don't kneel and that her eyes will look down and through you until dies irae and beyond. Down and through the clown with blood on his sleeves they called James Carroll. *Exit*

CARROLL It's true. I couldn't club down their eyes. After it was over

I had to leave Biddulph. I never went back there. You people here'd used me like a piece of dirty paper to wipe the Donnellys off your backsides. I died out West alone. Grave whereabouts unknown. I hate William Donnelly. I hate William Donnelly.

CHORUS End of Act Two.

The St Nicholas Hotel Wm Donnelly Prop.

Act Three

A gravel train with Mike Donnelly as brakeman backs into the audience. Three whistles for stop after Mike has signalled this with his lantern. Switch light and the two red lanterns on the back of the train move accordingly. Song over and Nellie to one side as commentary.

MIKE & CHORUS

I want to be a brakeman
And with the brakeman stand
A badge upon my forehead
A tail rope in my hand

With links & pins & bell cord
And signals red & white
I'd make a freight train back up
Or slack ahead all right.

When ere a train I shunted
At St Thomas so fair
I'd not forget my darling wife
But keep the crossing clear

NELLIE My husband Michael Donnelly, was a brakeman on a gravel train out of Waterford on the Canada Southern Line, division point St Thomas where I live with our children in a house on Mill Street—two nights he spends alone boarding at Waterford; tomorrow is his day off and he'll be home with us for four nights. But this is Wednesday, December 9th 1879. There's no snow yet. About four o'clock it begins to rain. His mate afterwards told me this is the way it went with Michael and the train, I wanted to know every crossing they came to before when their work was over they walked into the barroom at Slaght's Hotel. *Two blasts. The journey establishes itself then goes under her speech.* That means the engineer is ready to go. From the hind end of the train Mike gives him the highball so he whistles two short blasts meaning "I understand." Yes, I understand—that in the months before my husband was murdered in that barroom at Slaght's Hotel—there was a train, there was another sort of train that started out just after that election 1878 and every crossing it blew its whistle for was a crossing that was closer to my husband's death and I wish I could be clear in my own mind what that First Crossing was but I think I can see you there in cold blood talking about how you'll kill him and I run towards you to stop you but I meet the glass of mystery and time and trickery. I fall down and only know that I must listen for all the other four crossings Mike's train whistled for before the last time he walked out of the rain.

The barroom of the City Hotel fades in: Carroll, Sid Skinner & a Trainer.

CARROLL Well, shall we get started? We've got the job set up for you, Sid.

SID That's good of you. And then what do I do?

CARROLL What's the matter?

SID It's a great thing I'm to do, kill a man and go to prison for God knows how long. All today, all tonight at this bar I've been thinking about it and I have to pinch myself to wake up—this is happening to me, this is happening to you, Sid. Sid is getting out of here.

CARROLL Suit yourself, Sid Skinner. Maybe, and Bill here would agree with me, it'd just prove what Mike Donnelly said about you as he boasted about the girl he took away from you.

SID I don't want to know what he said. Just the last few days I realized what a duck I was going to her mother and saying I was going to kill Mike Donnelly. I'm not a fighting man.

CARROLL Then what kind of man was it who handled the bar in here tonight, eh Bill? That was a fighting man, but a fighting man that's not all just fight, but some brains in his head as well, eh? If Mike had seen you tonight he'd have had to eat his words—

SID What words?

CARROLL That you were a man of no prick. Yes, them's the dirty words he used about you, auh, he's a little fellow with no prick on him at all—**that** little fellow

SID Teach me how to kill him then. What dirt do I have to go through to wipe that off his mouth, yes, what's the false name you're giving me?

CARROLL After the lesson tonight, Sid, if you learn it well, you'll have a new name. Now, you're lucky you don't have to deal with the whole tribe the way I have to up in Biddulph. I wish I just had the one desperate character to clean up, but I've got six or seven of Mike's relatives to deal with every day and do you know who's the worst?

SID You're afraid of them?

CARROLL The mother, she's the one I'm

SID You're most afraid of an old woman?

CARROLL Well, what would you have done? If you can do it, maybe I can Sid, I don't know. On Monday morning last, Bill here saw me just after in Gallagher's yard and I was shaking like a leaf, for not an hour ago I'd took my life in my hands and dared to walk down the road past the Donnelly's place—was going to get some notes from a man I'd sold a fanning mill, Jack Donnelly was out plowing, Mrs Donnelly was milking a cow by the gate and Tom had just cursed me—Jack said—

JOHN Now there's that fighting man, Mr Jim Carroll. Jim—I want to talk to you. What were you saying about Bob and our family at the sale last night?

CARROLL I don't want to talk to you, Jack Donnelly, I've got too much respect for myself. Meet me this afternoon at Whalen's Corners.

JOHN Let's have no mobbing at Whalen's Corners, Jim. I'll fight you, right now, I'll make your big head soft right there on that road. What business is it of yours how light a sentence Bob got?

CARROLL Don't want much to fight, but if you'll meet me at Whalen's Corners I'll fight you. I'll lick all the Donnellys. Well, Jack drops his plow and he strode at me. I'm an inofffensive man. You come at me and I'll shoot you. Keep off *Tom throws stone*

JOHN Tom—get out on the road and thrash him—the coward, the thief.

CARROLL Now listen to what she said.

MRS DONNELLY You son of a bitch, you thief, you rogue. Give it to him, Tom, on his big head. Point a gun at an old woman milking a cow would you, you bastard, you should be arrested, Jim Carroll, and when they arrest you they should put you back down into the devil with thirty tails you belong to.

CARROLL Oh—the dirty names she called, calling my mother a dog and saying my father never married her, she made me feel so jumpy I just walked on, oh—I need someone to show me the way, I wouldn't dare shoot any of them now or ever. It's her, Sid, do you understand me, she's a witch and we'll never get rid of any of them unless there's someone brave enough to just—But there isn't. The mad dogs have won.

SID No, they haven't.

CARROLL Oh, well then, Bill to the bar please and just let on that you're Michael Donnelly taking a drink. Now, Sid—

Sid goes up to the trainer, hauls him around by the shoulder; they fight, but the trainer soon pins Sid to the ground.

BILL It's no use, Jim, all we've taught him doesn't put the weight on him Donnelly has and I'm doing just the things Donnelly does.

CARROLL Let's add something. Sid, watch me. Bill. Stop shooting off your big mouth, Mike Donnelly

Bill is stationed by the bar again. Carroll draws a jackknife which he holds in his left hand; he hits Bill from behind and draws Bill into chasing him behind the bar. In the clinch, Bill has hold of Carroll's shoulders but Carroll holds him by the vest and with the other knife hand stabs him below the belt.

BILL Do you want something from me. Holy name of God, Jim Carroll, go easy with that open knife. Do you want to try that now, Sid? And I think, Jim, the first few times with the Sid here we'll have the knife closed.

SID Stop shooting off your big mouth, Mike Donnelly.

BILL Do you want something from me?

Sid & Bill go through the new business. Exhausted but livened up & confident once more, Sid leans back against the bar while

Carroll unlocks the bar and pours them all a drink . . . even for the privy cleaner who now comes forward with shaving mug & lather.

CARROLL The mad dogs have lost.

SID Who's he? He's been watching all this.

CARROLL He's Mr Nobody, Sid, a retired barber, well semi-retired, he'd like to start shaving you just to rearrange your face whiskers a bit as well as your topknot

SID He smells!

CARROLL Well, when you enter the world where you have two faces under the one hat, Sid, you can't be too choosey about your barber any more. Cleans out privies for a living now because the razor hand got rather unsteady there one famous time, oh nothing to fear, Sid, by the way we've got to start calling you by your new name.

SID What's my new name.

CARROLL You've got a new name with the new job you're going to take tonight—you'll be a navvy for the Canada Southern near Waterford where your friend from Biddulph is a brakeman on their gravel train right now and everything is fixed up, don't worry, remember borrow the jackknife a few days before from some chum at your rooming house, let's go back in here to shave him.

SID What's my name.

BILL Same as my name, Bill Lewis.

SID But that's your name. I'm not a bit like you

BILL Sure it is. Sure you're not, but look here don't start wanting some other name. Jim, he doesn't like my name. I'm getting sore.

CARROLL Ah, darling, you like his name really don't you at heart. It's a stout little plain little name for a stout little plain little—you'll be like St Patrick, "Bill Lewis"

Laughing then both singing the St Patrick song as they escort him out behind the bar

BOTH

When blind worms crawling in the grass
Disgusted all the nation,
He gave them a rise which opened their eyes
To a sense of their situation.

So, success attend St Patrick's fist
For he's a saint so clever;
Oh! he gave the snakes and toads a twist
And bothered them forever...

The toads went pop, the frogs went hop,
Slap-dash into the water;
And the snakes committed suicide
To save themselves from slaughter.

So, success &c.

The clock in the St Nicholas Hotel strikes eleven: wind—establish this well before the other scene quite fades and we are back with the Minister & Will.

WILL Mr Donaldson, the next time the clock strikes, I know that I will have come to that part in my story I promised you—my brother Michael's death

DONALDSON You were telling me, Mr Donnelly, that the new priest formed a society against your family from among your fellow parishioners.

WILL Oh he turned them against us. But the man who really worked at turning people against us, and you see we were not to be trusted because we had led the parish in not voting the way that Bishop and Sir John A would have had us vote—the man who really worked at it was a drifter named James Carroll. I'll show you, sir, how our family first met him. We became an obsession with him, I think he was hungry for land, our land, our eyes, our clothes, our mother. They'd just lost the election, we'd won and down the road he came and my mother was milking a cow by the gate.

JOHN Oh I was on speaking terms with him. But he was a queer fellow

CARROLL Jack, what's this you were saying about me.

JOHN Nothing yesterday, Jim Carroll, but what I could say today.

CARROLL I wish you'd come out of that field and do it. You meet me at Whalen's Corners at two o'clock and we'll fight there.

JOHN There's none here but the two of us. We'll have it out here, Jim Carroll, and have no mobbing about it.

CARROLL *draws revolver* You son of a bitch. If you come one foot further, I'll blow your brains out. *Tom comes with stones*

WILL Tom—throw the stones down, he wants law, not fight.

MRS DONNELLY Go back, John, don't mind the blackguard or he'll shoot you.

CARROLL I'd as leave shoot you as him. *She rises, looks at him & turns her back on him.*

MRS DONNELLY Go away and mind your own business. I don't want anything to do with you.

CHORUS The Queen against Julia Donnelly

CARROLL Using abusive and insulting, grossly insulting language

MRS DONNELLY And I was convicted of doing so and fined one dollar and costs. He dragged me into court and into one of the newspapers where it was printed that I had thrown stones at him. Why, sir, are you hunting me down. Yes, I must be a beast if you can draw a revolver and aim it at me and no one says no

CHORUS The Queen against James Carroll

MRS DONNELLY Making threats to use revolver with intent. *pause* Well, I see that we get nowhere with that charge so that next time he walks by our house it may be with a mob who will—Jim Carroll, when I looked into your eyes I could see your mother's eyes and I could see you hating me long ago because you were fat and we'd killed your brother, on your deathbed you must have sharpened his teeth for me *Fat Lady's ghost crosses to her chair.* And if you have got some mud on the mother, the next crossing is to chase her sons and his friends about as if they were wild animals and the next crossing is to bring a mob to their father and mother's door, but first we have come to the *train journey up with crossing signal*

CHORUS Third Crossing.

Actors form Roman Line leaving their chairs unguarded. Tom Ryan, Tom Donnelly, James Carroll with cheesecloth over their faces play tricks, steal props from chairs, spin tops illegally, pick pockets, gallop up & down the road after they've gone asleep, snoring—whole Puck episode, ladies on their bums from chamberpots sort of thing.

WILL *after a silent build* Soon after this there began in the neighbourhood a whole parade of little mischievous things—Little, they began to get bigger and bigger and they told stories that my brother Tom took out horses, their horses at night and rode them up and down.

CHORUS From tollgate to tollgate

FARMER Until they're nigh dead and you know what Tom Donnelly's tied to her tail. *He holds up a placard saying "Vote Grit & Vote Right."*

FAT LADY *a scream of rage at this* That's Cripple's beautiful handwriting.

WILL There were stories that Tom Ryan in the middle of the night let people's cattle out of their fields and drove them up into Blanshard township.

VOICES IN SUCCESSION Who stole my disk? Who stole my pig? My tea chest is gone. Who done that? I know who done that. Who shaved my horses' tails? Who put stones in my threshing machine and iron pins? We know who done that

WILL Do you now and who done that?

CHORUS Who? stole my disk and stole my pig
rode my horses and drove my cows
cut out their tongues and cut off their ears?
repeat softly

The three mystery faces whip them like tops humming: Donnelly!

WILL Until my father said one day; If a stone fell from heaven they'd say

WILL & CHORUS Donnelly done it.

WILL We were blamed for everything and people shunned us, **would** not talk to us. Three times Carroll arrested my brother Tom on the charge of stealing

NED One hundred dollars from me—Ned Ryan and three times the case fell through

WILL But one fall night Carroll got a new warrant from the Grand Jury and he was out at our house at dawn to serve it

MRS DONNELLY Yes, you should look behind the stove, Mr Carroll, and why not look right in the stove while you're at it.

CARROLL I could not find him. I went over as far as Skinner's in Usborne and where Will lived at Whalen's Corners before I turned back.

MARY DONOVAN I was spinning opposite the doorway in the house that day—could see the concession from where I was working. Saw Thomas Donnelly in his father's potato field picking potatoes. I went upstairs for yarn rolls and I saw William Donnelly drive into his father's place and signal to Tom in the field

CARROLL I went over the fence into Mr Donnelly's field—went across a fall wheat field expecting to get in his tracks to follow him

MARY When I saw Carroll & Thomas Donnelly running they were both near the stable. Saw John Donnelly come out with a horse. Tom Donnelly came up running, got on the horse and ran away.

CARROLL If you'll stay away out of the county it's not particular if I catch you, Tom Donnelly. *To John* I'll make it hot for you when I get to Lucan, John Donnelly. You'd no business giving him that horse to escape with.

JOHN Jim, you never told me you had a new warrant for Tom.

CARROLL What do you think I was running all over that wheat field for?

JOHN Jim, Tom's not running away on you, sure he hardly seen you, he's going up to Kenny's blacksmith shop to get us some

CARROLL I went over to Quigley's and stopped the thrashing. They got their horses and we chased Tom Donnelly into the bush all around the township from tollgate to tollgate all that night, but by the holy name of God could we *helter skelter pursuit of Tom Donnelly*

CHORUS We've got him who stole my disk and stole my pig
rode my horses and drove my cows
cut out their tongues and cut off their ears

NED RYAN It's my son, Tom, dressed up in Tom Donnelly's clothes. Tom why would you play such a trick on us? Why would you side with the family that won't let the thrashing machine come to thrash at your father's farm and the crops are rotting in the field, why

TOM You old ruffian—I'll tell you why I side with the Donnellys. And you clodhoppers and you drifter—trying to pull them down. Three reasons. Because they're brave. They're not afraid. They're so little afraid of living here among you that this morning they started sowing their fall wheat. Two. They're handsome. Look at your faces—your faces'd fit into the hoofprints of forty old cows hopelessly lost in a bog. Yes, high & mighty one with your dirty linen scarce covering your hippopotamus rump and your hair like Third. When pa here took the axe to mother and Bridget and Sarah & me who was the only family on the whole road with enough sand to take us in? *pause* So that's why I side with them, Pa, and if you want to know who's doing all the mischief on this road it's him over there—Jim Carroll.

CARROLL Is it Jim Carroll for sure now, Tom Ryan?

NED RYAN Stand back from him all of you, let a father deal with his begetting. Come here my darling. I want you to be my boy again not the Donnellys' boy.

TOM You're going to beat me, aren't you, Pa.

NED No. *pulling open his shirt* Look at my heart in my chest now beating with love for you. Come to my heart—don't the rest of you lay a hand on him. Tom.

His arms are extended although we do see the club in his back pocket ready. Tom pauses, then runs at his belly with his head down and knocks him down, escapes. Everyone feels out of fuel; gawk listlessly, even Carroll. All at wits' end then cowbell and spinning sound before it, leading up to it.

MARY *ear shattering* My cow! The Donleys have stolen my cow. On Sunday evening my cattle were all at my gate when I came home. On Monday morning I went to look for her. I cannot get a trace of her. Who's man enough here to come and help me look for my cow? My cow! They're skinning and eating and cooking my cow right this very minute now and you just sit on your backsides and gawp at me, you gomerils. My cow's hidden somewhere at the Donleys.

CHAIRMAN Mary Donovan, Magistrate Stub says we can't have a warrant now because it's night time, but we are to keep watch and at dawn we can search. Will all members of the Peace Society who plan to visit the Donnelly homestead tomorrow come into the schoolhouse and take turns watching for dawn?

MARY *whispering as she exits with the others* It'll be too late by daybreak, they'll have eaten my cow all up, my cow! I had good reason to suspect the Donleys of taking my cow. The reason I suspected the Donleys as I had heard things spoke against them.

Silence as the night passes; crickets of early September, a bell rings matins, a wagon passes, train whistle, a clock strikes an early hour in the Donnelly house.

MRS DONNELLY The air was hollow so that you could hear things far away that night. Or did I dream it that first I was on a coach and then a train and I was taking an empty coffin to a tavern where they were going to kill one of my sons. Their leaving the school and tramping down the roads towards our place must have wakened me, but as I lit the stove and went to wake up my niece Bridget they were quiet enough.

CHORUS There's smoke coming up now from their chimney.

Whispers offstage under the audience. We are part of the mob.

MRS DONNELLY The sun comes up, there's my shadow long—getting shorter already, turn earth another morning and noon and night I wish I could stop it Bridget take out the pail and pump us a fresh pail of water, yesterday I could hear Mary Donovan spinning in her doorway, watching us, I wonder

Bridget screams and runs in

BRIDGET Aunt Judith, where shall we hide, there's a mob in the yard with sticks in their hands.

John sleeps behind the stove

MRS DONNELLY Augh! what has possessed them now. Go tell Mr. Donnelly. John, get dressed. I stood behind the door and looked through the crack at them. Why is it getting so dark in our house. Because the light of each window is shut out by the people there.

BRIDGET Uncle Jim, the yard is full of men with clubs. Johnny, you'd best get up

Mr Donnelly hitching up trousers, goes to the door and addresses a mob whose presence we feel rather than see.

MR DONNELLY Good morning, boys, what's up with you?

CARROLL We want nothing but to tell you Donnellys that we're not afraid of you

MRS DONNELLY Look at the dark bunch of them and he alone, what is it, it's

VOICE We're not afraid of you anymore, Donnelly.

MARY I have lost a cow

MRS DONNELLY A cow they say has been stolen from Mary Donovan's farm and we are suspected

VOICE We're through with being scared of the Donnellys.

MRS DONNELLY Why 'tis only right the cow should be found. If you think the cow is here, Jim Carroll, don't leave one straw on top of another

JOHN Turn the strawstack upside down. There's no stolen cow here, but I see the man who stole your cow in your crowd

Searching sounds, pails getting kicked, doors slammed &c.

VOICE We'll make you keep quiet, Jack Donnelly.

JOHN If you go up to the priest he'll curse the man who stole the cow and you'll find the cow before night.

CARROLL How'd you like a good stiff kick in the ribs?

MR DONNELLY And you can all kiss my backside. And I was a man, Jim Carroll, when you were not able to wipe your backside.

CARROLL We could break your bones at your door and you won't be able to help yourself.

MR DONNELLY I'll be here if the devil would burn the whole of you. I'm not in the least afraid of you. *He comes in the house.*

MRS DONNELLY They're kicking over hencoops and looking down the well, yes, fall down it if you can, John Macdonald, what is it I hear him begging them to do, they're putting forks through the strawstacks we thrashed yesterday, he's saying—

MR DONNELLY I wish John would stay in closer to the house, do you see that?

MRS DONNELLY Yes, they've circled him and they're saying things like

CHORUS Who stole my disk

JOHN I don't know who stole your disk

CHORUS Who stole my pig

JOHN How the hell would I know

CHORUS

who stole my disk and stole my pig
rode my horses and drove my cows
cut out their tongues and cut off their ears
who shaved off my horses' tails

JOHN I don't know anything at all about your horses' tails, all I know is that you're trespassing and my father's farm has a fence, my father's land is enclosed, by the way you're acting you'd think it was a public path

MARY I have lost a cow.

CHORUS Don't you tell us to get out Jack Donnelly. We're not afraid of you I'll get satisfaction if it's for twenty years. This work'll be put down and it'll be put down by us.

A roar as they find Tom Ryan. They rush on stage with him & now we & the Donnellys look out at the mob.

CHORUS Here's one thing found.

CARROLL Sit up there in the wagon and don't you move

CHORUS Harbouring this young horserider and cattle driver, eh Donnelly.

MR DONNELLY I'd harbour your father's son, O'Halloran, if all the world said no

O'HALLORAN Little do you care Donnelly for my father's sons. Tie his hands, it's off to jail with this one.

TOM RYAN Mr Donnelly wasn't harbouring me, I slept in their strawstack last night, they didn't know I was there. *pause* And I sat up there on the wagon. She came out. I was handcuffed. She came out and looked across at me. Between me and her was them with their clubs. What have I brought down on you, or would it have happened anyhow? Mrs Donnelly She was tall. If I could have I would have died for her. The wagon took me off to jail. I never saw her again.

Carrying Tom Ryan on their shoulders the mob circle and depart

MRS DONNELLY Yes, I stood there and I watched them tie up that lad and cuff him and knock him about. They were leaving, they hadn't found Mary Donovan's cow, but I was so glad they were leaving that I didn't dare try to help the boy because for the first time in my life I felt old and small & afraid. There were so many of them. Is this not a pretty way we are treated Mr. Donnelly?

MR DONNELLY But we deserve it, Mrs Donnelly.

MRS DONNELLY In the name of Heaven how?

MR DONNELLY For we're Donnellys.

MRS DONNELLY Yes, and I also heard Will's brother in law say they were going to his place at Whalen's Corners next. John, hitch up the driving horse for me, please.
There is a slight tug of war over the whip with Mr Donnelly. Haven't they gone up the road by Keefe's Mr Donnelly?

MR DONNELLY Yes. If you must go, Mrs Donnelly, then you can cut over on the sideroad.

MRS DONNELLY *pause* I **must** go.

What we have now is a bare stage with the bar as a place where Mrs Donnelly can coast up & down & around. A blacksmith should enter and stand near the bar which is going to be Will Donnelly's house. Mary Donovan should be sitting getting ready to spin & we need a girl who can simply fill in the choral replies to Mrs Donnelly, spin about perhaps supported by off stage voices. I'm in favour of a "Listen to the Wind" wheel & horse with Mrs Donnelly running behind. Simple & light.

JOHN Mother, what are you listening for? *triangle sounds*

MRS DONNELLY
I can hear the blacksmith who lives over at the village
where Will & Norah live
Closer and louder the sound of his hammer
Wheels take me Hooves draw me
Out of the yard of his father's house

GIRL
In the stream that I lie dreaming in I hear
A humming sound that fills me up with fear

MRS DONNELLY
My neighbour, Mary Donovan, cow lady,
I leave you behind me.

And Mrs Donnelly has done one circuit of the stage & vanished

MARY I heard a cow bawling over on Donley's place that sounded like my cow. I honestly believed the Donleys had my cow. The Donleys had my cow shut up. A great deal of pork & cattle stealing has been taking place in our neighbourhood. *A farmer enters with two pails which he sets down.* Dan Quigley, did you hear I've lost my cow? The Donleys've stolen my cow.

FARMER Mary Donovan, I just seen your cow.

MARY Seen my cow? Impossible. Where?

FARMER She's in our yard. I keep telling you the fence is down by McLaughlin's bush there and she strayed up to our yard with our cattle last night.

Mary kicks the pails & hits him off with either stick or spinning wheel or spindle.

MARY Who the hell's side do you think you're on, Dan Quigley. Are you telling me I didn't hear her bawling over at Donley's?

anvil

MRS DONNELLY
Closer and louder the sound of his hammer
Wheels take me
Hooves draw me
Gee Pilot! round the corner of Marksey's farm.
Down this road grown over with grass

Mob humming the tune of the St Patrick song & just about to burst out from beneath bar crossing down to us & meet schoolmaster

GIRL

In the spinning I lie dreaming in I hear
A humming sound that fills me up with fear

MRS DONNELLY

Look not this way, Jim Carroll, my enemy.
I leave you behind me

Circuit ends & she disappears

MOB

When blind worms crawling in the grass
Disgusted all the nation
He gave them a rise which opened their eyes
To a sense of their situation

SCHOOLMASTER I was the schoolmaster at the Donnelly School. On the morning of September 3rd, 1879 I met 40 to 50 men at half past eight in the morning. They had clubs and bludgeons in their hands in the name of God, where are you all going to?

CHORUS We are going away for a heifer that was lost.

SCHOOLMASTER Did every one of you lose a heifer?

CHORUS No, no.

SCHOOLMASTER Then it's time to bid the devil good morning when you meet him.

CHORUS Oh, we're a long time seeking him.

SCHOOLMASTER Would you know the old lad when you meet him?

CHORUS Would we know him, sure he's a cripple and lives near a forge. *anvil*

MRS DONNELLY

Closer and louder the sound of his hammer
Wheels take me   Hooves draw me
Haw Pilot! turn north on the Cedar Swamp Line!
What is the matter with that field of grain?

GIRL

In the humming I lie dreaming in I wake and hear

MRS RYAN Mrs Donnelly, have mercy on my children, tell your sons to please let the thrashing machine come harvest our wheat and barley. We'll starve this year if it rots away.

MRS DONNELLY *the anvil gets louder & louder* No! there's no time for the wife of Ned Ryan *and louder as she enters Whalen's Corners*
The first house, a shed, the second
A ditch, picket fence, gateway, a path, my journey is over
Will, Norah *she knocks* at my son's door.

But she has no sooner entered Will's house than we hear the mob already at the blacksmith's; the anvil stops and there are sounds of hammers and forges being tossed down:

MOB *offstage* We'll visit you at all hours of the night when you least expect it.

Now Will, Norah & Mrs Donnelly come out. Will can use either a fiddle or a gun—both are hanging behind the bar that represents his house.

WILL Mother, Norah—I'll ask them for their authority to search either my house or its premises. Did they show father any warrant to search?

MRS DONNELLY Nothing but their shadows

WILL Well then, if they can't show me a warrant, I'll shoot the first man who comes in the gate.

MOB

Nine hundred thousand reptiles blue
He charmed with sweet discourses,
And dined on them at Killaloe
In soups and second courses

The mob now slowly come towards the backs of the Donnellys. They are afraid. It's not the same as at the other house. Will's hand reaches up for his fiddle, he turns, tunes & then plays "Boney over the Alps" laughing at them. Some of them get into the audience by mistake. We should feel ashamed ourselves that we did not make a better showing against a lame man & two women.

MRS DONNELLY Are you looking for your mother Dennis Trehy? That you left to starve in the workhouse at Ballysheenan though you're rich here in Canada?

WILL My mother's taken the hunger off a great many of you in days gone by when your parents sent you to our school with no lunch.

MRS DONNELLY And I wonder at Martin O'Halloran being with such a gang as his father's the decentest man in Biddulph.

WILL Give them another, they're in full flight down the road. *She*

turns sharply away. James Carroll fell down and there's others tripping about the proud Napoleons they are. Mother, Norah, do you remember I told you how mother gave me this fiddle? Then they sold me to the brewer
And he brewed me on the pan,
But when I got into the jug
I was the strongest man. And it's right what you told me then. If you're afraid you should be. If you're not you'll live. Today I thank you. One fiddle you gave me a lame boy of twelve, has been worth forty men with rifles and clubs.

MRS DONNELLY Yes, I've marked you all with my foolish words

WILL Not foolish. You've been dreaming of a train. This fiddle stopped that train.

MRS DONNELLY Yes. But only in the daylight. The night, Will and Norah, may have—the dark has shoulders they can stand upon. To reach our eyes and our minds at last. Hush!

They stand again with their backs to the vigilantes who enter with a sick Carroll. It is as if Mrs Donnelly can hear them for she half turns. They stagger about as before. Carroll is stretched on floor.

VOICE What's the matter with him?

NED RYAN They've made him ill. *tends him with some restorative*

VOICE He's having a fit if you ask me and I don't want to have anything more to do with this. I'm leaving

They are all sitting down on their haunches.

CARROLL How's your old mother, Dennis, back in the workhouse at Ballysheenan?

NED RYAN How'd she get there ahead of us so fast?

CARROLL She's a witch, that's why. And she shall be burnt for a witch. *relapses*

VOICE Ned Ryan, I think he wants something. Bend over him and—

NED RYAN *pause* He wants you to bring him the Holy Bible out of the school cupboard.

It is brought & Carroll uses it for a pillow.

CARROLL Yes, Dennis, I ran like the rest of you. Now that's better. I ran like the rest of you—but there wasn't one of you behind me and there wasn't one of you I could keep up to—tell me, how many of yous are willing to draw lots— *They all shy away.* to see who will sue Jack Donnelly for perjuring himself when he says that we trespassed on his father's farm today. Because, you'll note the old man did tell us "If you think the cow is here, Jim Carroll, don't leave one straw on top of another." *They raise hands & come closer.* Well, who wouldn't dare to do that, but here's one more thing, and we'll just see who's man enough to raise their hands to this proposition. In this Bible someone has placed eight slips of paper each with the name of a Donnelly written thereon. Who is brave enough to come up and draw one of those slips of paper out?

VOICE Jim, what does it mean if we do draw the piece of paper out?

CARROLL It means that that Donnelly will be executed before the year is out. If it can be shown that one can be killed and the executioner get away with it how many of you are then willing to go on with me at your head against the rest of the family and I promise you there will be no risk involved.

VOICE Sure if this one is killed and no one is punished, sure.

CARROLL Let's take a vote then. Ned, take the vote will you?

NED Yeas? *hands are raised* Nays? *some hands go up* Forty-one to seven, Jim.

CARROLL The seven nays are to leave this room forever and I dare them to speak. When the execution takes place remember—you must help or join the Blackfeets. Come up and swear.

VOICE But, Jim, nobody's drawn the lot yet and I'm not.

NED I'll draw it. She took away my son, I'll take back one of hers.

CARROLL Remember what you're about to promise because yes a brave man has been found, not afraid of them, and he'll show us the way, the way I could not show you this shameful morning.

VOICE Who's he going to kill then?

NED RYAN Michael Donnelly.

Mrs Donnelly says the name too, screams "My son", train whistle, the train proceeds to the

CHORUS Fourth crossing!

The bartender at Slaght's Hotel slides a glass down the bar as Mike & Morrison, his mate, enter. "William Lewis" is waiting; an old man named Greenwood is standing at the bar, sometimes bending down to spin a top.

BARTENDER Mike, Jim. You're off early tonight. Still raining outside?

MIKE We both ordered hot whiskeys because we were cold & wet still. I could feel the heat of the drink coming through the glass into the flesh of my hand. There's that old fellow always in here spinning his top and going to make the same joke he always does about fighting dogs. My top against your top, Greenwood. You've been waiting for this all day, haven't you?

They both spin tops which fight each other.

GREENWOOD How's your big bulldog you got, Mike Donnelly.

MIKE Back home in St Thomas I've got a bulldog that can lick anything its weight in Ontario

GREENWOOD I ain't got no dog, just this top, but I can whip any dog myself, I'll strip off my clothes and commence anytime.

MIKE Ah, you couldn't beat my bulldog, you can't even beat my top with your old top it's got more than a few holes gnawed out of it, where do you keep it, old fellow, there's been rats biting away at this one.

GREENWOOD Here, don't you insult my top. Those holes are for balance.

LEWIS You don't want to hop on that man, Donnelly.

MIKE No one is touching him, and it's none of your business if there was.

LEWIS You are always shooting off your mouth, aren't you Donnelly. *takes off coat*

MIKE Do you want anything of me.

MORRISON Now look, you two, quit it. All he said, Bill Lewis, was that his top had holes in it. Turn around away from each other. Greenwood if that's your name, see if Mike'll do you a favour and have a return match with his top meanwhile where's the washroom around here? *A clock strikes six*

MIKE You do want something from me.

"Lewis" strikes Donnelly from behind; as Mike tries to pin him he leads him back behind the bar with the knife open & ready. Just as Morrison returns from the washroom, Mike is stabbed below the belt. Lewis glides away; Morrison catches Mike just as he falls. Train whistle.

MIKE My God, Neighbour, I'm gone stabbed Jim, that's our train!

The chorus comes—at the wake for Michael at the Donnelly farm —with four poles which represent the fourposter bed he was laid

on. Candles. People kneel by the bier, then retire to the sides of the room.

MRS DONNELLY Yes, his bed is ready. Bring Michael in here boys. Bridget, bring me the clean shirt I've got ready for him.

She takes off his old shirt, washes him & puts on a white shirt.

MORRISON We carried Mike to the washroom. I held his head for a while and saw him die.

CHORUS He was under bonds to keep the peace, and he was considered a desperate character.

MORRISON We were brakemen on that train together. I think he would fight if he was set upon, but as a bully I never saw him have a row.

CHORUS The first named testified that the deceased was a quarrelsome bully and started the row, but the others testified that he was not a disorderly character—

MORRISON I caught hold of Donnelly for the purpose of assisting him. I never heard anybody say anything against Donnelly, and I never saw him engaged in a row.

MRS DONNELLY I then read in the newspaper that the respective lawyers and the judge then addressed the jury, after which they retired and returned in a short time with a verdict of manslaughter. Since there was no defence offered at all, one supposes that if the lawyer for this William Lewis had offered a defence why my son's murderer might have got off completely scot free, but as it was the judge sentenced this man whom Michael had never even met before that night, whom none of us knows—two years in prison. In this forest there is now a proclamation that the hunting season on my sons is now open. There are only five of them left, the breed is rare, but do not let that limit your greed for their hearts blood. Michael. I wish that as I spoke with your oldest brother as he lay dying last summer I could have been there with you this winter. I told him what I tell you now—to look straight ahead past this stupid life and death they've fastened on you—just as long ago your father and me and our firstborn walked up over the last hill in Ireland and saw, what you will see now—for the first time in our lives we saw freedom, we saw the sea.

MR DONNELLY Mrs Donnelly, the sleighs have come to take our son to the church.

Candles, four poster, all sweep out of the room. We are in a barroom again. Slaght's years after; two chambermaids have just been assigned to clean out the barroom; outside the sun is just getting up. The old tramp is whistling "Buffalo Gals" as he walks up the empty Main Street of Waterford; train whistle. The one maid throws the pail of water over the floor and starts scrubbing. A clock strikes twelve. The ghost of Mike Donnelly stands behind the bar.

MAID ONE Ugh, clean the hotel from top to bottom would you. We won't be done in here till midnight, the old muck from their feet and mouths. What're you looking so pale for, it's only an old barroom, been closed up for thirty years till this fool thinks he can run it for a profit again.

MAID TWO I thought I saw someone standing by the end of the bar over there.

MAID ONE There's no one there I can see, Mary.

MAID TWO You don't know Waterford, this place too well do you.

MAID ONE What's there to know? There's that old man sloping off into the dawn, I wish I were free to walk the roads, not tied down like this to a scrubbing brush.

MAID TWO I wish you wouldn't pick that place by the bar to scrub so, Sarah.

MAID ONE There you go with your ghosts again. I don't believe them.

MAID TWO Would you please stop your damn scrubbing at the same spot, Sarah.

MAID ONE Are you against clean floors or something? There's something on the floor here that won't come out.

MAID TWO He's looking right down at you

MAID ONE I'll wet his feet for him then. Give me that soap, I'll...

MAID TWO Don't you know there was a murder in this barroom about thirty years ago, one of the brakemen on the Canada Southern, was stabbed right there where you're scrubbing. That's the blood from his wound you're trying to wash out and my mother says...

MAID ONE Mary, go up and start the sitting room if this is too... what did your mother say?

MAID TWO That's the blood of Michael Donnelly on the floor there. No matter how hard you try it never comes out.

A top spins across the floor. Scrubbing of the remaining woman; Ghost still there. Whistling dies away. "Buffalo Gals".

CHORUS

The St Nicholas Hotel
William Donnelly Proprietor
The Donnellys, Part Two

Three Songs used in the Play

ST PATRICK
(to the tune of *Pop Goes the Weasel)*

Oh! St Patrick was a gentleman,
Who came of decent people;
He built a church in Dublin town,
And on it put a steeple.
His father was a Gallagher;
His mother was a Brady;
His aunt was an O'Shaughnessy,
His uncle an O'Grady.

CHORUS
So, success attend St Patrick's fist,
For he's a saint so clever;
Oh! he gave the snakes and toads a twist,
And bothered them forever.

The Wicklow hills are very high,
And so's the Hill of Howth, sir;
But there's a hill much bigger still,
Much higher nor them both, sir.
'Twas on the top of this high hill
St Patrick preached his sarmint
That drove the frogs into the bogs,
And banished all the varmint.

So, success attend St Patrick's fist, &c.

There's not a mile in Ireland's isle
Where dirty varmin musters,
But there he put his dear fore-foot,
And murdered them in clusters.
The toads went pop, the frogs went hop,
Slap-dash into the water;
And the snakes committed suicide

To save themselves from slaughter.
So, success attend St Patrick's fist, &c.

Nine hundred thousand reptiles blue
He charmed with sweet discourses,
And dined on them at Killaloe
In soups and second courses.
When blind worms crawling in the grass
Disgusted all the nation,
He gave them a rise which opened their eyes
To a sense of their situation.

So, success attend St Patrick's fist, &c.

No wonder that those Irish lads
Should be so gay and frisky,
For sure St Pat he taught them that,
As well as making whisky;
No wonder that the saint himself
Should understand distilling,
Since his mother kept a shebeen shop
In the town of Enniskillen.

So success attend St Patrick's fist, &c.

Oh! was I but so fortunate
As to be back in Munster,
'Tis I'd be bound that from the ground
I never more would once stir.
For there St Patrick planted turf,
And plenty of the praties,
With pigs galore, ma gra, ma'store,
And cabbages . . . and ladies!

Then my blessing on St Patrick's fist.
For he's a darling saint, oh!
Oh! he gave the snakes and toads a twist;
He's a beauty without paint, oh!

HECTOR O'HARA'S JUBILEE SONG

(to the tune of *Perhaps She's on the Railway)*

Hark! the trumpets sounding
Proclaim this is the day,
With hearts so bright and bounding,
Thousands haste away;
To have a look on Salter's Grove,

The lads and lasses true
All thro' the day will shout hurrah,
For the Dominion's bonny blue.

CHORUS
Perhaps you've come to London
Upon this glorious day,
To Salter's Grove to have a lark,
You're sure to take your way.
The blues so true will stick to you,
So boldly they will stand,
The Grittish crew will never do,
No longer in the land.

The lads and lasses in their best,
Will ramble thro' the grounds—
The bands will play throughout the day,
In music's sweetest sounds;
The pleasant strains goes thro' the brains
Of each unhappy Grit,
It gives them all the belly ache,
And sends them home to—

From here and there and everywhere,
The folks have come today,
Darby and Joan have come from home
To see the grand display.
From east and west from north and south
There's people without end,
With frills and bows and furbelows,,
They'll do the Grecian Bend.

Elgin girls and Biddulph swells,
Each other try to please,
By doing the lardy dardy dum,
All among the trees,
From Westminster the pretty girls,
Are rolling in the hay.
Their mothers say they mustn't,
But their fathers say they may.

There's little Popsy Wopsy here,
From Ingersoll she has come—
She's doing the double shuffle
With the chap that beats the drum;
There's Bob and Jack, Sal and Pat
And Polly coming on,

Upon her head she carries a bed
And calls it her chignon.

Strathroy girls are here today,
So nicely dress'd in blue—
With chaps that come from Exeter,
The grand they mean to do.
Polly Strong, couldn't come on
For a nasty old tom cat,
Has got a lot of kittens in
Her Dolly Varden bat.

Then shout John A. forever boys,
That is the heading cry;
Every election we will win,
The time is drawing nigh,
The scheming Grits may bag their heads
That is if they've a mind,
Or go and dig up taters
With their shirts hung out behind.

BUFFALO GALS

CHORUS
Buffalo gals won't you come out tonight
Come out tonight come out tonight
Buffalo gals won't you come out tonight
And dance by the light of the moon.

1.
As I was tramping down the street
Down the street, down the street
I chanced a pretty girl to meet
Oh she was fair to view

2.
I asked her if she'd have some talk
Have some talk, have some talk
Her feet covered the whole sidewalk
As she stood close to me

3.
I asked her if she'd be my wife
Be my wife, be my wife
She'd make me happy all my life
If she stood by my side.

Handcuffs

HANDCUFFS: The Donnellys, Part III is written by James Reaney and was first performed at the Tarragon Theatre on March 29, 1975 with the following cast:

Jay Bowen	Miriam Greene
Tom Carew	Patricia Ludwick
Caryne Chapman	Don MacQuarrie
Peter Elliott	Keith McNair
David Ferry	Jill Orenstein
Jerry Franken	Gord Stobbe
Rick Gorrie	Suzanne Turnbull

Directed by Keith Turnbull   Designed by Rosalyn Mina

The original playing time was:

Act One—60 minutes
Act Two—60 minutes
Act Three—30 minutes

Handcuffs

Like slowly closing handcuffs *people* (priests, bishops, constables, farmers, tavern keepers, traitors, threshers, among others) openly and secretly, legally and illegally fasten the disturbing Donnelly family still so that it can murder them... Tuesday, 3 February, 1880.

But although no one was ever *legally* punished for this crime, there are stories still told of how almost a year later the ghosts of Mr & Mrs Donnelly managed to execute four or five of their enemies. Where the Donnelly house once stood the remaining family place four stones; it's hard to handcuff wheat.

JAMES REANEY

MARY I won't stop watching, Bill Donovan, till there's nothing more to watch.

Handcuffs

Act One

From somewhere behind a bare stage dominated by a large sideboard or buffet comes the sound of a family group singing to themselves Victorian parlour songs, some of them in four part harmony. Then they enter & cued by a visible pianist whose piano stands directly behind the cupboard they direct at us "When You & I Were Young, Maggie" (with tenor soloist) and then "Grandfather's Clock". Jennie Currie, nee Donnelly, comes forward and arranges four chairs or partners in a reel: she then winds up a gramaphone on Stage Right & places on it a record playing an Irish reel. She proceeds to dance all by herself. Having finished the Clock Song the rest of the cast form a "house" about this dancing figure and soon Thesesa O'Connor comes visiting with her children; they open the door and surprise Jennie who says:

JENNIE Oh, Theresa O'Connor, I never expected you'd catch me doing this. Dancing by myself. *The shebeen lady enters with Peggy and grandchildren, bonneted for a summer afternoon.*

THERESA Jennie Currie. We thought you were having a party in the middle of the afternoon. When I pushed open that door you children fully expected to see a fiddler and

PEGGY But there was only you, Jenny

JENNY And these chairs

THERESA And that gramaphone

CHILD Jennie Currie, what's in this box you've got on top of the buffet here?

JENNY Thesesa, do they know of my mother?

THERESA Children, Jenny's mother was Mrs James Donnelly

JENNY It's a piece of bone from my mother's arm.

Out of the corner of our eye we see a tall woman fling her arms up, turn and fade away

THERESA Your mother had arms like wings, Jenny, I remember you saying that at the wake.

JENNY I remember. Children, my mother what was left of her, was brought into your house, Theresa, your house and waked there

THERESA It was a rough wooden box the bones were in. I can

JENNY My mother, Thesesa had arms like wings. We'd be all alone in the house and she'd teach me how to dance

THERESA And the handwriting there'd be in that arm. Peggy, she sent a note in with Johnny once

JENNY You gave it to me at the wake and I've wrapped the piece of bone up in it

CHORUS November 23rd, 1879 *They sit on church pews on either side; enter as needed*

MRS DONNELLY Theresa O'Connor. I want Peggy over there to sew me—us nine—nine handkerchiefs edged with black in time for my son Michael's funeral

On Stage Left there is a sewing machine Peggy will soon be sewing at.

CHILD Mother, when did they kill her?

PEGGY & CHORUS Midnight, Tuesday, February the 3rd.

JENNY Oh Peggy, I asked your mother here at the wake as we stood looking at my mother's handwriting

THERESA We stood there, Jenny, and you asked me to tell you every last single time I saw your mother between the time she wrote that note

CHORUS November 23rd, 1879

JENNY And the time she died

PEGGY Tuesday, February the 3rd

THERESA Jenny, those last two months they were alive your brother Tom came twice, and I saw your brother John thrice and your father once and your mother four times and her niece

Theresa begins to take bottles out of the cupboard and puts them on top—changing Jenny's house into hers.

JENNY Oh Theresa, show me. Show me the twice and the thrice and the once and the four

Peggy goes to sewing machine. Its whirring sound rises and falls as part of the play's spirit.

THERESA At the wake you asked me, you ask me now and I tell you it was time flowing by in our little house we had no idea at first where time was flowing your mother on her visits to our house, you would be sewing over at the sewing machine more than likely, Peggy and—

JENNY It isn't summer any more outside my windows, it's snowing

THERESA The last two months went by like this: remember Peggy? I said one day to put up a curtain, now why did I tell you that—

PEGGY Well. Weren't they always saying that

THERESA Hush! Peggy, yes that I was running an illegal tavern, a shebeen

CARROLL *entering abruptly* There was a cupboard in her house made into a bar with bottles, glasses, whiskey, wine and pop in those bottles and she justified their presence by saying:

THERESA Aw for the love of Heaven, it's for the convenience of our boarders and roomers and I dare you to call me a liar.

CARROLL Theresa O'Connor, you've only got four rooms in this house. What boarders, what roomers?

THERESA Come this evening and you'll see them, Mr Inspector. We've small quarters but large hearts and—is he gone, children? Peggy, while you're sewing there could you just run me up a curtain there to hide our cupboard that they're— *kissing the sideboard—* darling cupboard—making such a fuss about?

PEGGY I will ma, but I wish you'd watch your tongue.

THERESA Heavens preserve us it's Mrs Donnelly coming to our door and she's got a strange young girl with her, who in the name of Heaven can that girl be? Peggy, darling, put on the kettle and we'll boil you's all a cup of tea.

PEGGY She wants to give Mrs Donnelly a cup of tea. Kitty, will you put the kettle on for ma?

KITTY Pat will you please put the kettle on for ma?

PAT Johnny, will you put the kettle on.

MRS DONNELLY Good day to you Theresa O'Connor, I would like you to meet my husband's niece Bridget who's just come over on the boat from Ireland. And we're back from town meeting her.

BRIDGET I'm very pleased to meet you, Mrs O'Connor.

MRS DONNELLY Theresa, Mr Donnelly was wondering if we could take Johnny back with us to the farm. We need a good boy like Johnny here to do the chores while we're away.

THERESA Johnny shall go with you as he has before and he likes going out to hear your boys talk and sing—Bridget, my darling, what's scaring you?

MRS DONNELLY It's the sewing machine, Theresa.

THERESA Bridget have you never heard one go that fast before?

BRIDGET I've never set eyes on a sewing machine before, Mrs O'Connor. Such a great fearsome roaring sound, what ever are you sewing on it girl?

PEGGY A curtain.

BRIDGET That's a very big curtain, is it Peggy O'Connor's your name?

Children are involved in shadowmaking.

PEGGY It has to be, Bridget Donnelly is that your name, it has to be a big curtain to hide the very big shame that my mother must keep a shebeen when you'd think it was only where you come from, girl that they'd have that kind of drinking place.

THERESA Peggy O'Connor, more sewing, less jawing. Bridget Donnelly, your aunt and uncle can explain better than I ever can why we must keep a supply of whiskey for certain of our friends. How would they get home on a cold wet night when by the time they leave one of the taverns on the Main Street and travel a bit they're half frozen through and that's where we come in—helping everybody we can the rest of the way home with the—you're scared again, girl. Sure have you never heard a piano before, it's hidden there where we store it for a friend behind the bar, whoops, cupboard, it's the piano belonged to old Mrs Flaherty who's in jail for poisoning Mr O'Flaherty, whoops—Pat stop strumming the piano and let Peggy here play a bit or perhaps you'd favour us with a song, Bridget, and Peggy would pick up behind you.

BRIDGET I do have a song. It's a song about coming here and how grateful I am to my uncle and my aunt for taking the weight of me off my father's family with times so hungry in Ireland. Aunt Julia, may I sing it?

MRS DONNELLY Yes, Bridget. You may sing here whenever you please.

BRIDGET

My heart's like a bird that has flown from her nest
For the harsh winter winds would give her no rest
Cross the seas and the wilderness she's rowed with her wings
Till at last in Ontario her freedom she sings.

I felt free, I guessed I would go on missing my mother and father back in Ireland, but I knew as soon as the horses' heads that afternoon pointed towards my uncle's gate that I was going to—it would be the happiest time of all my days.

Peggy has finished sewing the curtain and it is put up. It can be drawn completely across the stage, not only hiding the cupboard, but becoming an important, constantly moving character in the play as well.

THERESA The days of December, for that girl went out there to live with the Donnellys just before December began in 1879 and the first day of December was a

CHORUS Monday, Tuesday, Wednesday, Thursday, Friday, Saturday, Sunday, Monday, Tuesday, December the 9th, one of Mr and Mrs Donnelly's sons, Michael, was murdered in a bar room at Waterford. Wednesday—

PEGGY I sewed them all handkerchiefs bordered with black and took them out to them on

& CHORUS Thursday

THERESA The wake, and the funeral was on

& CHORUS Friday

THERESA Was it a large funeral, Peggy.

PEGGY Yes, but there were mainly Protestants at the funeral as many of their Catholic friends are afraid to go near them.

PAT & CHORUS Sunday,

PAT We had sore throats and stayed home from church,

Pat & Johnny are always playing with the shadows they can produce with a candle & cut out cardboard figures.

PAT & CHORUS Monday

Enter a young doctor: we may remember him as the tenor soloist in the family entertainment.

THERESA Jerome O'Halloran, Dr. Jerome O'Halloran, you're the new young doctor we've all been praying for as giving us some sort of choice away from that skull and cross bones that's been purging and amputating us all these years

JEROME Open your mouth, boy, till I get a look at this throat

O'HALLORANS *suddenly appearing* Jerome, what are you doing in this woman's shebeen? We happened to see you entering as we cuttered by.

JEROME Mother and father, what do you suppose I would be doing at Theresa O'Connor's. Her children are ill

O'HALLORANS A likely story. Theresa is more than likely leading you astray as she has many other sons, brothers and fathers by serving you whiskey and

Divide into Mr and Mrs after initial "solid" feeling is attained.

JEROME I apologize for the lunacy of my parents, Theresa O'Connor

O'HALLORANS And we apologize, my son Jerome, we have to apologize daily to the good people of the settlement for your shameless behaviour.

JEROME Father, what shameless behaviour?

O'HALLORAN William Donnelly was in your office yesterday.

JEROME William Donnelly hurt his shoulder lately. Am I not to heal

O'HALLORAN // Never a sick Donnelly. May they die in a ditch for his brothers Tom and John would let nobody thresh for me all fall and the grain rotted in the field

//= two stamps ()() will equal clappings. Generally speaking friends of the Donnellys clap their hands a lot, while their enemies stamp their feet.

JEROME) Oh you're mad with hatred of them.) I love the Donnellys.

O'HALLORAN Get out of here you miserable ingrate, get out

Jerome leaves

THERESA) Wait a minute, Mr and Mrs O'Halloran, whose house is this anyhow I love the Donnellys too.

O'HALLORAN No one lives in a proper house that loves the Donnellys.

Theresa gives a derisive "Hah!"

O'HALLORANS As the godparents of Peggy and Johnny, Theresa, we cannot help but notice how evilly you are bringing them up. You still keep the shebeen here, clandestinely, don't you, and if you do not mend your evil ways we will as the children's godparents see if we cannot get these children away from your influence.

THERESA Mr and Mrs O'Halloran, what is it you really mean? That I'm friendly to the Donnellys whom all you church proud people have taken to hating so much, go away with you O'Halloran, you're a total abstainer now, but if you don't go away and mind your own business I'll tell the children's godmother here about the time you puked all over my front steps and all the way home as far as the church

PEGGY Mother!

CHORUS Tuesday. Wednesday.

THERESA Johnny, you're back.

PEGGY It's a letter from Mrs Donnelly, mother.

She & Peggy are revealed in the Donnelly kitchen by the Stage Left curtain being drawn back

MRS DONNELLY Theresa, Bridget and myself would appreciate your sending out Peggy to sew for us—2 dresses & a quilted petticoat.

PEGGY Johnny, what else did you bring from their place?

JOHNNY Some apples, some loneliness.

THERESA Why loneliness? They've heaps of friends out that way.

JOHNNY Oh, no one comes to neighbour with the Donnellys any more.

THERESA What about the Keefes and the Feenys and the Macdonalds.

JOHNNY Only those three families.

THERESA I do not understand it, only.

JOHNNY They are being hounded out of the township, mother, and no one will come near them after what the priest said about them after mass last Sunday.

THERESA Speak of the devil, here comes the priest to our door—children! *they quickly close the curtain* Your reverence, Father Connolly.

PRIEST Good morning, Theresa O'Connor. Theresa O'Connor, I have heard bad things spoken about the use you make of your house and I have descended like fire from Heaven to see if it is so what

I've heard. Draw back that curtain, please. *A statuette of Mary is revealed.*

THERESA We like to keep her on top of the cupboard, sure it makes the whole room like a chapel and with a curtain in front of her there's a greater power to her mystery and greater mystery to her power. Would your reverence not take a cup of tea with us? Kitty...

PRIEST I have no time for tea, Theresa O'Connor, and I want you to know that I am by no means satisfied in this matter of the curtain that hides what's on the cupboard and I also want you and your children to be at mass next Sunday and every mass from now on.

THERESA Sir, they had the quinzy till their throats were puffed up like bladders, his throat's still...

PRIEST You're good at sewing up curtains, Peggy O'Connor, what else do I see you sewing?

PEGGY A dress for Bridget Donnelly, your reverence.

PRIEST Oh, their niece from Ireland, yes, her you may sew for, for she is innocent, but I would not waste my time if I were you sewing shirts for the sons or shifts for that mother of theirs. Good day to you Theresa O'Connor, no do not ask for my blessing.

CHORUS Tuesday, Wednesday early evening...

A young woman comes for a dress fitting.

THERESA Children, you'll set fire to the house playing with the candles that way. Peggy, perhaps you'd be wisest to give Miss Johnson her fitting up in my bedroom, I see someone coming to our door and it's a man.

JOHNNY They say there's a secret society formed against the Donnellys.

PAT What's a secret society, Johnny?

Dr Jerome O'Halloran enters. The boys retreat behind the ½ drawn Stage Right curtain.

JOHNNY Well, Pat—it's swear drink midnight attack

& CHORUS swear drink midnight attack

THERESA Dr O'Halloran, you've come back to look at the children's throats.

JEROME Yes, Mrs O'Connor. Even Father Connolly said I should look in.

THERESA Oh well then, your mother and father cannot take offence.

JEROME I know for a fact they're not in the village. Open up Patrick. Johnny. Now that's an awful shadow you're casting, my boy. Go to the druggist, Theresa, take this and he'll give you a bottle of the sweetest tasting nasty looking stuff you ever swallowed, children.

A curious pause.

THERESA Jerome O'Halloran, what is it you really want?

JEROME Theresa O'Connor. I saw Miss Johnson come in here and I did not see her leave. I can't help it, I've got something very important I'd like to say to her.

THERESA She's upstairs with my daughter, but you should knock on the door first for they're trying on a new dress.

Jerome hurries off behind the curtain.

JOHNNY There was once a man dug a tunnel out to his haystack so that when the secret society attacked, why he was able to get away and they...

THERESA Hush, children, you make my blood run cold, Peggy, what's the matter?

Peggy bursts out from behind the curtain.

PEGGY Mother, this is the worst yet you've done to us.

THERESA What on earth do you mean?

PEGGY Dr O'Halloran came in to the bedroom upstairs and just looked at Miss Johnson, and she just looked at him.

THERESA And what did you look at?

PEGGY I looked at them.

THERESA They're a handsome young couple. You should have stayed by as chaperone. They shouldn't be left alone in a bedroom together, they've been hopelessly in love for years.

PEGGY I can well believe it, mother, chaperone. Chaperone! I always feel that when people start unbuttoning their clothes and falling into each other's arms it's a bit late to play chaperone, so I ran out. Mother, what are you going to do?

THERESA Nothing.

PEGGY Your house is well known for its cupboard, now it's getting a reputation for its bed.

THERESA Oh Peggy, run off with this up to the drugstore, it's some medicine for the children and think as you're going up that sure

Jerome O'Halloran and Katie Johnson have been in love since they were sixteen and she the daughter of the Grand Master of the Orange Lodge and he the beloved son of the most pious Catholic family in the settlement and they've waited long enough for their hardhearted parents to melt so I said yes, I said to him yes ... go up and see if she's in the room, but if you'd had the courage to stay this'd never happened.

PEGGY They'll come and burn down our house for a bawdy house, mother, and don't you dare ask me to sew you up another curtain!

THERESA She's right, and yet I don't know how I let this happen. Uh, the poor young lovers there's little chance they'll ever get together again—go easy on the bed O'Halloran, men are always like that, shaking and shaking you till the bed starts squeaking and the bottom right leg is half broke as it is, I always felt like asking Mike when he was alive and he'd be on top of me, or under me sometimes what it was he was trying to shake out of me, the truth? Rattling you away like a box with a piece of bone in it when if the truth were known they would have just as much pleasure if they just held you in their arms and were still for a while. Jerome O'Halloran and Katie Johnson I hope you've come to the little garden you're knocking at the door of before Peggy gets home from the drugstore...

CHORUS Monday, Tuesday, Wednesday, Thursday....

JOHNNY Mother, I just seen a man tramping round the house.

THERESA It's the new constable, Jim Carroll, children! Good evening, Constable Carroll, and what can I do for you?

CARROLL You can serve me some of your old Hennessy, Theresa O'Connor and see if I know it.

THERESA And you can wipe your face on my arse, Jim Carroll if you think I'll fall for that trick of yours. There's not a drop in the house.

CARROLL Draw that curtain aside if you please. I want to know what is behind it.

A crucified Jesus is revealed.

THERESA There does that satisfy you?

CARROLL *afraid* Draw it again, Theresa. Theresa, if you'd only shun the Donnellys I might be able to do something for you.

THERESA Well we will not shun the Donnellys and there is nothing you might ever be able to help us with. Shut the door behind you, please.

CARROLL Didn't realize you had a door, Theresa. Most places like yours don't, they just have an old piece of sacking stretched across—a hole—in the wall.

CHORUS Thursday, December the 25th.

THERESA & CHORUS 26th, 27th, 28th, 29th, 30th.

THERESA Thirty days hath December.

PEGGY Mother, 31 days hath December.

THERESA, PEGGY & CHORUS Friday, New Year's Day, 1880.

THERESA Oh excuse me for yawning so much.

PEGGY It's been extremely quiet lately, mother.

THERESA It's a humdrum day, all hum and no drum.

PEGGY No visitors is the best sort of day. There goes John Donnelly.

Window filled with kid's faces looking at John.

JOHN Yes, I was murdered on the 4th of February, early in the morning. On New Year's day 1880 that was still a month away. I forget why I rode into Lucan, the snow so deep. Some errand for my parents and as I passed Connor's—how was I to know they would hold an inquest on my body there with you, coroner, cutting open my body and saying:

his shadow on curtain

CORONER What a large and well formed heart John Donnelly had. Look!

JOHN And my brother Will saying:

shadow on opposite curtain

WILL This is more than flesh and blood can endure. *Pause* I will live through this circus.

THERESA Here comes the eleven o'clock freight. You can hear it blowing for all the crossings—that'll be the Cedar Swamp Line, now the Chapel crossing line, now...

CHORUS Monday Tuesday Wednesday the 7th of January, 1880 Thursday Friday Saturday Sunday Monday Tuesday Wednesday Thursday the 15th Friday...

PEGGY Oh Mother, such a strange thing happened out at the Donnellys' there was a barn across the road from them burnt down in the middle of the night. Patrick Marksey's barn, and in the morning he came over and accused the Donnelly boys of burning it down, but they'd been at the Keefe's at the wedding dance all night. So he couldn't say very well they done it, so he turned on old Mr Donnelly and said,

MARKSEY You burnt my barns.

PEGGY How could he have burnt the barns—there was fresh snow fell in the night and I looked out into the yard and not one track went from the Donnellys' house anywhere. Hark, mother, here's Tom driving Mrs Donnelly to our door.

MRS DONNELLY Yes, Theresa, is this not a pretty way we are used. But I have no time to sit down and tell you the full lunacy of it all. Peggy, I'll take the pillow slips with me now, for I'm catching the train this morning and going to visit my daughter Jennie in St Thomas. I'm promised to see her and my grandchildren since the wake for Michael. What is it, Tom?

TOM Mother, we're cutting it awful close.

MRS DONNELLY Goodbye Theresa. Thank you Peggy.

THERESA She's not herself. She doesn't want to stay out there where you are being accused all the time of doing things it would take an athletic hoyden of sixteen all her time doing let alone an old woman in her sixties.

CARROLL I've a subpoena here for Peggy O'Connor. You by the sewing machine over there, come here and sign this piece of paper for me.

THERESA What's this about, Constable Carroll?

CARROLL Well, your daughter consorts with the Donnellys doesn't she? So she was out there the night of the fire and when she appears at the hearing tomorrow perhaps she can tell us what went on that night when

MARKSEY They burnt my barns.

PEGGY Yes, perhaps I can.

CARROLL Remember Peggy O'Connor. Two o'clock sharp at the Council Chambers.

CHORUS Saturday Sunday Amen Monday

THERESA I'm waving goodbye to Johnny he's going out with the boys to the farm again. The Donnellys'll need him to feed the pigs and cattle while they go to the hearing at Granton they're now draggin them to

PEGGY Now they're saying Mrs Donnelly helped Mr Donnelly set the fire and she's arrested too.

THERESA What did you forget, child?

JOHNNY My cap, goodbye mother. Goodbye Peggy. Wait for me John!

CHORUS Tuesday Wednesday Thursday Friday the 30th, Saturday the last day of January.

THERESA They're still having the hearings drag on about the fire and it is Candlemas and now it's Tuesday.

THERESA & CHORUS February the third

THERESA and it's St Blaise's Day—keep that blessed candle near your throat, Pat, it's blessed by the priest today and is bound to drive the quinzy away Mr Donnelly is there no stopping them from dragging you all over the country side examining about this fire business?

MR DONNELLY No stopping them. They've adjourned the hearings three times now. Why, Theresa, they're advertising my wife and myself as if we were mad dogs. Johnny, button up that coat for it's a cold day out on the line and the wind'll whistle right through you. Good day to you, Theresa O'Connor.

THERESA And good day to you, Mr Donnelly. Now the next day was

THERESA & CHORUS Wednesday the 4th

THERESA Johnny, you've come back from the Donnellys all by yourself whatever happened to your cap where'd you get that big lady's hat and—Johnny, where's your coat?

Johnny has a blanket around his shoulders.

JOHNNY It's burned up in the fire. Mother, my hat and my coat got burnt up last night. Old Mrs Whalen gave me her hat to wear.

THERESA Burnt up—where?

JOHNNY With the Donnellys.

THERESA What?

JOHNNY It's burned in the fire, the house was burned. Bridget's dead, they're all dead and burned.

THERESA *scream*

JOHNNY Mother, there was a whole bunch of men came into their house. I hid under the bed while they killed them and then they set the house afire.

THERESA I don't want to hear anymore who did this! Did you recognize the men?

JOHNNY Yes! The Donnellys are all dead.

THERESA *scream* All dead?

JOHNNY Mother—what I want to know is should I tell the names of the men, I know three of them, should I....

THERESA If you tell the names they'll kill you. *He whispers to her* This is too wicked to go unpunished. Tell yes. It is too bad to let them go, Peggy, Mrs Donnelly is dead and Bridget—stop sewing the dress for you're sewing the dress of a dead woman. *the sewing machine rattles furiously*

PAT Mother, Will Donnelly wants to know if they can bring the bodies here for the wake.

THERESA *scream* (*loudest*) Oh my God, whoever burnt down the Donnellys will be after us next. Peggy I beg you to stop sewing that dress. She's dead. We'll have to get the house ready for the wake, children get those chairs out of the attic. *The sewing machine stops!*

PEGGY I've finished the dress. Now they're bringing in John's body and there is an opening of that body by the coroner and then an inquest and he is taken away to the undertaker's. Then he comes back in his coffin. Oh Jennie Donnelly, when you ask us to teach you what it was like to live in my mother's shebeen the last month your mother was alive, it was like—it was *holding out the dress as the wake abruptly starts with coffins entering. John's coffin has a candle in it; the other coffin—a rough wooden box—contains four stones.*

PEGGY Those that love them clap (those that hate them stamp /

CHORUS

De profundis clamavi ad te, Domine
Domine, exaudi vocem meam
Si iniguitates observaveris, Domine, Domine, quis Sustinebit
Five dead people lying in a house[3]*
These four stones once were people and this candle
Once was he who held it—John Donnelly
Five dead people lying in a house
Five dead people are coming to this house
Five dead people have come into this house
On Alice Street near the tracks in Lucan
The last tollgate before harvest in God's eye

---

* To be repeated three times (likewise throughout).

The bridegroom's thigh, the Holy Spirit's sigh
//((//((//((//((//((//((//((//((//((//((//

Vary with toe taps and fingersnaps. The five dead people, their eyes bandaged with gauze, enter from behind the curtains, present themselves and fade away.

Who has entered this room whom I cannot see
Five dead people have come to this house
Mourn their collections, their sheaves of time
A stone for Bridget, a stone for Tom
A stone for James, a stone for Judith   we mourn them till dawn
And a candle for John
It's twelve o'clock, Jennie Donnelly, you're late, you're late

JENNIE My mother. Was it because she was tall that you hated her so much? And burnt her first with your words, then with your kerosene? Explain then why   she had to die

CHORUS It's half past twelve, Will Donnelly, you're late, you're late Cripple. Here comes Cripple! Cripple Cripple hey Cripple!

WILL *(* and who the hell are you over there *((((*

STAMPERS *////* We're we were we are their enemies */*

WILL And who the hell are you over there?

CLAPPERS *(* We are we were we will be—their friends?

In and out of the clapping & stamping, William Donnelly takes up the stone that represents Tom and presses it against O'Halloran (*Will is backed by clappers*) *and asks:*

WILL These are the bones of my brothers, O'Halloran. Tell us why you killed them or I'll beat you to death with them

CLAPPERS

Bones of my brothers, O'Halloran
Or I'll beat you to death with them

O'HALLORAN *//* You'll remember that last summer—this is Malachi O'Halloran speaking—my big field of wheat ripened and was cut and bound and we stooked it and it stood there and it stood there yes because of the quarrel between us and two of your brothers, yes two of your brothers dead there—yes, John said Tom said— *The brothers with eyes bandaged enter abruptly. People at the wake are smoking and drinking from bottles.*

TOM & JOHN O'Halloran, you will, we swear by the Holy Name, you will never thresh that grain.

TOM You've had me up in court just five times too often. You and your neighbours on their horses after me one whole night too many.

O'HALLORAN Curtin's threshing machine came up the front road and you stopped him off

CURTIN I came down the back road and you

TOM & JOHN No one threshes for O'Halloran do you hear, Marty Curtin? No one do you hear? After what he has done to us may your grain rot in your fields.

O'HALLORAN And I watched it do so. If I killed the mother and father, helped kill them, I killed the source of the men who meant that my seed was spilled on the ground.

TOM O'Halloran, what's this my ghost found in your granary today then? *throws the grain at him* Grain? We let you thresh after we'd shown you we could stop you forever if we wanted to. *The brothers throw the grain hither and thither.*

O'HALLORAN Yes, in the end my big field was threshed, but we'll see just how. But I still had to kill them for there was never any peace with them around like I'll show you, I'll show you what Tom was like—there's a tavern at Elginfield called Glass's Hotel and he rode by it once with his pal who's more here than I am tonight—Jim Feeny. Mrs Glass came out for some water and she saw Donnelly about to

MRS GLASS *We see her shadow—her mobcap silhouette* Don't water your horses there, Tom Donnelly. There's no water for Donnelly horses at this tavern, your friend there can have a drink if he must. *She comes out from behind the curtain.*

O'HALLORAN She went inside again. Micky Glass her husband said to her:

MR GLASS Who was that in the yard, missus?

TOM *from behind curtain with hobbyhorses* It was me Tom Donnelly and my horse Ploughboy and Jim Feeny and his horse—Whirlwind, *They enter on their horses* and we'll teach you to say no Donnellys get a drink at your horse trough, my horse is very upset, we'll drink your cellar dry, Mrs Glass and Mr Glass. Jim, start drinking. *Slurp*

MR & MRS GLASS Not if this poker—and this axhandle—can persuade you to do otherwise. Out of here out of that out here out of that. Don't you touch that cask tap. Get your damn thumb off that bung. *Their pursuit of Tom & Jim turns into the boys' pursuit of them!*

CHORUS *with bottles*

The table and punch was upshot
And the row it commenced in a minit, shure.
Niver a tast of a shtick had he got
So he picked up a piece of the furniture
Gurgle gurgle gurgle gurgle gurgle gurgle gurgle[32]

the Glasses are stuffed into a cubbyhole

A concrete sound chorus ending with an exhausted slurp

JIM This is Jim Feeny's arm. When we were boys he made me cut my name—no, his name, he made me cut his name into the flesh of my arm and he cut my name Jim Feeny into the flesh of his arm:

JIM & TOM My blood, your blood/Sealed in brotherhood[2]

JIM I've always liked being with him, except he sometimes goes a bit farther than my nerves can stand. Like now. And he knows that when I'm drunk I cannot stand the mention of Hell or devils, so why does he—Through clouds of tobacco smoke at the wake his sister Jennie comes towards me and she says:

JENNIE Jim Feeny. Jim, my brother tells me you almost stayed the night at our place.

JIM Yes, Jennie. Tom wanted me to stay, but I'd been told not to sleep at the Donnellys' any more.

JENNIE And, Jim, what's this I hear about Tom drinking again. I took him to the priest and he took the pledge, for oh that was much of his trouble.

JIM It was when his horse was denied drink, Jennie, that he started up again. I told her what happened at Glass's Tavern, but oh not all of it. She has the look they all have, commanding you to tell it all, he had it, well I won't, they're all too bossy, Tom was too bossy, especially right after breakfast the Donnellys are too bossy, and yet I'd have given anything to've been raised by his parents. You should see my father and mother—always fighting, always drinking with the farm dribbling through their fingers. We're poor. We need money.

TOM What's the matter, Jim. You're—stop drinking, you're getting into one of those sulky fits again where—you want to kill Tom Donnelly your only friend.

JIM Stay away from me, Tom Donnelly, or I'll shoot your friggin knees off.

TOM Come on, Jim. Try to kill me. That's great fun

JIM Try to kill you, why you nearly killed me.

TOM Jim, the silly girl never thought what she was doing and I can't share everything with you and besides your leg is mended.

JIM Yes, my leg's mended. Give me an ax and I'll chop off your feet —Oh I hear the dead men tramping by.

Bearing the coffins, the people at the wake march away with the coffins.

TOM That's right, Jim, the graveyards are on the march.

JIM Oh Tom, I'll—I know I'll die a hard death.

TOM Home. Let's go home so Mr and Mrs Glass can go to bed. *groans from the cubbyhole*

JIM Well, I'm not going home, you bugger, because you pushed me off the ladder.

The curtains swag back to reveal a girl lolling on top of the cupboard like a barroom picture.

GIRL What they're got onto is me. I was in love with Tom Donnelly once. When I was fourteen on the Main Street of Lucan I saw him go by and I took a *about to jump down* scissors—Tom Donnelly, kin I have a lock of your hair!

TOM Kin you, you just have.

GIRL I was crazy about the Donnelly boys, I'd have danced naked for Tom and told my parents of this desire which prompted them to move from Lucan as fast as they could to Brooke Township. But there was a man owned the swamp there decided to cut her all down, so that who should show up at my window last winter out of the lumber camp but Tom Donnelly with Jim Feeny holding the ladder. *This scene is played on top of the cupboard.*

TOM Look, my pal out there, Jim Feeny wonders if he can come up too.

GIRL Jim Feeny your pal, eh. Well, I told you I'd do anything for you, Tom, call him up he looks cold.

TOM Wait a minute I might just marry you. If it's a boy. But if my friend lies with you how will we know if it's his or mine?

GIRL That's very true, Tom Donnelly, said I and I tipped the ladder over with Jim Feeny halfway up it. *He crashes over.*

TOM Jim how was I to know you'd break your leg, and you start pounding me and I'll start hammering you. Let's get out of here, the constables are coming. Now come home.

A demon holds two moons in front of Jim.

JIM Do you see the moons, Tom?

TOM Yes, Jim, I'll bet there are two of them tonight.

JIM Do you see the devil peeking out at us from behind that bush?

TOM No. Yes. Oh, Jim Feeny, let's get it over with. I always say if you're going to vomit, vomit and if you're going to have the D.T.'s damn your heart, the sooner you have them the better and you're over with them.

Nightmare devils attack Jim Feeny.

JIM Don't you tell me when to have the D.T.'s! I'll kill you.

TOM Jim, old pal, when I go to Hell, will you come along with me?

JIM I told you not mention Hell or devils.

TOM I see the one that's about to pull your guts out. I'll fight him for you.

JIM I told you, Tom Donnelly, not to mention Hell. Hell. Oh God, there's a tree after me *One of the demons does pull Jim's guts out—a long magenta ribbon & dances away with it. Up in the air & over the demons lift him!*

CHORUS Hell hell hell hell hell hell hell hell hell hell[42]

fade to the Feeny house

JIM *screaming* Tom will you forgive me what I done to you if I can make you see what my soul was like?

Carroll is behind the bed listening. Use curtain as head of bed.

MATER Bless you, my son, *the demons whisk away!* it's not Tom Donnelly, it's your very own mother, *hiccough.*

PATER And your very own father— *hiccough.* Tom Donnelly brought you home to us two days ago and you've been raving in your sickbed now for

JIM Tom Donnelly sneaked away did he when the devils came to get me did he, well I'll get him. I'll kill him.

MATER Son, son I always thought that you liked Tom Donnelly quite a lot.

JIM I hate him, he makes me see devils

CARROLL Now Michael and Bridget Feeny, this is a very interesting thing you're telling me about your son when he was ill in bed with the D.T.'s. You see something awful is going to happen to the Donnellys, so tell your son not to sleep there anymore, Bridget Feeny, not to sleep there anymore when Tom invites him to stay the night—why are your crying, Mrs Feeny, Jim Feeny's mother? You see the whole plan for ridding us once and for all of this disturbing family depends a great deal on getting inside their house without their knowing it so that, we need someone to—someone that used to be, well used to be Tom Donnelly's friend.

PATER Jim Carroll, how much would you be willing to pay for this getting inside the Donnelly house?

CARROLL For the key to the Donnelly house, the skeleton key? Well, it's a pretty sick and feeble and used up looking and undependable key lying there, isn't it.

MATER For $500 his mother and his father might clean some of the rust and the cobwebs off it, Jim Carroll. They might.

Fades away. A prim, strict knocking comes from behind the curtains which part to reveal:

MR O'HALLORAN Mick Glass, open up your tavern, it's Malachi O'Halloran and his wife and we want a dish of hot tea on this cold night at the bottom of the hill coming in out of town.

MR GLASS We can't serve you, for Donnelly's locked us up in the cubbyhole over here.

MRS O'HALLORAN My soul, Malachi O'Halloran, the place looks as if a hundred devils had run through it.

MR O'HALLORAN Mickey Glass. Mrs Glass. What on earth's footstool has happened here?

MRS GLASS Donnelly. Donnelly came along and he brought his horses in to drink at our bar and

MR GLASS *crawling about* Oh if this is what Hell is like, what can Paradise be up to?

MRS GLASS You must excuse my husband, Mr and Mrs O'Halloran as I know you're the most upstanding people we've ever had in the settlement, but as the whiskey kept pouring in on us in there in the cubbyhole there he couldn't help but lick a few drops of his own whiskey off his very own floor.

MRS O'HALLORAN *loud* Can no justice, can no constable do nothing, anything, about this?

MR GLASS Malachi O'Halloran, I am a justice and I know for a fact that no constable of mine would dare arrest Tom Donnelly for this. He's got them all scared—if this is one corner of Hell called Mickey Glass's Tavern, what must the other corners be like?

MRS O'HALLORAN Well this carnival has gone on too long, husband. Sober up Mr Mickey Glass *stamping her foot* Is there no end in view? That family has bought law and used it like gipsies. And like gipsies that family must leave this parish, what hope of that, eh?

MR O'HALLORAN Honoria O'Halloran, the only hope is that—the bishop is moving his palace and see back—back from the border, back to London which is but 18 miles away and now—he's close enough to see what's the matter and to sort the wheat from the chaff. *Bells, big & little. The O'Hallorans ring handbells*

CHORUS Ash Wednesday. The Bishop that was always far away is now close by. Amen *sung*

Organ peals as curtains part to reveal Bishop preceded by proud hobbyhorsemen drawing him in his carriage.

BISHOP And I consulted with and visited every priest in my diocese until I felt as if I had become a shepherd striding across the field where my sheep grazed and my sheepdog priests kept them from straying. Father Girard, what is going on in your parish? I see from my tower the twinkling lights of burning barns. I see crops rotting in the field, I hear a constant gnashing of teeth, and of one family I hear—I see in the daily press constant reference.

FATHER GIRARD Your Excellency, in my parish there is a feud between certain families. I am not Irish as they are and you are, your Excellency I do not understand the feud, but my impression is that this family of the Donnellys is slowly losing ground.

BISHOP Losing ground.

FATHER GIRARD For example, your Excellency their reputation is far worse than they actually are. Even I who do not listen to stories, I am aware that outrages are purposely committed which will be blamed on them.

BISHOP And what do you yourself think of them, Father Girard?

FATHER GIRARD The Donnellys are like lions attacked in the desolate wilderness by a pack of wild dogs.

BISHOP Father Girard, there are changes, certain changes I wish to initiate in your particular parish. Two changes. The first is the pattern your parish has of voting for a Liberal candidate. I hope to change that.

FATHER GIRARD Your Excellency the second change must be involved with the first, for it is my removal from the parish is it not?

BISHOP Down in Belle River where you will have a French speaking parish you will still be able to drive your flock into the Liberal fold, but up here—you see we are hoping for a Catholic Conservative member of Parliament. So the Donnellys must change their voting pattern.

FATHER GIRARD They will not change, your Excellency.

BISHOP Will they not? Well, it is unfortunate for them that this riding cannot be won unless a party takes a majority of the votes, the Catholic votes in their ward, and the Conservative party shall take a majority of those votes. They must kneel with the rest of the parish.

FATHER GIRARD Your Excellency, what Conservative priest will next be the shepherd of my erstwhile flock?

BISHOP A very strong man. Even now I see his loving parishioners in Quebec bidding him farewell.

Father Connolly faces us with his flock kneeling in front of him. Organ.

CHORUS

Advent shadows in December
Violet branches on the snow
Help the Christian to remember
This babe returns to judge us now.

PRIEST My dear people of Kelly's Corners, tears fill my eyes as I hear for the last time your sweet voices. Oh no, this is too much, you are all kneeling with a parcel, no, no, what can be in this parcel?

CHORUS & SOLO We, the parishioners of Saint Malachy's Parish take this opportunity, Father Connolly, to make you a farewell gift as well as the purse we have made up for you. The winters of Biddulph we hear are even longer and colder than those here at Kelly's Corners, Quebec. It is a coat, Father Connolly.

PRIEST What warm thoughts you have had towards me, my dear parishioners. Of what animal is this extremely thick and handsome fur?

CHORUS & SOLO The wolf, Father Connolly. It is a wolfskin coat.

PRIEST *dressed in the coat which radiates a strange elegant power.* I think I was sent to this neighbourhood of Biddulph up in Ontario partly for the purpose of putting all lawless conduct down. There was no time to know the people at all; there I was, here I am, having said my first mass in St Patrick's and I barely know the alterboys' names. *The kneelers imperceptibly change to the Biddulph congregation with the Donnelly family on Stage Right.*

SOLO In their hands they shall bear Thee up, lest Thou dash Thy foot against a stone.

CHORUS Thou shalt walk upon the asp and the basilisk,

PRIEST and Thou shalt trample under foot the lion and the dragon.

CHORUS Amen.

PRIEST Now, what was I going to say to you, people of St Patrick's, Biddulph? Why it is simply this—before the week is out I hope to have visited each and every one of my parishioners.

JENNIE Father Connolly was as good as his word and soon one heard that Father Connolly had

CHORUS

visited Barry	visited Trehy
visited Feeny	visited O'Halloran

O'Halloran under or over this gestures and tells the priest of his troubles with the Donnellys.

O'HALLORAN	CHORUS
At night—someone takes out my horses—after we've gone to bed, father, and after we are sound asleep, and they ride those horses from one toll gate to another all night. But in the morning I find my horses back in my stables again—out of breath and nigh death.	Domine, non sum dignus/ut intres sub tectume meum:/ sed tantum dic verbo/et sanabitur anima mea[3]

CHORUS

visited Cahill	visited Cassleigh
visited McCann	visited O'Halloran again

O'Halloran is seen telling the priest an earful.

O'HALLORAN	CHORUS
Father Connolly, this summer my big field of wheat ripened and was cut and bound and we stooked it and it stands there and it stands there yes because of the quarrel between us and two of the Donnelly family, the brothers John and Tom. Father Connolly, they have sworn that I will not thresh that grain. Must my grain rot in the field and must my granaries cobweb because so says Donnelly?	In thine infinite goodness, we beseech Thee, O Lord, to watch over Thy household, that even as it relies solely upon the hope of Thy heavenly grace, so it may ever be defended by Thy protection. Through our Lord. In nomine Patris et Filii, et Spiritus Sancti. Amen. Visited Donnelly

PRIEST Mrs Donnelly, I have been hearing about your boys' bad doings.

MRS DONNELLY Let us their mother and father hear of them too, Father Connolly.

PRIEST They will let no one thresh the grain belonging to Malachi O'Halloran and it lies rotting in his field. Your son Will, I want particularly to visit him. Where does he live?

MRS DONNELLY Father Connolly, he lives in a house by the blacksmith's at Whalen's Corners.

PRIEST I understand he is harbouring a youth who has been taking out Mr O'Halloran's horses and

O'HALLORAN	CHORUS
At night—someone takes out my horses—after we've gone to bed, father, and after we are sound asleep, and they ride those horses from one toll gate to another all night. But in the morning I find my horses back in my stables again—out of breath and nigh death.	Domine, non sum dignus/ut intres sub tectume meum:/ sed tantum die verbo/ et sanabitur anima mea[3]

PRIEST Mrs Donnelly, your boys shall change their ways, or I'll straighten them.

MRS DONNELLY Father Connolly, there are worse than my sons in the neighbourhood, but the biggest crowd is against them. Father, we are being persecuted.

PRIEST I have also heard that your niece, Mr Donnelly, has come out from Ireland to live with you. Bridget Donnelly how long is it since you were in Ireland?

BRIDGET I was still there last harvest, Father, and I have not seen spring here in Canada.

PRIEST After I see your son William, Mrs Donnelly, I will make up my mind about what you have said, I wish you good day.

WILL But when Father Connolly in his visiting tour came to my house only my wife was there to receive him. We had a sick boy in the house; I was away in the village waiting at young Dr O'Halloran's office.

DR O'HALLORAN Will Donnelly, you appear to be the last customer this afternoon. How's the healing process going on with your shoulder?

WILL My wife was dressing it last night. Norah thinks it needs some more probing. You see, Jerome, when my stallion tried to pin me against the walls of his box stall he picked a rather slivery four by four to grind me against.

O'HALLORAN What makes this horse do things like this, Will. You usually get along well with all your beasts, don't you?

WILL There's been someone throwing stones at our house late at night. I've taken to locking his stable, but he gets nervous at the stones and the shouting.

DR O'HALLORAN What are they trying to do to you, Will?

WILL Jerome O'Halloran, I'm not going to tell you, you were whistling when I came in here, why should our miseries interrupt your happiness?

JEROME Yes, Will, I am very happy.

WILL And I bet I know why you're happy.

JEROME *Laughing* I suppose the whole village knows that I spent the night at Theresa O'Connor's with

WILL with Katie Johnson

JEROME It happened so suddenly, Will. Our respective parents will have to let us get married now.

WILL Jerome, I also need some medicine for the sick lad we have staying with us. He is hot with fever, but feels so cold he clings to our stove.

JEROME *Opening drawer of cupboard. Then writing prescription.*

Half of the people in the township have the symptoms you describe, Will. *A curious pause* What are you thinking, Will?

WILL That you and Katie Johnson will never be happy inside the tollgates of this township, Jerome.

JEROME *Emotion* Oh Will, we're sick of being afraid of them. No, no. We're staying where we were born & where I practise. Tomorrow I'm to see Father Connolly about our marrying

PRIEST *in wolfskin coat* Yes, it was after my attempt to visit Will Donnelly at Whalen's Corners that his friend the young doctor came to me with his miserable adventure at that woman's house with the curtain over the cupboard. Stephen, that is William Donnelly's house, why is their dog barking so ferociously at me?

BOY Your reverence, I don't feel that it's barking at you.

PRIEST You'll have to tie the horse to that tree or it will bolt. What a bitterly cold day and this is the last visit I have to make. They do so sic their dog on me, listen to it. Why do they not open the door. Open the door at once. Call off that beast of a dog!

GIRL Good day to you, sir.

PRIEST Is your husband at home? I pray do not bar me from entering your house, your dog is snapping at our heels.

GIRL Joe, off with you. I am their hired girl, sir. Joe! My mistress is lying down just at present and my master is away. Yes, Mr Donnelly is away from home and he warned me not to let any stranger into the house while he was gone. Gipsies and other such mountebanks are rife in all sorts of disguises.

PRIEST Get down on your knees, girl, when you address your priest with such nonsense.

GIRL Norah Donnelly, do I have to get down on my knees if this fellow in the great big fur coat says?

PRIEST I am not a gipsy, I am not a mountebank. You could not have been at mass last Sunday, I am the new priest of the parish.

NORAH Father Connolly. Pardon us, Father. We did not know who you were... if you are... what kind of fur is that?

PRIEST What business is it of yours what kind of fur—

NORAH It's wolfskin, isn't it?

PRIEST Yes, Mrs Donnelly, it is wolfskin, what of that? My parishioners presented it to me as a parting gift and I wish I were back with them now.

NORAH Your reverence, forgive me. I honestly did not recognize you as a priest dressed—it's very dangerous to wear that fur when there are so many fierce dogs about, they smell the wolf, Father Connolly, welcome to our house.

PRIEST Thank you. And you are Norah Donnelly, then, William Donnelly's wife?

NORAH Yes, your reverence. The reason I was not at mass last Sunday is that I was ill. And my husband is not at home. He is out looking for some medicine for the sick boy we have here behind the stove.

PRIEST Who is this lad? What name is upon you, boy?

NORAH I doubt if he hears you, father. He has been so feverish.

PRIEST Surely he is no boy of yours, what is his name then?

NORAH Tom Ryan.

PRIEST I was told by the O'Hallorans that you harboured a lad here who is accused of stealing a horse of theirs.

NORAH Your reverence, he is an outcast boy thrown out of his home by his father. Sometimes he makes his home with us and I have heard another side to the story about O'Halloran's horse.

PRIEST Young woman, are you calling the most respectable family in my parish liars?

NORAH No, father, I am simply saying there are always two sides to a story.

PRIEST Well, Mrs William Donnelly, in that supposition you are wrong. There are not always two sides to a story. There is one side, mark this, and one side only *he climbs into the pulpit (step ladder) & the scene dissolves into a church scene* Last Sunday I spoke of making things better in this parish. Have they been getting better? No. No, they have been getting worse, for last week someone whose name I think I know although no one will tell me his name because they are terrified of a certain gang of roughs and toughs in the neighbourhood, that someone took out one of Mr O'Halloran's horses in the dead of night and rode him from tollgate to tollgate until the poor beast was nigh dead. I told the culprit to come and see me. He came to see me and brought with him his lame friend who on finding me out left me a threatening letter.

The congregaton are kneeling in front of him & cower in terror, beating their breasts when he starts "cursing".

WILL It is not fair, Father Connolly, that you should ask this lad's master to discharge him.

PRIEST He is a drifter, one of the young ne'er do wells who hang out at a certain house not three miles from where you are kneeling and I am standing.

WILL First prove that he took the horse, we can give you proof of the lad's innocence.

TOM RYAN *lounging on the cupboard which has lately been used for an altar* By the way, in this particular instance, I, Tom Ryan, did not take out O'Halloran's horse, although at three other times I had—just for the hell of it. But whoever this time did take out O'Halloran's horse picked just the right moment to do it.

PRIEST I curse the man or boy who took out the horse and nearly killed it.

WILL *at first as a silhouette, then slowly out with the congregation on this side of the curtain* You have paid his master twenty dollars to let him go; you had him put in a buggy and driven to the borders of Biddulph where I met him, drove him back to Lucan and got him a job with a threshing gang.

PRIEST Who is the priest in this parish? I tell you I curse the man or boy who did this deed. I ask the congregation to mark this prophecy of mine—the guilty party shall be a corpse inside a month. Whoever took out O'Halloran's horse—shall be a corpse inside a month.

WILL Everybody stand up. Father Connolly ... what are you saying—that the person in this community, the person who dies within the next month is the person who stole O'Halloran's horse?

PRIEST I have received a threatening letter from a cripple and a devil notorious in this parish.

WILL Are you all alive now? You alive, Tom Ryan?

TOM RYAN Yes, Mr Donnelly.

WILL At the end of thirty days let us see, Father Connolly, who has keeled over. The month of June has thirty days;

CHORUS Four Thursdays four Fridays four ... One day, two days, 3/4/5/6/7/8/9/10 days11/12//////////14/15/16/17/18/19/20/21/22/23/24/25/26/27/28/29/ thirty days ... Saturdays, Five Sundays, Five Mondays, Four Tuesdays, Five Wednesdays

PRIEST I ask this congregation to mark this prophecy of mine – the guilty party will be a corpse inside a month so now that thirty days have passed – who is dead? And who is dead is he or she who took out O'Halloran's horse?

SOLO MAN Phil Flannery, aged pauper. Too weak at the time to steal a horse.

SOLO WOMAN Old Mrs O'Flaherty. After a year in the county jail on suspicion of poisoning my late dear husband, and I'm seventy seven years old.

WILL Tom Ryan, are you still alive?

TOM RYAN Still alive, Mr Donnelly.

O'HALLORAN And so you are mocked, Father, in their rathole tavern by that William Donnelly and that ne'er do well Tom Ryan whom we cannot seem to get expelled from the township and who has not even the grace to die when he has been cursed from the altar.

PRIEST Mr O'Halloran is it true that no thresher is brave enough to thresh your grain for you because of the Donnelly boys' threats

O'HALLORAN All too true, Father.

PRIEST Who has the nearest threshing machine in these parts?

O'HALLORAN Oh Marty Curtin has one, but he won't use it. He doesn't want it destroyed.

The congregation form a threshing machine & are led offstage by the thresher, Curtin, and followed by Fr Connolly.

PRIEST I personally, Mr Curtin, with cash of my own will guarantee any damage to your machine even to complete destruction. We shall just see who is the priest of this parish, a lame man who trades horses and leads around a stallion in the spring for she mares, or he who has been vouchsafed the sacrament of ordination.

MRS DONNELLY *revealed in her kitchen by the drawing of Stage Left curtain* How quiet it is on the line tonight, Mr Donnelly. I can hear Bridget ironing handkerchiefs and you mending harness and Tom polishing it, but there's nothing else to hear.

TOM The leaves are all off the trees, that's why. And there's no wind, mother.

MRS DONNELLY When's John coming home?

TOM RYAN When the threshing's through at Trehy's unless they have a dance. If they have a dance then – daybreak.

MRS DONNELLY Oh well, then I'll lock him out and he can knock on the windows if he wants in.

TOM Mother, you've taken such a fancy lately to locking up the house. What's got into you?

MRS DONNELLY Fewer and fewer people are neighbouring with us. Back in the old country that sometimes meant they visited you at other times. What's that sound?

MR DONNELLY Mrs Donnelly, read that paper out you found hidden under Tom's mattress this morning. I want to hear that again.

MRS DONNELLY Northern Sparks. A hotel wrecked by roughs in London Township. A few of the natives deliberately took possession of Glass's Hotel, Elginfield, London Township and commenced a fearful scrimmage. Poor Glass had no chance whatever. The table and punch was upsot/An' the row it commenced in a minit, shure. Niver a taste of shtick had he got,/So he picked up a piece of the furniture. Probably it was a bad job for him he did so, as they soon made splinters of all and sundry of the bar furniture, and Glass fled in all directions . . .

TOM Aw they left out the best part. We shoved them in the little cubby hole they have under the stairs and we let the whiskey barrel bung out right beside so you could hear old Glass getting drunk, sad, wet, mad and glad all at once.

MRS DONNELLY How would you like it Tom if someone put you under a stair and drowned you in whiskey?

TOM Mother, how would you like it if you were riding along with your friend and old Mrs Glass comes out into her yard and says: Donnellys must not drink from our trough. Her trough's too good for Donnelly horses is it, well I'll show her, her decanters aren't good enough for our horses.

MR DONNELLY It's true. At your age I'd have done something. I don't think I'd have taken my horse into the bar though. Your horse might have hurt his feet in the barroom, Tom. What are you rummaging about in the cupboard for, Tom, don't you see they partly know they'll get a rise out of you.

TOM I think I hear a constable coming to arrest me. Oh it's John. That's none of our horses though, I knew it was a strange horse.

JOHN Tom! I caught them trying to sneak the threshing machine into O'Halloran's through the back of Trehy's farm. Listen you can hear it. Tom, they've got the priest with them.

Threshing machine slowly approaches with Priest intoning the following litany as the machine is elaborately cranked & set going by Curtin. This human threshing machine should behave with busybody solemnity led in by the cleric chanting from a small black book:

Holy Mary, *pray for us.*
Holy Mother of God,*
Holy Virgin of virgins,*
St Michael,*

fades into O'Halloran's speech & under the noise of the machine

St Gabriel,*
St Raphael,*
All ye holy Angels & Archangels,*
All ye holy order of blessed Spirits,*
St John Baptist,*
St Joseph,*
All ye holy Patriarchs & Prophets &c.*

O'HALLORAN
We got it nearly all threshed. Well more than half way. And they stood on the road looking over at us with broad grins. I guess they knew what was going to happen. One of the sheaves I was pitching in felt a bit heavy.† By the name of God they had hidden horseshoes and iron pins in the sheaves by the road and small stones that—

* *pray for us*

†TOM Lift it Malachi, heavy though it be.

JOHN There's a saying O'Halloran, heavy in the sheaf, full in the granary.

As the machine breaks down, Fr Connolly's face is blackened by an inner explosion.

PRIEST *pulpit* Things will be better in Biddulph. *Congregation kneels in front of him.* I do not care if I get a bullet through my head, but they will be better. I propose to form a Peace Society. I have stated the purpose here at the head of this paper. *The paper is the same prop scroll used to represent the petition for Donnelly's life in Part One.* I want all the men who are interested in preserving peace and order in the parish of St Patrick's, Biddulph, to sign their names. All those who do not sign I shall consider backsliders, blacklegs and sympathizers with this gang of evildoers and ruffians in our midst. Any of you who do not sign if they take sick they may send for William Donnelly. Do not send for Father John Connolly. As an indication of who is with me and who is against me will those that intend signing—kneel

This leaves the Donnellys standing. They leave the church and the paper is signed as in Part I with congregation intoning the Roman Line names.

CARROLL For those of us who had some time ago decided that handcuffs must be forged and plans must be made this was the moment we had waited for over a year. *cartwheels & yells!* Now we had a screen to work behind and a petition was soon forwarded to the Court House too—we had the Priest and the Conservative Party behind us. Now we needed the law. For years the Donnellys had been using the law, protected by the Grit Sherriff, pampered by Grit magistrates—so we said:

CHORUS *they face us in a compact line* To the Judge of the County of Middlesex. We the undersigned inhabitants of Biddulph humbly pray, humbly petition. Whereas for some time past evil-minded persons have robbed us, slashed our animals, burnt our barns, broke my threshing machine, deluded our females, bullied us, tormented us, stole my cow, laughed at us, looked right through us, mocked us ... we want James Carroll to be of said Township Constable therein and the following respectable farmers and landowners to be magistrates: Messrs Cassleigh and O'Halloran.

CASSLEIGH & O'HALLORAN Mr Carroll, you're in a position to catch them now.

CARROLL Yes, yes. I'll be the cause of the Donnellys being banished out of Biddulph or lose my life in the process.

CHORUS *joining hands, dancing & singing about him* There came one day to Lucan town/A man of mighty frame/His beard was black, his shoulders broad/James Carroll was his name. *fiddle*

CARROLL Then we went after them ...

BISHOP Father Mahoney, let us go up in the tower of my cathedral—higher, higher, higher yet till we see?

At the huge step ladder behind everything, the Bishop & his secretary climb up to survey what is happening.

MAHONEY I see a mob invade the Donnelly farm in search of a lost cow. I see them drag the Ryan boy off to jail at last ... I see the Donnelly family cleaning wheat at their kitchen door.

BISHOP Are they looking dejected?

MAHONEY Not very. Some, your excellency.

BISHOP Now that we have punished them, we will show them some kindness in some unexpected way. You will see, we will bring them round. First severity, then love. And then—they will kneel.

MRS DONNELLY John! John and Tom Donnelly, don't sow this wheat! Have you been sowing any of it?

JOHN Yes, mother. We have.

MRS DONNELLY What's the use of sowing wheat in a township that hates us?

TOM Shall we go about the front field picking up all the grain we've sown then, mother?

MR DONNELLY Your mother's tired of Biddulph, John.

MRS DONNELLY I'm sick of Biddulph. Why don't we take our wheat with us somewhere and sow it there. Not here.

MR DONNELLY When there's children to this, we will.

MRS DONNELLY I'll never see this harvested. James, you'll never see it harvested. John I thought you were to sow the wheat tomorrow, I never dreamed you were...

JOHN Mother, we were, but then the boy came to tell us not to bother going to his father's threshing today.

TOM and not to neighbour with his father anymore because of what the men said to his father last night—

JOHN so Tom started sowing and I did too,

TOM tramping up and down the field right out there, I thought you looked dreaming about something,

JOHN was it Bridget talking about the old country, or—time passing by without your noticing until the wheat is nearly all sown except for this.

We are back at the wake again. The coffins return; all lie asleep by them.

MRS DONNELLY Into the ground with them, then, John. *she throws a handful of wheat at us* And burn these bad seeds, Mr Donnelly, burn them over here. *A brazier of bad seeds is burnt.* November! November I shall say to you, John, your wheat's up. *Her form towers & fades in & out behind the smoke & fire of the brazier* Next month I'll go to see Jennie in St Thomas. She used to ask me to lift my arms like this and then bring them down like wings and lift her up in them, until she got bigger and instead I taught her to dance when we'd be all alone here, my daughter and myself. Even if she's dancing all alone she's really dancing with me.

JENNIE That clock strikes the hour nearest dawn. Am I only left awake to watch? No. William's gone to look after the horses.

CHORUS Five dead people lying in a house
The last tollgate before harvest and heaven

JENNIE But at dawn comes a sleigh to bear you away

CHORUS Five dead people are leaving this house

The blindfolded dead come out from behind the curtain & follow their coffins but—

JENNIE But at dawn comes a sleigh to bear you away

CHORUS Five dead people are leaving this house

The blindfolded dead come out from behind the curtain & follow their coffins but—

JENNIE No, not yet

Mrs Donnelly, her eyes bandaged, dances with Jennie to the gramaphone & then leaves.

CHORUS *record* Five dead people are leaving this house[3]

JENNIE

At dawn comes a sleigh to bear you away
The snow has come down
To cover the ground
Where you will lie buried today

Two times cross each other—the morning of Friday, 6 *February,* 1880 *and the summer afternoon in* 1900. *We hear sleighbells, then the chuff-chuff of the gramaphone.*

CHORUS End of Act One

Handcuffs

Act Two

Organ. The coffins arrive at the church. Fr Connolly comes to meet the Donnellys. The scene shifts to the Bishop's Palace.

CHORUS *sung*

Exsultabunt Domine ossa humiliata
They shall rejoice in the Lord, the bones that have been humbled
Requiem aeternam dona eis, Domine. Et lux perpetua luceat eis.

CORCORAN Two years before the Donnelly Tragedy if tragedy it can be called, I, Timothy Corcoran, was almost their member of Parliament, and after the results came out I paid a visit to His Excellency the Bishop, Francis McSweeney

BISHOP Appointments, Father Mahoney?

MAHONEY Mr Corcoran is soon here to see you, Your Excellency. And the chimney sweeps are coming at half past. In these few spare moments might we, Your Excellency, just go through your speech at four o'clock at the Academy of the Sacred Heart.

BISHOP My dear children I have assisted at this annual distribution of prizes with much gratification. Father Mahoney, weren't our chimneys just swept?

MAHONEY Your Excellency, the bird, the wild bird that has been trapped in the fireplace chimney here for three or four days now.

BISHOP Ah yes, Father Mahoney. It's not making much of a sound this morning, is it? The child when brought to school is not only an ignorant being but it is also a being inclined to evil. How important, therefore...

MAHONEY Your Excellency, I beg your pardon. I forgot that Mr Corcoran is already here.

BISHOP Timothy Corcoran. May I congratulate you, Mr Timothy Corcoran, on your victory at the polls yesterday. We Conservatives who are Catholics are marching forward to greater and greater strengths.

CORCORAN *who has kneeled & kissed the Bishop's ring* Your Excellency, there's

BISHOP Who says this is not an age for miracles, Mr Corcoran? Sir John A Macdonald waves his magic wand—good Catholics every where vote for

CORCORAN Your Excellency, there has been a final tally of the votes. I lost by seven votes.

BISHOP By how many votes? Mr Corcoran, are you telling me that you lost the riding by just seven votes? Then the Protestants did not vote for you as they promised. Some Orangemen. Although you were the Conservative candidate you were also a Catholic and they

CORCORAN Your Excellency, it was some Irish Catholics who did not

BISHOP Where?

CORCORAN By a large margin I lost in Ward Three, Biddulph.

BISHOP That should have been the safest spot in the world for an Irish Catholic candidate. Whatever has gone wrong?

CORCORAN There is a family there that is Catholic and Irish, but we cannot persuade them to vote Conservative. They influence the whole neighbourhood to vote the Protestant ticket. Grit.

BISHOP What name is upon them?

CORCORAN Donnelly.

BISHOP Father Mahoney?

MAHONEY Your Excellency may remember that a letter came to you from a member of that family—William Donnelly. *draws the curtain aside to reveal this person*

WILL & BISHOP Your reverence. Our new parish priest, Father Connolly, has formed a Peace Society in direct opposition to our family. I wonder if Father Connolly knows that the members

BISHOP What beautiful handwriting.

WILL & BISHOP of this society are sworn to each other? I wish that you would bring Father Connolly and me face to face before you and decide who is in the wrong.

BISHOP The man should have been a priest.

WILL & BISHOP Our name is continually referred to in church in connection with crime, but the names of others known to have committed crimes are never even hinted at. For God's sake, do something before it is too late.

BISHOP But he doesn't know how to address his bishop. No, I am not your reverence, William Donnelly, I am your Excellency. And. He doesn't know that before you can stand you must learn to kneel. Seven votes. *Rescues the bird at the fireplace* (*sewing machine*) So, Mr Corcoran, this William Donnelly did not vote for you then, and he is just one of a whole family of such people?

CORCORAN Your Excellency, yes. He is the very worst one of all the Donnellys.

BISHOP You said just now that they influence the whole neighbourhood, why would you say that now?

CORCORAN The kind of influence they use is to ride the horses of my supporters all night until they are nigh dead and leave tied to their tails if they have not cut them off—Vote Tory, Be Sorry.

BISHOP Father Mahoney. You may tell the chimney sweeps to go away. We have no need of their service now the trapped bird has fallen down into the grate.... *Bird shadow on the curtain now.* Black with soot, ashes. Dead? No. With the warmth of my hands, the pressure of the ring on my finger, the bird revives. Its heart is beating; its wings flutter:—open that window if you please— *both Mahoney & Corcoran rush to obey* and after four days and nights in our dark chimney off the wretched bird flies, free out of my palace, away from my cathedral, trapped in our flues no longer. *Gesture of arms up* Free, yes free. But black marked, dirty with soot and ashes. He flies to his familiar or her familiar branch in the grove—oh Father Mahoney, this is the turn I shall give the speech this afternoon, *Wing Shadows on Curtain.*

MAHONEY Your Excellency, this is the trope we have been searching for.

BISHOP Does this sooty bird resemble its fellow birds now? Is it as it looked before? No. The other birds turn away. What bird is this so different.

MRS DONNELLY Shure, don't you see how my family is being treated. We are being shunned. No one neighbours with us any more.

BISHOP All the birds of the grove give it a roost by itself, a wide roost

Mr & Mrs Donnelly are about to be surrounded by a mob and killed.

MRS DONNELLY at first	*Vicious chirping*
MR DONNELLY They are using us worse than mad dogs.	*Bird starling sounds*

BISHOP At first, then the other birds can bear the stranger no longer. Cruel are the laws of nature. At first a peck. And then a buffet.

MR DONNELLY I was not in the least afraid of them.

BISHOP Peck peck peck Buffet buffet buffet

CHORUS A gang of masked men murder an entire family. Intense excitement.

Birds attack the "different" bird & kill her & him with chirping sounds.

BISHOP My dear children, would you have joined with those cruel birds driving away the stranger who was after all their brother but only changed by the soot of our chimneys? Tree cross roost Arimathea work that around some more, Father Mahoney and let me see it at eleven.

A servant pours water into a basin and brings it to his master. The bishop washes his hands.

Mr Corcoran, we have been chastizing this family, we have been trying to teach them not to be so different—or else. Now when they have had time to think it all over, we will show them the other side of our power, the power to overlook, to forgive. Be patient likewise, Mr Corcoran. We are working with the government to free the son who is in prison—Robert. I want you to take him home to his father and you will see and we shall see—if that does not change matters with this family cleanse the soot off their feathers as it were. Ah, your wrath against this family can only with difficulty be assuaged. Timothy Corcoran, try to forgive them, have you forgiven them? Can you forgive them, ever?

He nods his head after a long pause

And when the next election, the provincial one is held in your riding and you run again, this time you will win, by a large margin. You will win because you have swallowed your pride and helped us give this family one more chance. *Crossing and climbing as in the diocesan walk scene to Fr Girard.* Father Mahoney, did I write to Crinnon, Bishop of Hamilton, a short while ago?

Jim Feeny takes a rope & starts to hang himself from another stepladder.

MAHONEY Yes, your Excellency, and you asked him this question: Why did you not invite Father Connolly to your thirty-fifth anniversary celebrations?

The two prelates climb the two sides of the great stepladder at the back of the stage.

BISHOP You invited all the other priests from all the other missions to which you had once ministered, except Father Connolly, and he is the priest of St Patrick's, Biddulph, your very first pastorate. It was noticed by many too and even hinted at as a scandal that you did not send an invitation to the incumbent at your very first mission, St Patrick's

CRINNON McSweeny, he will never get one. I consider it one of the duties of a pastor to keep his parishioners alive.

BISHOP Spiritually alive.

CRINNON Alive. Why there is the son of one of my old parishioners throwing a rope over a tree branch in the forest.

BISHOP The Feeny boy. A difficult case. How can Connolly help him when he is too weak and drunken and generally besotted even to come near the church.

CRINNON McSweeny, it is not only Feeny who is sick of life. Go down the steps of your steeple with its bells and see what you find stretched out at the foot of your altar.

BISHOP Crinnon, I know, I know. Father Connolly came into town this morning from Biddulph and he has been mysteriously praying at my altar ever since.

Connolly at foot of altar. Young lovers in doctor's office

CRINNON Do you want me to show you why he is doing this?

BISHOP No. I know. It concerns that wretched young doctor, Jerome O'Halloran. How on earth, Crinnon, could Connolly have foreseen that turn to events. Yes, a few days ago, I know, you do not have to tell me, this young man met his—concubine in his office and

KATE Jerry, I slipped out through the back door of the milliner's. They will all think I have gone home, but of course there I cannot go.

JEROME Why what have they said?

KATE Not to come home again.

JEROME Home here then. Kate, my hands. These hands have just examined a dead man at the inquest.

KATE I don't care. I'll kiss away the death.

JEROME So there's that and there's also the fact that I kept my appointment with Father Connolly. I went to see him at his office.

KATE What did he say, Jerome.

JEROME He says that if I marry you he will excommunicate me and that I will be damned. He says that ... I told him of what we had done at Mrs Connors', that in effect we are married already, and he called me a fornicator and you were called such a name that I struck him. I struck him. He then told me that I was a disgrace to my pious old mother and father, and that I was even worse than the very very worst of the Donnellys—that cripple and devil, Will Donnelly. Later at the inquest as I was cutting open that man's body in order to get at the heart it suddenly came to me that tonight when you came—why *Gets both poison and wine from altar* we would drink this in some wine—from this glass and we would at last be free. What are you thinking?

KATE Yes. Jerome, you know I will go with you wherever you go.

They drink, he first

JEROME Do you want to know where we are going now, Kate?

KATE If you know, tell me.

JEROME We'll put on our coats because the thing works through various stages of increasing drowsiness and we'll walk down the the road to the tollgate. *They walk toward us*

KATE Once past the tollgate we're out of Biddulph, Jerome. Jerome, may I turn back just once?

JEROME When we get to the tollgate. *They have disappeared.*

BISHOP *down from ladder now & bending over the abject priest* Connolly, I want you to come with me to my study. What happened then?

CONNOLLY They were found dead just this side of Kelly's toll house, Kelly brought them back into the village in a cart. Tell me, your Excellency, where I am to bury him?

BISHOP What does the church say with regard to the burial of those who take their own lives?

CONNOLLY The gravedigger without waiting for my authority went ahead and dug the young man's grave in their family plot by the chancel.

BISHOP Tell him to dig another one outside the fence. He must not be buried in consecrated ground.

CONNOLLY You tell him, because I'm not going back there ever again.Here's the key to the church.

BISHOP Connolly, I am going to get Father Mahoney to walk over to the Huron Hotel and get you a hack. He will tell the driver to take you back to your presbytery and the first thing you must do is tell the sexton to fill in the grave by the chancel and dig the new one outside the church yard. Don't you realize the good that will come of this severity? Now if you go back you will be respected as you have never been respected before. Connolly, who has the key to that church and the key to their souls, you or William Donnelly? It is a battle, lives are lost in battles, but to save men's souls we must fight on. The unfaithful shepherd

CONNOLLY Wolf. Yes. Your Excellency, you are sending a wolf back to them. I am one, I cannot sleep, I hear both sides of the feud confess opposite things until I, I feel graceless.

BISHOP Get up Connolly

CONNOLLY How much longer do I have to stay there then if I do go back.

BISHOP If! Until you die, Connolly. Get up and out of here. Father Mahoney!

He beats Father Connolly with his crozier out of the church—towards us as Tom races across to the tree where Feeny is hanging himself.

TOM Jim Feeny, you young bugger, what are you trying to get away with this time? I'll hang you. Just because Jerry O'Halloran did himself in you feel it's the fashionable thing to do, do you, hang yourself? Jimmy. God you've been drinking.

JIM A man can't even die around here anymore. Let me have my rope back.

TOM Nothing doing. I'm hiding this rope on you. *Exit behind curtain to hide same*

JIM Why was I hanging myself anyhow? The time I was so sick after Tom and me smashed up Glass's Tavern there was somebody at my bedside, no not my mother

CARROLL It was I, Jim Carroll, when your mind was open like a cracked egg, I suggested

JIM That I should change sides! Well. And yet to all the world and the Donnellys I'd still appear a Donnelly man

CARROLL Oh, you want to join us, do you? Well.

JIM Yes, Jim Carroll, if I am to change sides just where is the other side and how do I join?

CARROLL Let's put you through your paces. I sent him one of my anonymous notes. Towards the end I got rather famous for these, my stepmother's hair fell out after one I sent her.

JIM & CARROLL Shun the Donnellys, or you will be used in the manner they will be used. Signed—Vigilant.

Suggest the Donnelly house with small windows held up by actors.

JIM I spent the next few weeks hanging around the Donnellys as I never hung around them before. And

CARROLL I've a warrant here for your arrest, Jim Feeny, but if you leave the township nothing more will be heard of it.

JIM My feelings were hurt, they didn't want me to join their society after all. He wanted me not. He wanted me to leave the township. Well, I like Tom again. To hell with you Carroll, I'm never leaving this township.
Now's your time to arrest me:
Here's my hands and here's my fists
Put them round my dimpled wrists

CARROLL I have an object of my own in view just now, Jim Feeny, but I will arrest you the first time I find you in Lucan.

JIM Then Jim, I'll walk into Lucan with you and here, everybody, *much pursuing of Carroll in & out of the curtains which part, sway, close* in front of the Post Office, Constable Carroll, arrest me. *and move as of themselves to suggest a whole day's chasing of Carroll by Feeny* Am I not even worth arresting? *The citizens of Lucan freeze in surprise.*

POSTMASTER Letter for you, Jim. That's a good pair of lungs you have there, almost blew all the stamps and telegraph forms we got in here out of their respective drawers. Woke the baby.

JIM & CARROLL So you're tired of the crowd you're with, come to the dance tonight.

JIM Dance tonight. There were dances all over the township. *Three Dances. These dances whirl about Jim Feeny without letting him join.* I must have visited three of them before I finally stumbled *The last dancers disappear behind the curtain.* into the deserted house on a side road not far from the Donnellys. The house was under a big elm and you'd see a flock of crows fly in one window of the house and out another.

The curtains draw back: organ chord out of horror movies; a row of heads rise slowly up from behind the altar—the Secret Society in council.

CHORUS Here, you can't come in here. You're not a member.

JIM If this is the Peace Society I'd like to join. My father signed the book in the church, why can't I join?

O'HALLORAN Prove you're an enemy of the Donnellys.

JIM How can I prove that now, tell me how.

CARROLL Bring us a pair of Tom Donnelly's old shoes, an old shirt of his and some pants and a coat, a coat he used to wear a lot.

TOM & JIM *Tom quietly crossing to him*
But—Your blood, my blood/Sealed in brotherhood

TOM When he remembers me signing his name on my arm, he loves me. But when he remembers the sting of my knife signing my name on his arm he hates me

JIM I was like a girl who couldn't make up her mind. And I said no.

CARROLL Yes

JIM No!

CARROLL Yes, the trouble with Jim Feeny is he never has and never will be able to make up his mind, so we'll make it up for you. Handcuff him. Because a girl that can't make up her mind, but has gone this far with her petticoat up and the man has it out

He handcuffs Feeny who is hanged behind & over the altar this time by his wrists.

JIM I'm not that much of a whore yet that you'll get me to get you Tom Donnelly's clothes.

CARROLL Well, we'll see about that, and here's a bell you can ring when your wrists feel ready to steal Tom's clothes. Don't let it drop now, we'll tie it to your hand.

JIM Carroll, I'll never ring it. You haven't broken my backbone yet, I won't give in even if it's to old Christ himself.

The curtains fold over to conceal Feeny.

CARROLL That's the spirit, Jim. Me, I had got what I wanted behind me. All the things I mentioned before, priest, law and this group of men sworn to each other, but there were still one or two gaps to be filled – our strongwilled friend back there and the fact that there was one strong man in the land just around the Donnellys' place whose help we needed. Patrick Marksey. *We hear the cane of an old, yet tough, strong farmer tapping on the frozen ground.*

TOM Patrick Marksey. Yes, behind my back they strung up my friend in a deserted house they had no permission to occupy.

MARKSEY Who the hell do you men think you are trespassing on my property?

CARROLL Good night, Pat.

MARKSEY Get out of here, Jim Carroll and take your friends with you. Get out!

CARROLL Pat, it's a great deal of trouble you'd be saving us if you can let us use this old place. Sure there's nobody living here before we came except Mrs Wind and Mr Rain, are they such better tenants of yours?

MARKSEY I don't want any of your secret people money, and don't ask me to join you or to swear your oath or help you in any way. O'Halloran, I'm surprised to see you in this gang, has God not punished you enough?

O'HALLORAN Marksey, the Donnellys have insulted us for years till it's now we have marked them down and God punishes them through us. I swear it was them misled my boy who killed himself and is now lying in a ditch, yes God will punish those whose strength and place was needed in the holy work and they hid their talent, Patrick Marksey.

CARROLL We can't move without a man of standing like you, Pat, in on it.

MARKSEY I know you can't, Jim Carroll, and I'll say this: I have not got a thing against the Donnellys. I'm tired of your always being after them. Leave them alone or I'll advertise you and this old house even if the crows nest in it it is my house, not your house, Jim Carroll. Good night to you, boys. *They Leave. Crow sounds.*

Ah, I'll clear the rest of you vermin out tomorrow and break up your nests—Jim Feeny. What have they got you strung up there for, tinkling a bell like a blind beggar. *He lowers Jim & Carroll enters to seize him.*

CARROLL Pat! Jim. I can leave the handcuffs on you and it's the lock-up or— you can come with us forever and I'll take them off.

JIM Take them off.

MRS DONNELLY *from her kitchen* It was late in the fall now, the roads iron with frost, and the men were sitting in the kitchen mending harness. Bridget was baking. I was knitting and listening to the quiet outside as I had begun to more and more. I thought *we hear a tiny bell tinkling; so does she* that at a great distance I could hear—there it is again, a tinker's bell, no not a tinker's bell, but a leper's bell. Some story my mother read me by the fire a very long time ago—about a saint who was a leper and had to wear a bell to warn people that he was coming... *Sudden noise at the door. Horsemen have thrown a briefly dressed Feeny on to their doorstep.*

TOM In the name of Heaven, what happened to you, Jim Feeny. Stand back, mother and Bridget. He's not decent. Jim, here's a pair of my old shoes. An old shirt of mine and some pants.

JIM They strung me up, Tom, and left me hanging. Then they stripped me and burnt my clothes and when I said I wouldn't join them they brought me here and threw me at your mother's door.

MRS DONNELLY And a coat. A coat Tom used to wear a lot, Jim. Put it on.

JIM And I put them on. Then it was like clapping drowned out by stamping for I went back to them with Tom's clothes and they took them off me—made me watch while they gambled for them.

Card game with vigilantes smacking cards on floor and reciting Romàn Line litany sotto voce. Leave clothes on Feeny, have identical Tom's clothes on dummy. This takes place in silhouette behind the curtain.

TOM When Jim would stay at our place some nights I'd wake up and look at your face beside because something had changed about you

JIM Couldn't you see what was happening?

TOM Stuck eyelid! *He draws back the curtain to reveal the card game.*

VIGILANTE You're it, Barry! You've won the clothes of Tom Donnelly

CARROLL Wait a minute, according to the rules—it's O'Halloran who's won!

ALL O'Halloran!

O'HALLORAN Jim Carroll, what am I to do with Tom Donnelly's clothes.

CARROLL Dress up in them.

O'HALLORAN I'm too stout

CARROLL But your servant Jim Purtell is Tom's size, is he not?

O'HALLORAN Yes, and dressed as Tom Donnelly what does he do?

CARROLL Don't you see? He burns down Patrick Marksey's barns.

The curtains close cutting us off from the vigilantes.

TOM And so the clothes my mother and myself gave you when you were naked, Jim were used to bring in Marksey on their side. In fire or flood or field or air where we wander now I ask you, Jim Feeny.

JIM Yes, Tom, I helped close the ring around you. Then it was the day before Christmas and seemed as good a day as any, so I found a rope in my father's driving shed and walked into the Donnelly's woods to hang myself. And all is done as you have seen. *Tom's now coming back from hiding the rope* I the whore told you they were always like that, bossy, try to hang yourself and they won't let you, what'd you do with the rope?

TOM Hid it on you, Jim. Look, Jim, I want you to come home with me, it's Christmas Eve.

JIM If you hadn't interrupted me I'd have been all right by now.

TOM Not by a long shot, you'd have been choking for hours, I never seen a hangman's knot tied more ill, you just don't know how to do it, Jim.

JIM I could see the door of the Donnelly kitchen getting closer and closer. Mr and Mrs Donnelly and John were all dressed up for church.

JIM That's a new suit, John.

JOHN Yes, it's the first time I've worn it.

TOM Whatever happened to your old suit, why everything you're wearing is new?

JOHN Burnt them

MRS DONNELLY Now why would you do that now?

JOHN I read something in the newspaper made me do it, mother, if you must know. If you remember that woman I was married to for a week and twice she said bad things about us, and I said once more hurt us like that and I'll go back, and so she did it the third time?

MR DONNELLY John, your mother and myself are sorry we asked.

JOHN Well, she got married again, father, and I burnt the suit I married her in.

MR DONNELLY Tonight, John, confession and mass. And the old year is ended.

JOHN Father. Mother. *Kneels and receives their blessing*

MR & MRS DONNELLY Bless you my son. In nomine patris et filii et spiritus sancti. Amen.

JIM They left the house when Mr Keefe's sleigh called for them. Tom and Bridget went out to the barn to do the chores. *Pause, kissing the cupboard* I love the house of the Donnellys. *Caressing other pieces of furniture, curtains, invisible tables* I love their chairs and their *John's mother and father still kiss him. Some emotional cry or scream or choked anguish as the love turns to hatred at his arm being cut, probably by the cupboard again, kicking cupboard* Burn to the ground, burn to the ground. *Pause before leaving* I leave. Only saw Tom Donnelly once ever again, saw him the night they got him.

Curtains

CHORUS *sing "The snow lay on the ground" under*

PRIEST Who is next? *He draws the Stage Left curtain in front of himself, then ducks down behind altar and stands behind Stage Right curtain. Mrs. Donnelly knocks at the Stage Left curtain; Fr Connolly opens his curtain.* Come in, Mrs Donnelly. *She opens the Stage Left curtain*

MRS DONNELLY Father Connolly. *She shuts the curtain in front of her*

PRIEST Father Connolly. *He shuts curtain in front of himself* She says it as if she were my equal. Father Connolly. Mrs Donnelly.

MRS DONNELLY Mrs Donnelly. He is afraid of me, I can tell by the way his lips purse my name. *She opens Stage Right curtain and appears at it: he opens Stage Left curtain and appears.*

PRIEST To see me about? Yourself, your husband, and your son John were just at confession, were you not?

MRS DONNELLY Are you sure John came to you? *The priest draws his curtain shut*

PRIEST Yes

MRS DONNELLY What I should have said was—yes, John came to you, but did you receive him.

PRIEST Ah, but you didn't ask that you see.

MRS DONNELLY So that I went on for an hour with you *she comes out and goes over to confront his curtain after closing her curtain:* telling you the story of my life ever since *she draws aside the curtain: he has vanished* yes, the story of my life has been this *she draws the Stage Left curtain too and he is not behind it.* If you could see my face and I could see yours, but no

PRIEST *appearing at Stage Right opening his curtain* Mrs Donnelly, when people have a hard name, as a priest, having the charge of souls, I must set my face against their deeds.

MRS DONNELLY Why is it that you have a face for our deeds but no face at all for the lives that are explainers of these deeds. *He draws the other curtain sharply in front of him. The curtains both wave out at her; she touches them to see who, if anybody, is behind.* Is it that when you first came to our neighbourhood—her farm on the road is before our farm and with her sable coat and her sable muff and her fur hat driving down to the church to suck the toes of Jesus in her jet black cutter, the soul of respectability ... Mrs. O'Halloran. *Mrs Donnelly reveals her by sharply drawing aside the Stage Right curtain.*

MRS O'HALLORAN *in her usual regalia* Father Connolly, my mother was sitting in her parlour when my infant brother came running in from the road.

BOY Mammy! There's a strange woman coming down the street out of Connors' shebeen and she's drunk!

MRS DONNELLY And so, Father Connolly—when you see me you don't see me you always see—this! *Drawing the Stage Left curtain aside to reveal the Ax woman—James Carroll dressed up as the Mrs Donnelly of the vigilante version: coarse, pipe-smoking rough, jug-toting and a giantess to boot!*

MRS O'HALLORAN It was Mrs Donnelly, Father Connolly, walking! down! the middle! of the

AX WOMAN My husband's got seven years in Kingston, and my seven sons'll each kill their man for each year their darling father's in the cage.

MRS O'HALLORAN Shut up the shutters, my mother then said. Shut them up till Mrs Donnelly goes past and away. *Axwoman draws Stage Left curtain across her face and Mrs O'Halloran draws her shutters.*

MRS DONNELLY I am not like that. Keep that curtain away from your face, Father, when you talk to me—stop that! *Every time she gets one curtain open, it is shut. The space before the altar fills with worshippers. She has a piece of cloth in her hands.*

PRIEST *rapidly drawing aside, then shutting the Stage Right curtain* Good evening, Mrs Donnelly.

CHORUS Sanctus!

MRS DONNELLY Yes, good evening Father Connolly. Perhaps at mass, Mr Donnelly, John *She and the Donnelly men are now at the back of the church, Father Connolly is celebrating mass and we cut to his administering the sacrament. The Donnellys with others proceed to the communion rail, but John hangs back.*

MR DONNELLY John. Why are you not coming forward with us?

JOHN Mother and father, Father Connelly refused me confession—I cannot go up.

MRS DONNELLY WHY?

JOHN Because, because he said I probably intended to confess a lie in order to shield Tom at the trial when the case comes up about Glass's tavern.

MRS DONNELLY *Tears her veil apart. She turns away. The Donnellys leave the church* This is the last time we come to your altar, Father Connolly. Oh no—we will come once more. Once more!

MUSIC *"I Dreamt of Marble Halls" & Wedding Dance at Donnelly School. The mandolin plays the tune very coldly & the dance is sluggish.*

BISHOP Father Mahoney, my hand is stained with ink. Ask the servant to bring me a basin of water. I look down from my tower and over my diocese. There is Corcoran driving down from Biddulph. Are all these people at the wedding party friends of the Donnellys, Mr Corcoran?

CORCORAN And vote as they vote. If they vote for me tomorrow I win the riding.

BISHOP And will they vote for you? *From the stepladder he views the dance & washes his hands.*

MARIA It's not like my wedding dance at all at all if the Donnelly boys don't show up at it, father. Does anyone know if they're coming?

MR KEEFE Maria, darling, the Donnelly boys may not be anxious to come to the dance with a brother dead just a month ago.

GIRL There's some say their good shirts were out on the line drying all afternoon, and they've disappeared.

WOMAN They've trouble finding handkerchiefs, they had no handkerchiefs but ones edged in black

GIRL They're still in town getting proper handkerchiefs, they couldn't dance with those in their pockets.

MARIA Can they hear the music from the dance up at their house there? Sure, they can, I used to hear Will playing at the Donnellys' when I was a girl at school here, but you aren't playing loud enough, all of you put your heart into it, open the windows and the doors so the sound of it makes their feet tap and their father and mother say, go—mourning or no, get out of the house and off to Maria and Nick's wedding party.

This sequence is a reprise that brings together the musical & dance themes of the whole trilogy. What the dancers are trying to do is make enough noise to attract the Donnelly boys to the dance. What they don't realize, of course, is that if the boys do come to the dance Carroll cannot accuse them of burning down Marksey's barn which is about to go up in flames; he will then in desperation turn upon their mother and father.

We hear Will's fiddle and soon the four Donnelly boys appear and each performs a solo dance "The Haymakers' Reel"

DANCES

1. *Schottische*
2. *Buffalo Gals*
3. *Elgin Girls*
4. *John Barley Corn*
5. *Sticks & Stones*
6. *Schottische*
7. *Stamping & Clapping*
8. *Jig with Solos*

The feeling of this sequence should be of a last desperate fling on the part of the Donnellys and their friends. As Corcoran speaks the dances become shadows and the fiddle music weakens.

9. *Curtain Dance "The Haymakers' Reel!"*

CORCORAN Oh your Excellency, I went to the prison. I showed them your letter, I received Bob Donnelly, I drove with him towards his father's farm and could see in the distance Old Donnelly waiting at his gate

MR DONNELLY I saw Mr Corcoran driving towards me, my son Bob beside him.

The Bishop washes his hands, scrub, brush his nails

CORCORAN Jim, I know you and your sons worked against me last election. No hard feelings, Jim, we've got Bob out of prison six months before his sentence

MR DONNELLY He should never have gone to prison in the first place.

CORCORAN Jim, you're glad to see him back, aren't you?

MR DONNELLY Bob

BOB Father, forgive me. They pried me loose. *He kneels to his father*

MR DONNELLY Mr Corcoran, on Sunday last after mass Father Connolly told the parish we should all vote for you. He said you were a good man.

CORCORAN Mr Donnelly, Father Connolly is a good and wise man. As much as the bishop he worked for Bob's release.

MR DONNELLY We didn't go to mass, Mr Corcoran. On Christmas Eve Father Connolly refused to confess another son of mine, John.

CORCORAN Mr Donnelly

MR DONNELLY Mr Corcoran, all my life men have come to my door both here and in Ireland and asked me to do something I do not want to do—you and your pals have taken away from us half my farm most of our reputation. But he has a few friends left.

CHORUS Seven votes!

MR DONNELLY Yes, we lost you the riding, so what you're really saying, Mr Corcoran, is—Donnelly, you've still got something left, some votes and we want them too and if you don't give me them votes, out of the township, I won't vote for you. I'm not in the least

BISHOP Corcoran, are you quite sure of that

CORCORAN Yes, your Excellency, his answer was

MR DONNELLY *Directly up to Bishop* No!

MR DONNELLY & CHORUS *Directly up to Bishop* No!

BISHOP You know I must have signed a hundred letters to get that man's son out of prison. Here, take this water and throw it away.

Continue with dance scene which comes out from behind the shadow curtain once more threading through it will be Mahoney descending with basin to servant who passes basin to another servant who passes basin to another servant until the basin cuts across the dance and its water is thrown out in the centre of the dancing floor.

DANCERS *whispering* We've danced till dawn. That's not the dawn that's the moon. That's not the moon, that's a barn burning, it's Pat Marksey's barn! *A blazing model of a barn is brought in.*

MARKSEY I got my horses and cows out, I had enough time to do that, but there's all my grain and tons of hay and implements and the new buggy my son Morris bought last summer and waggons, the new buggy.... There they are going by on the road, I saw them, Tom and Bob and John and Will. I said—they burnt my barns!

BRIAN Father, they couldn't have. I'm just home from the dance at the school and the Donnelly boys were there the whole night. Tom and Bob and John and Will.

MARKSEY Was Tom Donnelly at the dance, Brian?

BRIAN Father, ask others than your own son if you must, but I swear you are wrong—why would they want to burn down your barns.

MARKSEY I swear I saw Tom Donnelly come out of our granary with a lighted torch, it's the old man then, for who else but the Donnellys

BRIAN Why would old Donnelly burn you out, give me one reason.

MARKSEY If he didn't who did? Where's Jim Carroll, well where is the man, he's generally skulking at their gate. Carroll!

"Sweet & Low" hummed under—first line under of Bridget's speech only

Use the human house convention

BRIDGET I waved goodbye to Mrs Donnelly who that morning was off on a long promised visit to her daughter in St Thomas. Tom was driving her to catch the train at Lucan Crossing. I was sweeping the snow from the doorstep....

CARROLL Out of my way girl, I've business inside this shanty. Mr James Donnelly, the Elder, I've a warrant here for your arrest.

MR DONNELLY *smiling* Jim, you haven't visited us for over two months now. Where have you been?

JOHN Get those handcuffs away from my father. Read the warrant first, Carroll.

CARROLL You, James Donnelly, are charged with—the burning down last night of Patrick Marksey's barns. Where's the old woman, where's your wife, Donnelly?

JOHN It's not our job to hunt down our mother for you, Carroll. *"Sweet & Low" Bridget's speech under again.*

BRIDGET By that time my aunt would have been at the O'Connor house in the village where she *we suddenly shift to the O'Connor shebeen and for the first time repeat verbatim one of the scenes from Act One.*

MRS DONNELLY Yes, Theresa, is this not a pretty way we are used. *The audience should now begin to grasp the structure of the play and experience a "double" feeling about the next events. The sewing machine sound here should help us transfer our mind back to the earlier shebeen scenes.* But I have no time to sit down and tell you the full lunacy of it all. Peggy, I'll take the pillow slips with me now, for I'm catching the train this morning and going to visit my daughter Jennie in St Thomas. I'm promised to see her and my grandchildren since the wake for Michael. What is it, Tom?

TOM Mother, we're cutting it awful close.

MRS DONNELLY Goodbye Theresa. Thank you Peggy.

THERESA She's not herself. She doesn't want to stay out there where you're being accused all the time of doing things it would take an athletic hoyden of sixteen all her time doing let alone an old woman in her sixties.

CARROLL I've a subpoena here for Peggy O'Connor. You by the sewing machine over there, come here and sign this piece of paper for me.

THERESA What's this about, Constable Carroll?

CARROLL Well, your daughter consorts *Humming of "Sweet & Low" under & on. This Victorian tune is Mrs Donnelly's mind thinking of her grandchildren as she takes the long complex rail journey to St Thomas; a lullaby, a world so different from the Biddulph world she is escaping from.* with the Donnellys doesn't she? So she was out there the night of the fire and when she appears at the hearing tomorrow perhaps she can tell us what went on that night when

MARKSEY They burnt my barns

PEG Yes, perhaps I can.

CARROLL Remember Peggy O'Connor. Two o'clock sharp at the Council Chambers.

The actors sit as if on a gaslit train (the L.H.&B.) going down to London

TRAVELLER Gaslight. I was asleep, but at Lucan Crossing an old woman in black got on and sat beside me. Snowflakes on her bonnet. Gaslight.

MRS DONNELLY All the fields covered in snow up over the fences. Snow. *Train whistle as train enters London station & screech of brakes.* At the station in London I suddenly realized how sick I was of Biddulph and when no one was looking I put up both my arms just to see I still could. *The actors get off the train & become the Market Square at London; silhouettes of the hotels and halls there.*

STATION AGENT I saw her when I was putting more coke in the waiting room stove. I could see her reflection in the mica windows. All dressed in black and— *Imitates her but he can't get his arms up as high as she can.*

MAN Who is that old woman? Crossing the Market Square where only snow is being sold this day at one gust of wind a peck.

CHORUS I saw her...Sam Kelly, Thomas Varley, Thomas Hodgins—

MAN See the old woman go into the dining room at the City Hotel.

WOMAN She's somebody from Biddulph isn't she, Tom?

Use a "held" window to establish the dining room.

HOSTESS Good day to you, Mrs Donnelly. Are you all alone in town or are you expecting some other members of your family

MRS DONNELLY I'm all alone, Mrs McMartin, for I'm going down to St Thomas to see my daughter, Jennie. I'll have a glass of port, and a piece of seed cake, if you please.

CHORUS & PAPERBOY Through the thick glass of the dining room window and the snow comes

PAPERBOY My voice selling papers. Great victory in Zululand, Burmese Rebels Routed and.... Incendiarism in Biddulph, the barns of...

MRS DONNELLY There was time before the other train to St Thomas to buy the children a toy, and then my tracks in the deep snow behind me

Now the London & Port Stanley train is mimed; Mrs Donnelly walks toward us down a line of kneeling passengers.

CHORUS
John Wood William Ramsay
Hugh McDonald Andrew Mc-
Causlin
Pond Mills 3.30
North Westminster 3.40
Westminster 3.57
Glamworth 4.05
Yarmouth 4.09
St Thomas 4.15

train whistle & brake screech

GRANDCHILD I can remember her visiting us. I said to my mother— *at Jennie's house* was looking out the window in the front room down the street and there was this old woman coming up the street with her footsteps behind her.

JENNIE That old woman is your grandmother, children. What do you mean at all, old woman. Mother. At last you've come down from Biddulph to see us. At last at last.

GIRL Then she picked us up and whirled us around—it was then that she seemed to change—

BOY She wasn't a grandmother any more, boy she was strong and if she'd ever let you go *stop humming "Sweet & Low"* it'd been like a cannon or an eagle.

GIRL I remember she asked us a riddle.

MRS DONNELLY I have seven sons and each of them a sister. How many children have I?

BOY Grandmother, two of your sons are dead.

MRS DONNELLY Oh yes, but they're still my sons. Seven sons have I, and each of them has a sister. How many in my family? I'll fly through the air with the right answer.

CHILD I: Fourteen

CHILD 2: Fifteen, grandmother.

BOY Eight! *She picks him up and whirls him about.*

MRS DONNELLY Right. Eight is right, your mother is sister to seven brothers. Now fly over my head, for eight children, seven boys and a girl have I. *Clock strikes seven.*

JENNIE Mother, sit down and rest yourself now. They won't go to bed until they see the toy you brought them, and it's dark enough now—it's a magic lantern. Hush, your grandmother's gone to sleep. Nellie, could you see who that is at the door, I'm terrified to leave this thing shining by itself, flaming away in there, well I guess it's.... Who are you and what do you want? *The shadow of the hand and the handcuffs comes on the screen.*

The magic lantern should show a brightly coloured garden scene, the garden, as a matter of fact, mentioned earlier by Theresa O'Connor in connection with Jerome & Katie

CONSTABLE I have a warrant for a Mrs James Donnelly. Where is she?

JENNIE My mother. Asleep in that chair over there.

CONSTABLE Constable Carroll, is this the woman you mean.

CARROLL Yes, and I told you what a hard lot she is. Wake her up.

MRS DONNELLY There's no need to wake me up. I'm just keeping my eyes closed so as not to see your face, Jim Carroll.

CONSTABLE Mrs Donnelly. You are to come along with me to the police station, and from there Constable Carroll will take you back to Biddulph.

MRS DONNELLY Read the warrant first, if you please.

CONSTABLE Constable Carroll will do that. Mrs Currie, tell your mother she must get up out of that chair.

JENNIE I will tell her no such thing.

MRS DONNELLY I know my law. If he has the warrant then let him come in here and read it.

CARROLL Mrs Donnelly, you are charged with incendiarism. Patrick Marksey alleges that

Handcuffs her. There is a struggle. She tries to embrace

on January the 15th you aided your husband in burning down his barns. *her grandchildren, but her wings have now been clipped.*

JENNIE No! you're not taking her back there alone with you. Nellie, you'll have to take care of the children for a few days. Slow down your sleigh. Wait up. Mother. I'm coming with you. I'm coming with you. *Use Roman Line Convention with its litany of names which imprisons Mrs Donnelly once more* When we reached home, my father and brothers had the bail papers ready and he took off the handcuffs. *Mrs Donnelly falls to the ground on her face.* Mother, I've talked to William and he says there is nothing to worry about. It is only their law and they are making fools of themselves, but I won't leave you unless you raise up your head. *Mrs Donnelly doesn't*

MRS DONNELLY Oh God, I thought to myself, If I said so despite her children she'd stay with me and they'd get her too, so raise your head Judith Donnelly although when you raise it and my head is so heavy, it is to *Slowly she gets up: she & Jennie come towards each other—but the lawyer's voice interrupts.*

LAWYER *at the Lucan Council Chambers* Mrs Donnelly, at the preliminary hearing today as your lawyer I want you to promise me one thing

MRS DONNELLY Very well, Mr McDiarmid. What one thing?

LAWYER Even if what you and your husband say is true about these magistrates and your accuser, do not even dream of telling them so to their faces.

MRS DONNELLY Mr McDiarmid, do you mean to tell me that Squire Cassleigh is to sit in judgement on us when it is he murdered a man on the road, oh years ago now, and they could never pin it on him, and do you tell me that this knife which I myself took away from him, oh years ago now at the bee, this knife—do you not want to know what he was doing with this knife? yes, torturing a man, clipping off his ears, am I not then to give him back his knife—and shame him? Or is it that I tell you what is not true about him.

LAWYER Mrs Donnelly, I do believe you, but with persons of power it is wise to be discreet

CONSTABLE Oyez, oyez, the court is in session,

CHORUS Will all those present rise.

MAGISTRATE CASSLEIGH Patrick Marksey versus James Donnelly

and Julia Donnelly who are charged with incendiarism. The Prisoners are called and answer to their respective names.

He enjoys this hugely; perhaps we do remember his activities in Part One where his gavel did more than just tap a magisterial table.

MR DONNELLY I am James Donnelly

MRS DONNELLY I am Julia Donnelly

JUDGE How plead you, James Donnelly

MR DONNELLY Not guilty.

JUDGE How plead you, Julia Donnelly with regard to the charge that you helped your husband burn down Patrick Marksey's barns on the night of January the 15th.

MRS DONNELLY Not guilty

MARKSEY My name is Patrick Marksey. My reasons for suspecting the Donnellys of burning my barns was—That I heard a neighbour, Mrs John Carroll told my daughter Mary that my son would not be long riding in his new buggy—and this buggy was burned in the barn, the driving shed. Further she said that Mrs Donnelly made this threat. Yes, this threat alarmed me.

LAWYER Have you any other reason, Mr Marksey?

MARKSEY No.

MRS DONNELLY *Advancing down stage* Oh of course, Mr Marksey, no other reason and who dared to speak in my defence, who dared to say that I, who dared to say that we had not scampered through the snow drifts to light this man's barns, why who but three woman—Peggy O'Connor who had been dressmaking at our house that evening

PEGGY Donnelly boys went to the wedding just before dark. *At the sewing machine* Prisoners and Miss Donnelly and myself remained afterwards in the house, went to bed about 11 o'clock *Clock strikes* all of us did

MRS DONNELLY And my niece Bridget said:

BRIDGET Mrs Donnelly slept in the middle of the bed between me and Miss Connors and was not out of the bed all night.

MRS DONNELLY And the neighbour, Mr Marksey, Mrs John Carroll she was brave enough to stand up in court and say that

MRS JOHN CARROLL Mrs Donnelly visits with me sometimes. Mr Marksey, Mrs Donnelly did not say that your son would not have his buggy long I am positive of this. What she did say was that

MRS DONNELLY I'll put a blush in his face and make him lie back in his grand buggy because that particular Marksey boy had been part of a mob trampling through our yard in search of the famous cow that was lost

MRS JOHN CARROLL No, I have not heard Mrs Donnelly say anything against the Markseys since.

JOHN & TOM The magistrates adjourned, this time to Granton for February the 4th

MR DONNELLY They are treating us like mad dogs. We have been dragged all across the township to make us laughing stocks, an old man and an old woman over sixty years old. We are being advertised as barn burners.

MRS DONNELLY Good evening, Mr & Mrs O'Halloran

MR DONNELLY My wife said good evening, Mr & Mrs O'Halloran.

MRS O'HALLORAN Malachi, let us leave this room where we won't be bothered by barn burners. Father Connolly should tell this family to leave the parish. *This snub is the breaking point and*

MRS DONNELLY *turning back* Mr Cassleigh. Magistrate Cassleigh, your honour.

CASSLEIGH Why, Mrs Donnelly, are you showing me this knife?

MRS DONNELLY Because I once was the woman who stopped you from tormenting a man with this knife and I am now the woman who tells you that with the exception of Mr Lindsay over there my husband and myself are being tried, accused and judged by thieves and murderers. *She throws the knife at his feet; he picks it up.*

CASSLEIGH *Starts to whet the knife on a stone.* I'm not facing that woman again, Carroll in daylight. I'll show her who's master of this neighbourhood get me a calendar. Marksey, we've been through this before. Can we use your old house to meet in?

CARROLL We'll need some whiskey. Better make up a list of our men.

CASSLEIGH Everybody got a pen and some ink, O'Halloran. Here's some paper.

CARROLL Sunday's out. There are only two possible days—this and this.

MARKSEY Why?

CARROLL Unless you want to wait until after the hearing which is going to fall through and then they're at our throats for malicious arrest.

MARKSEY Tell us what to write. No, Ash Wednesday would be bad luck, you're

CARROLL *directly to us* "Tie up your dogs tonight. Keep them inside. If you hear any noise outside, pay no heed." We'll need fifty copies of that

MARKSEY When do we hand them out?*They tear paper.*

CARROLL Not until after we hear what this priest has to say at mass.

CHORUS Amen!

PRIEST Then at the harvest-time, I will order the harvesters: "Collect the weeds first, and bundle them up to burn. But gather the wheat into my barn."... Bundle them up to burn. And I say to you that whoever has burnt down the barns of Patrick Marksey, their house—a ball of fire from Heaven shall fall on that house before this month is out.

CHORUS February the third dawn *clock strikes five* And there was a house built by James Donnelly on the Sixth Concession it was filled with living people and on the last day on which this house stood the following events happened. Nine o'clock *clock*

JOHN After breakfast my father asked me to get ink and pen and we wrote a letter to a lawyer in town

MR DONNELLY I want you to attack them at once, as they will never let us alone until some of them are—made an example of.

JOHN James Donnelly, X his mark

CHORUS Ten o'clock *clock*

JOHN My brother Will came riding up to borrow the cutter. As he left I called after him: Will, expect me this evening, I'll ride over and get the cutter back to drive them to Granton tomorrow.

CHORUS One o'clock *clock*

TOM After dinner I took my father into Lucan on our sleigh. We posted a letter to the lawyer, bought some tobacco, and then went to Connors' place to pick up Johnny.

THERESA Mr Donnelly, is there no stopping them from dragging you all over the countryside examining you about this fire business.

MR DONNELLY Apparently not, Theresa O'Connor. They're advertising my wife and myself as if we were mad dogs. Johnny, button up your coat, for it's a cold day out on the line and the wind'll whistle right through you. Theresa, we'll bring Johnny back tomorrow if we have no more hearings ahead of us. If he's not back they've put us in jail, you'll know....

THERESA Oh Mr Donnelly, sufficient unto the day is the evil thereof. Be a good and helpful boy out at Donnellys', Johnny. Goodbye now.

CHORUS Six o'clock *clock*

CASSLEIGH, MARKSEY & CHORUS There they go. Tom and his father. Going a bit fast, Tom's drunk. Bags of grain under the buffalo robe? Tie up your dogs tonight. Keep him inside. If you hear....

CHORUS A quarter past six

JOHNNY Good evening, Mrs Donnelly. May I take my outer pants off and dry them by the stove?

MRS DONNELLY Shure, Johnny. Bridget, watch the stove for me. Boys your mitts'll burn there. Up here with them. Did you post the letter, Mr Donnelly?

JOHNNY It got dark, and just after dark, after we had tea, John Donnelly put the harness loose on his pony, and he rode off to Will's place at Whalen's Corners to get the cutter.

CHORUS Seven o'clock *clock*

JOHN *on hobbyhorse* As I went up to the Town Line and then down to Whalen's Corners the moon went behind a cloud. I tied up my horse in Will's stable, the one next to the locked one where he kept his stallion.

William's house at Whalen's Corners should be established in front of the closed curtain.

CHORUS *Humming until William's speech*

NORAH Through this doorway my brother-in-law John came into our house. Just after dark. I went to bed about nine. Will and John stayed up talking with their friend, Martin Hogan. John was to sleep closest of all to this door.

CHORUS Midnight, midnight *clock*

WILLIAM Gentlemen, I'm winding the clock, *he winds up the gramophone whose chuff-chuff sound continues until the end of this act* and then I'm retiring. Talking about the Vigilantes or the Secret People or the Happy Gang as I prefer to call them is never as much fun as slumber. Norah's been in bed these last three hours.

NORAH Give the men the buffalo robe. It's cold in that room, Will

JOHN Good night, Will. Hey, Martin, what're you putting your mitts on for?

MARTIN I'm staying the night at Morkin's, Jack. We're threshing there tomorrow.

JOHN Martin, it's all hours and Mrs Morkin's got all those children, wake one up and the whole house wakes up, poor woman, stay with us, Martin. Will, tell him to stay the night.

WILLIAM I did, in there Martin. Goodnight.

MARTIN Lots of fresh air in here. John Donnelly, there's someone cut off a swatch of your hair lately.

JOHN Good night Martin. *Looks at him. As in the case of Tom's girl, people are getting relics of the Donnelly boys while there is still time.* I went right to sleep. But when you sleep there's a part of yourself that wakes up, the cat's whisker two miles long inside your brain comes twitching out fishing and although you are asleep it roams the yard and road outside Will's house, then the fields so that deep as the dreamsea was that waved over me I knew that something was wrong. There were no dogs barking in Biddulph, but the dogs in Blanshard were, why? Someone is coming up the road to spy on us. At one o'clock part of me knew already that a tall narrow light had sprung up over my father's house and that mother and father were walking in a fiery furnace. A greasy, sweaty blood ball of *We see rifle-bearing silhouettes waiting at the door,* humanity was rolling towards us now and at a quarter to two early ones were whispering to each other

CARROLL Get the stallion. When he hears it kicking he'll come running out. *Use hobbyhorse head for stallion*

JOHN But Will's sleep was too deep for their line, my sleep began to flow back and more and more of me knew that they wanted my brother Will to come to this door. It mustn't be Norah because her brother, John, and three other men were pointing at the door with guns, no—it's the Cripple they want, my lame brother I love with all my heart, and I swam up on top of the dreamriver and made my eyes open

MARKSEY Give over that. You'll never wake him up that way. Call him by name.

CARROLL Kick at the door. Fire, fire. Open the door Will. Fire, fire. Open the door, Will

JOHN I got up out of the bed, I began to open the inner door, they had opened the outer one, and I said: I wonder who's hollering fire and rapping at the door? ///// Will. Will. I'm shot and may the Lord have mercy on my soul.

MACDONALD Brother-in-law is easy at last.

CARROLL What next?

MARTIN Don't move Will, it's you they want and they think they got you.

Martin and Norah drag in John and place candle in his hand. Will walks down stage towards us and draws aside an invisible curtain which is repeated by a curtain motion upstage revealing just disappearing vigilantes.

WILL When I woke up to John's voice, then the shots ///// I reached up to the window and pulled the curtain aside. I saw Carroll's hand and heard my brother-in-law's voice.

MACDONALD Brother-in-law is easy at last.

CARROLL What next?

NORAH *Rises from John's side and screams at the door* Murderers!

WILL When I raised the curtain again they were gone. *Clock strikes two.* It was all over in five minutes.

NORAH As I walk back and forth the window gets bigger. Then smaller.

Clock strikes the hours.

WILL Just before daybreak it began to snow.

NORAH At eight o'clock Will asked a neighbour to drive over to his father's place and see if anything was the matter. If not—to tell them that John was dead.

WILL I stayed at home till my neighbour came back.

NEIGHBOUR Will Donnelly, your mother and father are dead. Last night. They were all murdered last night and their house set fire upon them. *We look directly at William's face.*

Train whistle. Will Donnelly is remembering a train whistle a very long time ago when his father came home to them one summer evening after being seven years away.

ALL End of Act Two

Handcuffs

Act Three

We open in the graveyard of St Patrick's, Biddulph in the early 1970's. *On the anniversary of the murder it is the custom for crowds of people in cars to come up, park and wait for a possible ghostly appearance at the Donnelly grave. In the centre of the stage stand the ghosts of Mr & Mrs Donnelly behind two cloths representing their first and second gravestone.*

CHORUS February the third, 1974, St Blaise's Day falls on Shrove Tuesday this year.

A car radio blares out "At the Hop"

CHORUS This is the night the Donnellys got killed.

GIRL Oh Verne, let's drive up to Lucan and go out to the graveyard and see if we can see their ghosts.

OLD MAN I am the sexton of St Patrick's Church and I draw my churchyard with a stick on this floor. Yes, the Donnellys are buried here.

GIRL Tonight's the night they killed the Donnellys.

CHORUS There are seventy five cars parked by the churchyard with two hundred people in them waiting for midnight when Mrs Donnelly's ghost will appear.

BOYS Waiting for what?

CHORUS For the Donnellys to appear. Smoking dope, drinking beer. Listening to our car radios. Blowing our horns. Hey. Look at him jump over the fence.

OLD MAN Get out of the churchyard. Stay clear off that gate. Get down off of that fence.

BOY Hey. Look at the old guy after him with the rake.

CHORUS Thaw. Violet thunder. *Use camera flash cubes* Ice on the roads. Rain.

BOY He's got to the grave.

GIRL The old fellow's slipped.

BOY He's standing on top of it.

YOUTH (TOM) *in hockey windbreaker* Johannah and James Donnelly. Rise up. Rise up and show yourselves. *He falls down drunk close by the gravestone.*

CHORUS February the third. 1974. St Blaise's Day falls on Shrove Tuesday this year.

CHORUS (PART) This is the night the Donnellys got killed.

GIRL Oh Verne, let's drive up to Lucan and go out to the graveyard and see if we can see their ghosts.

OLD MAN I am the caretaker of St Patrick's churchyard and with this stick I draw my churchyard on this floor. Get out of the churchyard. Stay clear of that gate. Stop taking pictures of me. Get out of the churchyard.

Use flashlights for headlights, kids' wagons. Underneath banners that have the 2 inscriptions on them lie the Donnellys.

MRS DONNELLY Who's that walking over our grave? Who's that screeching for us to rise from our tombs.

MR & MRS DONNELLY Well, young fellow, you may get the worst thing in the world and that is to get what you want.

MRS DONNELLY Get that false gravestone off us. – We weren't died, we were killed, we were murdered. That's better now heave that one up too till we get at this young bastard. Grab him Jim. For I am buried here, oh yes, with my husband and my sons, they buried what's left of me. Here's the coffin four of us lie in. Hear our bones rattling? *They have grabbed the drunken youth and are turning him into their son, Tom.*

OLD MAN Get out of the churchyard! Get down off that fence. Stay clear of that gate.

MR DONNELLY But they never finished the older gravestone that says we were murdered. My remaining sons wanted to put on top of it a statue of my son Tom whom they handcuffed before they butchered him. My youngest son in only his shirt sleeves, blood spurting from his wounds and on his strong arms they, all twenty of them were that afraid of—HANDCUFFS!

YOUTH Let me go you old bugger. Keep your hands off me. I dreamt then that they handcuffed me, you old harridan, don't look at me with your hell eyes.

MRS DONNELLY Yes, we've handcuffed you and we've handcuffed their church, they dare not leave it open because James Donnelly what happened the last time they did so.

MR DONNELLY Toughs from Grand Bend came in with their trulls in search of us into the house of God and desecrated the altar.

MRS DONNELLY And we've handcuffed their priest. Are you there, priest—no, the presbytery's not a good place to sleep at nights for there's a certain unused rocking chair that all by itself...

YOUTH Let me go, please let me go. Take the handcuffs off me.

MR DONNELLY Make up your mind what you want then, soft tough, is it too much when the curtain between you and us, between your life and our life, between life and death starts wavering and swaying and

MRS DONNELLY drawing back like a foreskin from the thigh of demon lover Christ himself.

MR DONNELLY like the mighty eyelid of God the Father's eye,

MRS DONNELLY like the wind from the mouth of the Holy Ghost that flutters her veil as she speaks:

BOTH UNDO THE HANDCUFFS, Indeed! First unlock the handcuffs in your mind that you make see us as

MR DONNELLY that fierce harridan

MRS DONNELLY that old barnburner!

BOTH We weren't like that/this! I take you by the hair down into our grave and beyond where

MR DONNELLY you'll be our son Tom

MR DONNELLY you'll see that

BOTH

I was a child once, a spring.
These speeches involve fluttering, waving curtains and the movement of the ghosts behind the gravestone curtains.

I became a river when my body united with his/hers
From that river came seven sons and one daughter
We were all right, they said, if you left us alone
But there was something about us that made people
Never able to leave us alone and we fought them
Until the river fell into the sea of Death and the Sun of Hell
Changed us into the fog outside this winter night
With our handcuffed boy—

& TOM

look we are everywhere
In the clouds, in the treebranch, in the puddle,
There. Here. In your fork. In your minds.
Your lungs are filled with us, we are the air you breathe
And you say—

MARY DONOVAN & CHORUS *in nightgown. A window is held in front of her. She is watching the Donnelly house go up in flames. A fierce red glow lights up her face.*

Mary Donovan
Watches the Fiery Furnace

MARY, MR & MRS DONNELLY & TOM

There burn four of her neighbours
James and Judith Donnelly, Tom and Bridget

MARY

Kerosene angel do not forget
To grind my enemies all to dust
In your fiery furnace, fiery furnace, fiery furnace &c.

MARY *knocking* Go see who's knocking at our door, Bill.

BILL *her husband who seems slow to understand the delights of revenge* Can't you tear yourself away from that window?

MARY I won't stop watching, Bill Donovan, till there's nothing more to watch.

BILL What are you looking at anyhow—just a house burning.

MARY Oh no, Bill. It's just not a house burning. Inside that house is the woman who once said that my mother was so fat she had to be pulled in and out of a bed with a pulley. There goes the chimney, Bill! And did you get him, Jim?

he enters still excited from what he has lately accomplished

CARROLL Yes, we got him.

MARY So Cripple's dead. How'd you get him?

CARROLL *laughing hysterically* We called Fire at his door. Will, Will, Fire, fire. And he came and we shot him.

BILL How'd you get them over here, Jim?

CARROLL Handcuffs. We handcuffed them.

BILL Jim, you're weeping.

CARROLL It's the first time I've wept since my mother died. I swore then—a lad of ten that I was—that I'd not weep again till the night I got them for her

BILL The flames from their house are reflected in your tears, James Carroll.

even in death the Donnellys still offend

CARROLL Will their house never stop burning? How can I get any sleep with it so bright all over your house, Mary and Bill?

MARY You'd better get some sleep, Jim. You have to be at the hearing over at Granton by ten, don't you?

BILL *stupidly* What's the use of your going to that. They won't be there.

CARROLL Bill Donovan, it'd be just like the Donnellys not to show up, wouldn't it. Just like them

MARY Jim has to go to the hearing, Bill. Otherwise people would say he knew they were dead. Bill, tie this around Jim's face. *She gives Bill a long white bandage* Lead him off to his bed. Lead him off to his bed. *He is led off with his eyes bandaged.*

CHORUS

Pillar of fire turns to pillar of smoke
Pillar of fire, pillar of smoke

LINDSAY I am one of the magistrates in the Marksey fire hearing. Squire Lindsay. Just before ten I showed up at Middleton's Hotel. The Donnellys had not arrived as yet. Way off to the west of the village there was a pillar of smoke. Good morning Cassleigh, Carroll. Mr Pat Whalen, what are you doing here?

WHALEN Ask Jim Carroll, Squire Lindsay.

CARROLL Pat's wife, Mr Lindsay, I've heard old Mrs Donnelly making some more threats about Marksey's barns and I came to Pat's house with a subpoena but Pat here saw fit to wave an axe at me when all the world knows his old woman is dying to testify. So—Pat is up for assaulting me.

LINDSAY Mr Whalen

WHALEN Squire Lindsay

LINDSAY You live across from the Donnellys, don't you?

WHALEN I do that

LINDSAY Any signs of them turning out. They're late and that's not their custom

WHALEN Oh, sir, it will be their custom this morning.

CARROLL I wonder what can be keeping them?

CASSLEIGH What do you mean, Pat, it will be their custom this morning

WHALEN I mean that smoke over there. Their place got burnt down last night.

CARROLL Cold day to be without a house

CASSLEIGH Seen Tom and the old man go by in the sleigh yesterday. Going fast. Drunk. They'd quarrel among themselves a lot.

WHALEN Yes, they'll quarrel no more then. Yes, they're dead. I saw their bodies burning. But not all of them that were in the house last night lie there with it snowing on them. Yes, there was a boy with them last night and he got out of the house and came over to our place sometime after one o'clock. In his bare feet.

CARROLL A boy. What was this boy doing there, Pat?

WHALEN Cassleigh, you didn't see him in the sleigh, did you, because he was there, still going to haul me up for waving the axe, Jim, because that boy was sleeping with Old Donnelly and he says there was a man came into the house to arrest the Donnellys and then there were thirty men came in and beat them to death, but he was hiding under the bed.

CARROLL Pat, what will you be telling us next. Did he recognize the man?

CASSLEIGH Where is this little firebug at this very moment, Pat?

They elbow Whalen out of the room.

CARROLL Join us at the bar, Squire Lindsay.

LINDSAY I couldn't take my eyes off their sleeves. They hadn't had time to change their shirts yet. *Carroll and Cassleigh re-emerge from behind the curtain with terror on their faces; something has scared them & they are getting away from it!*

LINDSAY What's the matter, gentlemen?

Enter William Donnelly who should play the Prosecuting Attorney's role in the coming trial scenes since in real life it was his intelligence that directed the prosecution

WILLIAM The matter, Squire Lindsay, is that when they came into the bar here they learned from the boy they sent over to spy on my house this morning that they didn't succeed in shooting me last night. My brother, not his brother. I'm very much alive still, and very much in their minds.

something darkens the stage

LINDSAY A wind from the west came up and drove the pillar of smoke over the village darkening the sun. The bodies of Mr and Mrs Donnelly lay open to the sky until someone came to rake them up.

We now move to the ruins of the Donnelly homestead represented by four stones. A long line of people representing the endless line of sightseers' cutters and sleighs that went by in the days after the murder circle the four stones. Sometimes when Keefe's back is turned they snatch at a souvenir, i.e.—a skull, a teapot lid or a piece of Mrs Donnelly's stove. Mr Keefe is collecting the bones of the Donnellys with the same sort of rake that the sexton held at the opening of this act.

KEEFE When I, Jim Keefe, told Father Connolly at Christmas that I would give Jim Donnolly rides in my cart as long as I had a horse to drive him I never thought I would be doing this.

Some choral funeral service round here: Amen or Ora pro nobis

PRIEST Dear Friends, you are in the presence of one of the most solemn scenes which I have ever witnessed, but I have witnessed many a solemn scene, but never like this. I am heart broken... I never suspected. *He is agitated, yet strangely calm.* The guilty men who imbued their hand in innocent blood will have to answer for this awful crime before the living God.

In other words on one level we are proceeding through the funeral service and its images sift in with images from the trials &c.

KEEFE Yes, before the living God, I seen Marksey ride by Donnelly's gate last night with a sword wrapped up in a blanket

NEIGHBOUR Oh Mr Keefe, you should never tell that to anyone.

KEEFE I should tell if it were my own son and he were to hang for it. Hhrrout of that, stranger, don't touch the bones of the dead. Before the living God, I am their only friend it seems left to guard their bones and there's not enough of me.

PRIEST I believed that there were men who would give a man a clout when half drunk in Biddulph but I never thought that they could commit such a Oh! God in Heaven, who would have thought it would I can't say anymore *He falls face down on the altar.*

PATRICK *standing up in the congregation* Father Connolly, I wish you to give a more detailed account.

PRIEST What do you ask me, Patrick Donnelly?

PATRICK I would like you to tell the whole matter, giving particulars more fully.

PRIEST Well, perhaps it would be better for me to tell. I remember saying that and then—I told this and I told that it was reported in the newspapers, but to tell *exaggerated gesture using the curtain* the whole matter, Oh God in Heaven, no, Patrick Donnelly, you don't know what you are asking—no,no—to circumcize this veil that hides each and every one of us from each other and from God?

He slides away from view behind the curtain. Suddenly we are in court and listening to Mary Donovan's testimony; she wears loud clothes, an awful bonnet and is supremely smiling & confident.

MARY Yes, I am Mary Donovan, wife of Bill Donovan. Yes, my house is near the Donnellys

LAWYER Mrs Donovan, is there anything to intercept the view between your house and the Donnellys?

MARY Not a thing. We were next neighbours on the same side of the road. On the night of the murder James Carroll stayed at our house. He went to bed before we did and did not get up till after we did

CHIEF I am the Chief of Police for London. On the day following the murder I asked you if your bedroom door was shut.

MARY Yes, but I could hear if they went out.

LAWYER Did you sleep sound last night, Mrs Donovan?

MARY I slept very sound, always do nights. That's what I go to bed for.

LAWYER Did you hear any noise in the night?

MARY No, nor anything about the fire until we looked over in the morning.

LAWYER Surely Mrs Thompson, if James Carroll's brother says that he woke up at one o'clock having heard the clock strike would he not have seen the fire at Donnellys' through the window. Your honour, the window in question looked directly over to the Donnelly homestead. It would seem to me that when you see a house burning *A model of the Donnellys' curtilage (house, outbuildings and barn) is brought in and set down.*

MARY Ah, his brother didn't want to bother him about a little thing like that.

JUDGE May I ask this witness a question? Mrs Donovan, I suppose when you heard the next day that not three hundred feet away four people had been murdered the night before—I suppose you were greatly alarmed?

MARY Well, no—nothing extra.

CHIEF The first time I questioned her there was nothing down in front of this window which overlooks the Donnelly place. *The window in question is held up.*

MARY What was that question, again, Chief?

CHIEF Anyone lying on this bed could have seen the fire at one o'clock.

MARY —Not if they put up a blanket. Maybe they put up a blanket. *She places a towel across the window.*

CHORUS The Queen against James Carroll. For the murder of Julia Donnelly....

FRAMER I am a house framer by occupation. This is the Donnelly house ten years ago I built—one and a half storey log house.

JUDGE Who were the neighbours to this house?

4 NEIGHBOURS We are

Have the model set fire to and burning now by two Vigilante "ladies" with torches.

JUDGE And what did you do the night Neighbour Donnelly was murdered and his house burned over his head.

4 NEIGHBOURS Our houses were, our houses still are only a few rods, a few yards away

CAIN John Cain. I live on the south half of lot 18. I heard no noise all that night. There's been a good many fires in that neighbourhood and sometimes people get into trouble by being too quick to turn out to a fire.

JUDGE After you heard of their murder did you go over to the Donnellys?

RYDER No. I had some potatoes to take in and I went to take them in.

JUDGE Even though you knew that four of your neighbours had been killed and their house burned, you never went to see anything about it?

Four neighbours turn their back on a blazing house.

RYDER No, we had our work to do.

WHALEN Patrick Whalen, Ann Whalen

ANN We live just across the road from the Donnellys.

& PAT Concession 7, lot 18.

ANN I was waked up by someone rapping on the kitchen door. Who is it?

JOHNNY Johnny Connors.

PAT Who?

JOHNNY Call up the old man and the boys and quench the fire at Donnellys'. A lot of men—dressed in women's clothes and set fire to the two beds.

PAT It's not a fire... seems more like a lamp burning.

JOHNNY A lot of men came over

PAT Do you be dreaming boy? Why you're walking in your sleep.

JOHNNY Mr Whalen, I'm not. Mr & Mrs Donnelly. Tom murdered. Might still be alive.

ANN Pat, don't listen to him. You're a smart little fire bug. Don't call up the boys. They might get killed.

PAT Annie, his little feet are frozen. Now I'll get the fire going here and just get these poor little bare feet warm. Put them up on the oven door. That's the way. Why you're right. It is a fire, Annie. I'll go over and tell Jack.

LAWYER Did you know anybody there, Johnny Connors?

JOHNNY Yes, Jim Carroll.

ANN *slaps him* Be careful of what you're saying boy. You mightn't be telling the truth. We might all be brought to court and I wouldn't want that.

CHORUS It's a dangerous thing to find a dead man.

LAWYER Mrs Donovan again, please.

MARY William Donnelly? I can't think of anyone I hate more in the township. *She leans down over the model house & sings:*

Cain killed Abel, Donnelly killed Farrell
Your old man killed Farrell, Will
Where's your father they asked young Cripple
He's down at Kingston on the old treadmill

LAWYER Mrs Donovan, at the preliminary hearings the Chief of Police said that the window overlooking the Donnelly house had no curtain.

MARY No, he could not have said that. Because over that window there was always a curtain of double thickness. I put it up there when they were sowing their fall wheat to keep out the rain and the snow. So neither we nor James Caroll could have possibly seen their

LAWYER Then if the Police Chief says that the curtain was not there at his first visit, but only appeared some time afterwards, he says what is not true?

MARY No man can say I was mistaken in that. No one lying on that bed could see the Donnelly house burning down because it was a double thickness double thickness double thickness double thickness

CLERK The next witness, Johnny Connors.

LAWYER Coming to the boy Connors I would ask you to weigh very carefully his evidence because it is in the main upon this child's

MARKSEY That son of a bitch, he'd swear to anything.

All the actors available get on their hands and knees and crawl downstage to represent the pigs in the Donnellys' barn waiting for their nightly feed.

JOHNNY After tea, after John went over to Will's, Tom and I did the chores.

TOM Here Johnny. Take my whip. I'll show you how to keep the pigs back with one hand while your other gets the feed in the trough. Otherwise they'll get the pail away on you. Hrrout of that! Get back there you fat devil. Now Johnny, climb up in the loft and throw down straw till I tell you enough ... enough. That's for the cattle. Always check the blanket on my horse, Indian. Because he's always getting it off. There. Johnny will take good care of yous all.

JOHNNY Then we went back into the house. Then we sat for a

while. Mrs Donnelly was reading the paper. Bridget was knitting. Tom said

TOM Bridget, get some apples for Johnny. I can tell he's thinking of them down there in the cellar. Aren't you, Johnny?

Mr Donnelly is kneeling at a chair saying his evening prayers.

JOHNNY Then when we got the apples eat, the old man said his prayers.

MR DONNELLY World without end. Amen.

JOHNNY Then he said

MR DONNELLY Take off your boots, Johnny. You'll sleep alongside of me tonight.

TOM Johnny's staying out here with me, Father.

MR DONNELLY More room in my four poster, Johnny.

JOHNNY So I did. Mr Donnelly got into the bed first. I climbed over him. As I was falling asleep I thought I heard someone in the kitchen with the old woman, Tom and Bridget... I think it was Jim Feeny. Then I went to sleep.

MRS DONNELLY Are you off to the dance tonight, Jim Feeny?

JIM *wearing a peculiar coat* Mrs Donnelly. Only I can't make up my mind which one to go to.

MRS DONNELLY Tomorrow's Ash Wednesday. Don't the dances and weddings come thick and fast just before it comes. Well, there was a carnival you might have frolicked at up at Parkhill last Saturday.

TOM Jim, you should wear that coat to the carnival. I didn't recognize you in it I swear to God you've never worn that before. At least I've never seen it on your back before.

JIM Oh—I've just got this coat, Tom. Got it over in Michigan. Johnny not in tonight?

BRIDGET He's gone to bed with Uncle Jim.

JIM You're right Bridget, it is all hours. I'll be saying goodnight to yous all.

MRS DONNELLY Come here, Jim Feeny. Come and let me look at your wrists. Where did you get that nasty red welt around your neck? Bridget, bring this man a cup of tea, he's cold and trembly.

JIM Oh no thank you, Mrs Donnelly. I was only trying to get my cap out of the threshing machine a couple of days ago at Morkin's the silly old cap had blown off my head into all those moving up and down parts, for shure I didn't want to see my cap turned into a bushel of wheat, eh Bridget, and goodnight, Mrs Donnelly.

TOM Drink the tea! My mother says you're to have a cup of tea before you leave the premises.

MRS DONNELLY Tom, don't be so harsh with your friend. You might roll up your sleeve and show Bridget how you've got Jim's name carved on your arm, and he's got your name on his arm. It's years ago I caught them doing that out on the door step. Jim Feeny these red marks about your wrists I understand, but

TOM Mother, why don't we undress him, take off his shirt and we'll give him a scratch and bruise catechism.

MRS DONNELLY Jim Feeny, look me in the eye.

JIM You know I can't do that, Tom's mother. If only I could.

MRS DONNELLY You wore handcuffs for our sake, who made you wear rope for us too?

JIM Mrs Donnelly.

MRS DONNELLY She didn't hang you lately and give you a red necklace. No. Who? I know who—them. But why? Jim Feeny. All your life Jim Feeny you've been handcuffed and tethered by one fear or another. Tell me. Speak out! James Feeny, is it true what your mother once told me that you're still a child, that you can't raise your arms over your head. Try. Try. *she raises her arms but he cannot quite raise his*

JIM My nerves. My nerves.

MRS DONNELLY Tom, take care of your friend.

TOM What's the matter, Jim. Get hold of yourself. Stay the night and talk it over with me.

They are now in front of the model. We should glimpse Mrs Donnelly checking doors and saying her prayers before retiring. The curtains close.

JIM I'm promised I'd drop over at the Whalens' and walk Temperance Trehy home, Tom.

TOM Oh, it's Temperance Trehy is it. I wish you luck there Jim, shure she was born with her legs crossed.

JIM Tom she'll laugh at me in this coat. Could I leave it here and pick it up later on?

TOM Shure. Pick it up tomorrow.

JIM Tom, it's the sort of night when it's cold enough to wear the damn thing all the way home, but not to visit across the road.

TOM Come back this night, Jim, and get it then. I'll be in bed though. We're up early tomorrow to go to the trial.

JIM No Tom, I wouldn't want to wake yous. Give it here.

TOM Jim, I'll leave the kitchen door on the latch. Mother always bolts it, but after she's gone to bed, I'll fix it so you can let yourself in when we're all asleep. Don't make any noise though.

JIM Fine, Tom. Fine. I'll tiptoe so you'll never hear me. Goodnight, Tom.

TOM Goodnight Jim.

JIM Goodbye Tom.

JOHNNY Then I went to sleep and between twelve and two o'clock a man came into the house to arrest the old man and Jack.

LAWYER Today in court do you see this man?

JOHNNY Yes, there he is. James Carroll.

MR DONNELLY What have you got against me now, Jim?

CARROLL I've got another charge against you and Jack. Where is he?

MR DONNELLY He's not in.

CARROLL Where'd you say he was?

MR DONNELLY Didn't I tell you, he's not in. Hold the light now till I dress myself. Judy, where's my coat?

MRS DONNELLY Bridget, up and light the fire.

Carroll is whistling the "St Patrick was a gentleman" song.

JOHNNY I said, "Here's your coat, Mr Donnelly. I'm using it for a pillow."

BRIDGET Uncle Jim, could I have your knife to make shavings with to light the fire?

MR DONNELLY Tom, are you handcuffed?

"Ladies" are already prowling about.

TOM Yes, he thinks he's smart. Read me your warrant Carroll.

CARROLL There's lots of time for that

In shadow we see the confused forms of a massacre, what a child might see from under a bed. In front of the curtain four "ladies" beat the stones with pickaxes.

JOHNNY Then a whole crowd jumped in and commenced hammering them with sticks and spades. Tom ran out into the front room and got outside. Bridget ran upstairs and I ran after her. She shut the door and I ran back again in the room and got under the bed behind a clothes *Tom should pick up his stone & run away with it. We see Bridget on top of one of the step-ladders.* basket. I could see only their feet, but I got a look at some faces by

They carried Tom inside the house again. They said *Tom is dragged behind the curtain again.*

MARKSEY Hit that fellow with a spade and break his skull open.

CARROLL Here—hold the candle here. Get those handcuffs off of him

MACDONALD Where's the girl.

JOHNNY Then one of them said, Where's the girl?

Quite quickly we are at the trial again. Carroll collapses in front of the curtain.

DEFENCE LAWYER My lord, we crave the court's permission to allow the prisoner to retire. He has taken ill.

JUDGE What does the Gaol Surgeon say?

DOCTOR The prisoner is suffering from heart disease, my Lord, and is too ill to attend today.

JUDGE *pause* Very well. The court stands adjourned until 9:30 a.m. tomorrow *Carroll proceeds over to Bridget and takes the stone away from her.*

BRIDGET When I got upstairs I went to the window and knelt by it hoping to see a star if the one cloud that covered the whole sky now would lift. I knew they would come to get me and they did. They dragged me down the stairs. The star came closer as they beat me with the flail that unhusks your soul. At last I could see the star close by; it was my aunt and uncle's burning house in Ontario where—and in that star James and Judith and Tom and Bridget Donnelly may be seen walking as in a fiery furnace calmy and happily forever. Free at last.

The O'Hallorans dart out from behind the curtains.

MRS O'HALLORAN The boy is lying, lying when he says our hired man was present at the house.

JUDGE Mrs O'Halloran, if you do not keep quiet how would you like it if I put you in jail for twenty-four hours.

MRS O'HALLORAN Put me in jail for twenty-four years I will have my say. Jim Purtell our hired man could not have left our house without upsetting a chair which my father-in-law always puts against the front door.

DEFENCE LAWYER *blocking out the Judge with a skilful tug at the curtain.* Try that Mr O'Halloran, if you please.

MR O'HALLORAN The boy is lying, lying, lying when he says our hired man was present at the house.

DEFENCE LAWYER No. Mrs O'Halloran says it with more conviction. You see we've got to break the jury's trust in the boy's testimony. As one of your defence lawyers let me tell you that unless, O'Halloran, you put more conviction into your statements Carroll's bound to hang, so it's Mrs O'Halloran.

MR O'HALLORAN *he's getting mad!* Why don't you get up and testify yourself, McWhin, sure you're the lawyer that helped us plan so many of the things, but your foresight didn't deal with a boy under a bed.

DEFENCE LAWYER Well, patience. You see our difficulty is, O'Halloran, that the boy is telling the truth. And the jury knows that. But we have to...

MR O'HALLORAN *angrily shouting* Johnny Connors is not telling the truth. He's lying, he's been posted by Bill Donnelly, he's

DEFENCE LAWYER Bravo! That's it. Now don't be afraid to make a scene in court. Before they can stop you, Mr & Mrs O'Halloran—you should plant a few ideas in everybody's heads. Let's have it all again. *Draws curtains aside so as to reveal the Judge.*

MR O'HALLORAN My wife's statement I beg leave to corroborate and if this boy's testimony is wrong with regard to one person he says he saw at the Donnelly house

MRS O'HALLORAN They were not people, everyone knows they were fond of animal fighting among themselves, some of them got drunk, a lamp upset—if a mob came to the house as the child says then why weren't the barns burnt down too? Why just the house?

MR O'HALLORAN Many agree with the very believable theory that William Donnelly killed them. Half of the farmers in Oxford County believe this.

MRS O'HALLORAN What about the pair of pants in the basin of blood found in my back yard on a post. Well, with this a very laughable story is connected; we took the basin to a doctor in Granton to have it analyzed and it was, he said, red dye. Red dye not blood.

JOHNNY I am not lying. I saw him there. *Johnny yanks the curtains apart revealing people who seem involved in odd activities. They start when the curtain reveals their tricks.* I saw him, and him and Mr & Mrs O'Halloran—my own godfather and godmother as a matter of fact—I saw your hired man there and—but what is one clap of two hands against the thunder of hundreds of stamping feet?

A stamping & clapping contest between the O'Hallorans & the Connors. The others stamp too & march out with the model.

JUDGE There had to be a second trial because the jury disagreed. Four for hanging Carroll. One undecided, and seven for acquittal.

It is years afterward. Son and mother by the fireplace.

THERESA Johnny Connors, what are you thinking of, my God what are you doing with that toy train over and over again playing in front of the fire, you're a bit full grown to be still playing with such a toy.

JOHNNY Do you remember the O'Hallorans, mother, and how they fought so against my testimony that Jim Purtell had been at the Donnelly's killing them?

THERESA They were such a proud pair of them with their rich farm and their children all lawyers and doctors, oh dear, so respectable looking.

JOHNNY They were lying. I used to watch them in court and think—you're not really respectable at all, Mr & Mrs O'Halloran.

THERESA What does that matter—they looked so. Well. *The O'Hallorans with hobbyhorsemen prance through.* Look at them the proud ones that Christmas their sleigh prancing down the snowy roads.

JOHNNY The last time I saw the Donnellys—they were lying bleeding on the floor, smashed and battered. As I fled their burning house my bare foot stepped on Mrs Donnelly's face. Oh and the O'Hallorans had led the pack of the highflyers against the Donnellys. But I see them triumphant over their enemies. I see the ghosts of Mr & Mrs Donnelly, not their ghosts—them *Johnny should begin to walk about here—glorying in his Donnellys. Mr & Mrs Donnelly come out from behind the curtains; well, their ghosts do and they are waiting for somebody.* See them come from wherever the dead wait in fire or flood or cloud or field—I see them waiting in the ditch by the road where the O'Hallorans will come by. *The O'Hallorans drive up & the Donnellys hold their horses' reins so that the sleigh is pinned to the railway tracks. A train runs over them, but a baby is thrown free.*

FARM WIFE Mr & Mrs O'Halloran were coming to have dinner with us. *The farm wife puts 4 plates on the altar.* I had finished setting the table, it was Christmas 1880, dark and snowing heavily outside and I thought the train whistled oddly. There was a strange sound, the brakeman of the 6 o'clock freight train came to our door

BRAKEMAN Missus, I'm the brakeman of the freight train's just had an accident at the crossing over there.

FARM WIFE My God, what's that baby you hold in your arms!

BRAKEMAN Missus, I guess whoever was driving the sleigh we hit got trapped on the tracks and when we hit them the baby was thrown clear into the snow.

FARM WIFE This baby is my brother's youngest, Denis O'Halloran. I sewed this baby's petticoat, my God man are all the people on the sleigh dead then. All the O'Hallorans save this baby?

THERESA You make my blood run cold, Johnny, do you suppose it could be true?

JOHNNY Country people say the old man and woman then disappeared and that it was revenge on O'Halloran who was the secret leader of the gang that killed them.

THERESA They say they still walk it's true. Oh that was a good many years ago, Johnny.

JOHNNY *coming downstage & facing us with his arms held up* They held the horses, two strong horses just by with the reins of their eyes, my Mr Donnelly and my Mrs Donnelly. So that at the second trial there was not one O'Halloran left to call me a liar.

FARM WIFE Take these four plates away, Kitty, and break them. The O'Hallorans and their son and wife will never eat with us again. *We hear the first plate cracking and so to the others; the fourth is broken at the very end of the play. Organ chord. The coffins are brought in & the funeral service sweeps on to its conclusion.*

WOMEN *sung* Deliver me, O Lord, from everlasting death on that day of terror.

MEN Quando caeli movendi sunt et terra

WOMEN When Thou shalt come to judge the world by fire.

MEN Dread and trembling have laid hold on me

WOMEN et timeo, dum discussio venerit at que ventura ira.

MEN When Thou shalt come to judge the world by fire.

ALL Kyrie eleison. Christe eleison. Kyrie eleison

PRIEST Dominus vobiscum *sprinkling holy water on the coffins. The altar boy lights the candle which will also be used in censing the two closed boxes.*

ALL Et cum spiritu tuo.

PRIEST Oremus.

PRIEST O lord, do not bring your servants to trial, for no man becomes holy in your sight unless you grant him forgiveness of all his sins ... By the help of your grace, may they escape the sentence which they deserve, for during their earthly lives, they were signed with the seal of the Holy Trinity: you who live and reign forever and ever.

ALL Amen.

PRIEST Pater noster ... *While he silently prays and moves sprinkling about in the background we are also in the juryroom.*

JUROR #1 How many, Mr Foreman, here believe, just let me poll my fellow jurors, just how many of you believe the boy's testimony?

JUROR #2 And how many of you would hang Carroll even if you saw him doing it?

JUDGE Gentlemen of the jury

VOICES Vote for Corcoran or your barns burn.

JURY

Horace Hyatt	Joe Lamont
B. Francis	Dugal Graham
Jas F. Elliot	Jas A. Waterworth
James Dores	Hopper Ward
Asa Luce	Benjamin Kilburn
John Carrothers	William Hooper

Eleven yeomen and one baker, good men and true of Middlesex County.

JUDGE Is the prisoner James Carroll guilty or not guilty of having murdered Julia Donnelly? Have you agreed upon your verdict?

JURY We have.

JUDGE What say you then, guilty or not guilty?

Carroll appears behind the jurors.

VOICES We will visit you at all hours of the night when you least expect it. The only difference between them and mad dogs was in the face. *It is obviously Carroll who says this.*

JURY Not guilty.

CARROLL Before I got out of jail I wrote a song, when we were acquitted we hired an Italian band to go back with us to Lucan on the train. So ladies and gentlemen, when you hear me sing this—there's a harp! *Mandolin & Piano as in a John McCormack recording.*

The Vigilant boys, like heroes, from the prison dock will go
When the jury gives their verdict and the world their truth shall know
It is then they'll join their many friends whose hearts will jump with glee
We'll soon be all safe home again, for the Vigilant boys are free.
I now must take my leave of you
Tis all I have to tell
All those who chance to hear my song
I bid you all farewell.

One last thing! I remember the look on Jim Feeny's face when we told him that—Jim we can't pay you the $500.

This scene is a farewell close up of James Carroll.

PRIEST ...And lead us not into temptation

CHORUS But deliver us from evil.

PRIEST Requiescant in Pace

CHORUS Amen

The coffins are taken out of the church into the graveyard.

*Sung to**

May the angels take you into paradise
in tuo adventu suscipiant te Martyres
And lead you into the holy city of Jerusalem
Chorus angelorum te suscipiat

Three crouching forms are left on stage—Mr & Mrs Donnelly, James Carroll

And with Lazarus who was poor
Aeternam habeas requiem
May you have everlasting rest.*

The pall bearers, all actors—return to the stage miming the growth of a wheatfield.

March! the snow has gone
The green field John & Tom sowed
Still there green
April! growing again growing again
May! taller and longer with longer
Days until
June and July
July! until ready for harvest
August
Shivering and rippling
cloud shadows summer wind
cloud shadows

A golden light sweeps the stage. We should feel that around the Donnelly farmyard lies a big field of wheat ready for harvest.

CHORUS To the yard of the house which once had stood by this wheat field came the Donnellys who were left. Patrick Donnelly! tell us now something that you once did or wrote or said, Pat Donnelly. *pp* Four stones where there once was a house/ home

PAT *placing stone* I, Pat Donnelly, blacksmith from St Catharines, once heard James Feeny say that there was only one thing he ever done that he was sorry for. I asked him what that was. He said he sold Tom Donnelly the best friend he ever he had. *He begins to beat the handcuffs apart with his hammer.*

CHORUS Robert Donnelly

BOB *placing stone* Bob Donnelly, drayman from Glencoe. They told me it was the remains of my father. I knelt down and picked up his heart *Kisses it then slowly puts it down.*

CHORUS William Donnelly

WILLIAM Weep for one, not for four.

CHORUS Jennie Currie that once was Jennie Donnelly from St Thomas.

JENNIE My husband tells me that you, William, have preserved one of the bones of my mother's arms. If so, when you come to St Thomas let him bring it with him, so that I may kiss the loving arm that never failed to throw protection around and provide for all of us in the darkest day of our need.

CHORUS
Where there once was a house/home, four stones.
Handcuffs, The Donnellys, Part Three

THE END

Middlesex Tower
University College, University of Western Ontario,
London,
Ontario.
January 15, 1976

Concluding Essay

The 1973 production of *Sticks and Stones* was James Reaney's first play since the success of *Colours in the Dark* at Stratford's Avon Theatre in 1967. One might have expected that with this and several other plays behind him Reaney would have been ready to write a steady stream of dramatic work. But as Reaney the playwright became better known in Canada through the production of these works, he was also becoming engrossed in the fascinating tale of the Donnellys of Lucan, Ontario, and shaping their incredible story into dramatic form. He began working on a play about the Donnellys for the Stratford Festival and hoped to collaborate with John Hirsch on its production. When Hirsch left Stratford in 1969 the planned collaboration was dropped, but Reaney continued to research the Donnelly story and began to shape a play based on his own perception of the Donnellys as heroic figures unique in Canadian history and legend.

In 1972 Reaney completed a long first draft of the play. He realized, however, there was too much background for a single play, so he decided to rewrite it in the form of the now completed trilogy. He finished the first part in the summer of 1973 for a workshop production in Halifax followed by the full-scale production in Toronto that fall. *The St. Nicholas Hotel*, the second part, went through the same process of Halifax summer workshop followed by a Tarragon production in the fall of 1974. The third and final part, *Handcuffs*, was developed in workshops in Toronto prior to its opening at the Tarragon Theatre on March 29, 1975.

In many ways *Sticks and Stones* marks a new and exciting departure in the drama of James Reaney. It is the first of his plays that is based on events that have taken place in Canada and that are already familiar, at least in their broad outline, to a wide audience. Most of Reaney's earlier plays have a fairly distinct Canadian, and usually Southwestern Ontario setting. Some of these settings are left fairly vague, as in the case of *The Easter Egg*, which takes place 'somewhere in the English part of Canada,' or *Listen to the Wind* with its rural setting modelled on that of the Bronte children on the English moors, or *The Killdeer*, whose location is a cottage somewhere in rural Ontario. *Colours in the Dark*, once described by Michael Tait as 'a psychedelic excursion into the corporate Canadian consciousness,' has clear references to many of the locales and historical events that are familiar to Canadians. But none of these plays deals at length with characters and events from Canada's past. In some of the earlier works it seems as if Reaney did not want his setting to be too explicitly Canadian or Ontarian lest the play lose some of its universal appeal.

Nevertheless he has always been intensely aware of his own rural and national background and of the importance of using this background in his poetry and drama. He is also much concerned with how his plays can contribute to a distinctly Canadian theatre. In his 1966 note in *Listen to the Wind* he expressed the hope that out of this play 'a new theatre in Canada might grow.' It is thus no surprise to see Reaney using events surrounding the Donnellys as the basis for a new play. Indeed it is a natural development for him, as if much of his own dramaturgy were tending toward a native subject that would yield itself to his own imaginative growth. Seen in the light of his background and earlier plays, the Donnelly story appears ready-made for the Reaney world. There is a sense as we read or see *Sticks and Stones* that Reaney has finally hit on a subject that can give full scope to his regional, national, and artistic bent. One even wonders why the Donnelly legend did not draw his attention as a dramatist much earlier. After all, Lucan is a mere thirty miles from Stratford, Ontario, the nearest town to the farm on which Reaney was born and lived during his boyhood and adolescence. He had heard the Donnelly story many times as a boy, and refers to it in his 1949 poem 'Winter's Tales', republished in *Poems* (1972):

The farmer told them stories
That his father had told him
Of the massacre at Lucan
Where the neighbours killed all the McKilligans dead
Except one little boy who crawled under a bed.

When he did decide to write a play about the Donnellys he became so interested in the unexplored and unanswered questions related to the events and people of the time that his historical study delayed his creative work for several years. Today Reaney probably knows more about the history of the Donnellys than anyone, with the possible exception of Hamilton lawyer Raymond Fazakas and Point Edward pastor Orlo Miller. He is fascinated by the complexities and relationships that he continues to uncover and is constantly seeking out people who can tell him more about the Donnellys. He has recently carried out some reserch in Tipperary into the background of the Donnelly family and the antagonisms they inherited.

However, we must not get so caught up in the historical details that Reaney presents in the play as to forget that he is using history only as a starting point for a wider vision. In the hands of a great writer history becomes only one of the many tools at his disposal in the new creation he is fashioning. So we should not be surprised in *Sticks and Stones* to find that Reaney actually changes facts for his dramatic purposes. One obvious change is the use of names, some of which Reaney changes for humanitarian reasons. For example, the names of the Marksey family and Tom Cassleigh in the play are not the real names of the originals on whom they are based. The correct names of these and other characters can usually be found in Orlo Miller's *The Donnellys Must Die*. But Reaney is not trying to present a complete or totally accurate picture of these people.

An example of this shaping of history is the last sequence of the play, in which Jennie says:

A dozen years after this a mob led by Tom Cassleigh, and by this time he had turned nearly everyone against us, at night, this mob broke into my father's house, clubbed them to death and then burnt the house down over my mother and father's heads.

There is no evidence that the person on whom Cassleigh is modelled led the mob. He was not one of the six men charged with the murders, though two of the originals of the Marksey family were. But at this climactic point in the play it is dramatically apt that Cassleigh, the man who had been an accomplice in the murder of Brimmacombe, who had been refused absolution by the Friar because he had not repented of his crime, who had been prevented by Mrs. Donnelly from cutting the ears off Donegan, who then tried so hard to drive the Donnellys from Biddulph, and who later became the first Catholic magistrate in the township, should be the one to lead the mob. The irony in his leading the mob is so dramatically apt that Reaney is justified in the extrapolating from history to art at this point. Historians might object, living relatives of the historical parallel of Cassleigh might cry foul, but the answer to all of them is simply: *Sticks and Stones* is not history, it is drama. However important its base in history, the play remains a play, an artist's view of the possibilities these facts lend to his inner vision. However much Reaney is fascinated by the history, he need not and will not be bound by it in his play.

The importance of using history as a base for the dramatist is that it gives him a starting-point in common with his audience. The historic authenticity of a play like *Sticks and Stones* opens the inner eye of readers to the wider landscape that the artist wishes to paint. When the audience realizes that the events described have a base in history they are disposed to be receptive to the poetic vision. As Reaney says in his introduction to *Sticks and Stones*:

When you immerse yourself in this play, you may find that your experience matches my own when I immersed myself some eight years ago in documents which had lain for years and years in the attics of two local courthouses: after a while I couldn't stop thinking about them.

The awareness that 'these people lived', in a place we can identify, makes us open to Reaney's vision of the characters he brings to life from the bare bones of history. The heroic figures he has made of the Donnellys give us an insight into the potential that lies in the most unlikely places in our own past. Even if some later historian should come along and discount Reaney's facts, the dramatic vision would remain valid and would still have to be judged on its artistic, not its historic, merits. Kelley's *The Black Donnellys* can be criticized not only because it pretends to be history, which it is not, but also because it is bad writing.

Reaney has created in *The Donnellys* a new mythology for Canadians of a proud, heroic family, violent in a violent place and era of our country, who refuse to submit to the will of the majority when they know they are in the right. They refuse to submit to the physical and moral pressures either to join their enemies or be driven off their land. Several key speeches in the final act of *Sticks and Stones* typify their heroism, as when Mr. Donnelly says to Cassleigh, 'Donnellys don't kneel,' and when Mrs. Donnelly tells her daughter in the last line, 'Jennie, your father and I will never leave Biddulph.' As the play develops, the Donnellys take on larger than life proportions in keeping with the stature they will attain at the end. This is apparent from the first appearance of Mr. Donnelly, who enters and stands silently with his back to the audience while Mrs. Donnelly and Will speak of him and his troubles back in Tipperary. Then 'Donnelly turns to us for the first time. He is a small square chunk of will.' We see the uniqueness of the Donnellys in the contrast between them and the Fat Woman and her husband, who 'have a certain on the ground quality which materializes everything, while with the Donnellys there is just the opposite feeling.' There is an heroic aura about Donnelly even after he strikes Farl at the logging bee. Farl is hanging on Donnelly's back and at the blow, 'The burden drops off him, he stands straighter and still, then takes off his shirt. Bright sunlight.' The stature of both Mr. and Mrs. Donnelly is enhanced in the next sequence when he kneels for the first time. Significantly, the person he kneels to is his wife, his only equal in the drama. He 'plods up to her, kneels at her feet after catching up some dirt in his hand' and, as all the other players kneel in awe of him, says, 'this is what is left of our farm and I've killed a man for it.'

By the way Reaney relates the audience to the Donnellys we are made to feel that the enemies of the Donnellys are our enemies too, that the Donnelly figures on stage are our alter egos. An example of this is seen at Gallagher's bee when 'Suddenly we (the audience) and Donegan are faced by a gang of men with sticks.' The sticks, which stand for the foes of the Donnellys, are a reminder that they are our foes too even when Donnelly himself is not on stage. As the play goes on we realize that the Donnellys will never die, that they are part of the indomitable spirit of man in all ages. This is impressed on us most forcefully in the fantasy scene where Mrs. Donnelly, in the light of the moon and the stars, meets her own Ghost, a figure come from the future after her murder, 'another deep down dead leaf self', and says:

I stand. I'll stand here years after tonight—a seal in the air—long after my house and my gate and my curtilage have become dust. A lamp hanging in the air, held by a ghost lady.

The heroic nature of this family is further impressed upon us when

Mr. Donnelly returns from prison to meet his boys after seven years and we see 'the shadows of the seven Donnellys grow huge and by themselves towering over the theatre.' By the end of *Sticks and Stones* we are prepared for Jennie's tribute to those who were massacred:

from the eye of God in which you will someday walk you will see that once, long before you were born, you chose to be a Donnelly and laughed at what it would mean... You laughed and lay down with your fate like a bride, even the miserable fire of it. So that I am proud to be a Donnelly against all the contempt of the world.

The apotheosis of the Donnellys is not confined to this final scene of the play. We have been prepared for it at many points. Even the allusion in the above speech to the outcast Christ-figure of Psalm 22 ('My God, my God, why hast thou forsaken me?') has an echo earlier in the play when Donnelly proclaims: 'I killed and in turn you broke my bones, burnt my home.' The Biblical parallels to the action are made at several points in the play, as when Andy Keefe, on his departure from Biddulph, refers to it as 'this settlement of Cain.' Jim Feeney's swearing fidelity in blood to Tom Donnelly is a preparation for his Judas-figure's later betrayal of his friend, whom he will hand over to the vigilante mob. We realize that in this community of Christians something has gone badly awry when the Friar asks Cassleigh, in cathechism fashion: "What is the fifth commandment of God?' and the answer, in the Biddulph rite, is: 'The fifth commandment of God is: Thou, Brimmacombe—should not have seen me beaten so badly.' The recitation of the Angelus, and its association with the prayerful farmer and his wife in the painting by Millet, is an ironic comment on the lives of the farming community of Biddulph.

The institutional church becomes an important source of the religious symbolism in the play. One of the patterns on which Part One of the trilogy is built is the Christian sacraments of initiation. Baptism and Confirmation. But in *Sticks and Stones* there are churches other than the institutional one. There is the Church of Biddulph with its own initiation rites, and there is the Church of the higher world to which the Donnellys properly belong. The play opens with Will Donnelly, catechism in hand, preparing for his reception of the Sacrament of Confirmation at the hands of the bishop; it ends with the Donnellys having failed to pass the test for Confirmation in the Church of Biddulph, but ready for their initiation some thirteen years later into their own Church. Mrs. Donnelly questions her son from the catechism on the nature of the Sacraments of Baptism,

Confirmation, and Holy Orders, but very soon it is Will who is questioning her on the nature of the Sacraments of Biddulph: 'But what do they mean by Blackfoot?... Who were the Whitefeet?' Later he tells the Friar who is preparing him for the ceremony: 'There is a question, Father, I want to ask the bishop... why was I created lame? I'm going to ask him that.' In the final act, failure of the Donnellys to gain membership in the broader community is emphasized by Jennie, who uses the sacramental reference again:

we were up for confirmation in a church called the Roman line. No, it was a bigger church than that for it involved Protestants too. We were going to be tested for confirmation in a church called—Biddulph... Our confirmation came up and although we had known our catechism well, we failed.

This is followed by a series of questions asked by the Chorus in the peremptory manner of the catechism that build to a climax throughout the act and end with the chant: 'Why was I a Donnelly?' and the proud response: 'Because you chose to be a Donnelly.'

Jennie's Christening Scene in Act Two becomes a metaphor for the final consummation of the Donnellys by fire and a preparation for their marriage with their heavenly spouse, in the words of the ritual:

so that when the Lord shall come to call thee to the nuptials, thou mayest meet Him with all the saints in the heavenly courts, there to live for ever and ever.

Even the Confirmation card received by the child in the administration of the sacrament is given a wider significance by Reaney. Here it is paralled by the ticket Andy Keefe buys to get away from the township, by the tickets in Jennie's dream when she tries to persuade her parents to leave Biddulph with her, and by the Ghost of Mrs. Donnelly who speaks of her husband 'coming back to you as one day his ghost will come back to me—with a ticket that confirms us across the river and finally out of Biddulph.' The burning of the Donnellys' barn while they were at the dance becomes an image of the confirming bishop 'in his flame red robes (who) would appear to say whether we could join the church of Biddulph.' Explaining why she and Patrick had left the township Jennie says:

We could see that we could never join that Church that the bishop had finally come to with fire for a mitre and a torch for a crook and had not just slapped us all lightly on either cheek as token for the sufferings we must endure as followers of Jesus, no—the old ruffian had knocked us on the floor, to the floor and kicked us with his hooved boot and punched us with his thistle mitts and said: Get the hell out, you bugger Donnellys. No water for you, but we've fire.

It is a marvelously apt speech in which the colour of the religious rite, including the symbolic tap on the cheek by the mitred bishop with his gloved hand, evokes the heroic vision of the Donnellys that is the main theme of *Sticks and Stones.*

An important feature of the structure of *Sticks and Stones* is a series of opposites used to emphasize the fate of the Donnellys, who were caught and crushed between opposing forces. These opposites are typified in the title itself for in the course of the action the sticks and stones stand for the enemies and friends of the Donnellys. Other opposites included are Protestant and Roman Catholic, Grits and Tories, Whitefeet and Blackfeet, Church and State, the Girl with the Sword and the Fat Lady, and the false picture of the Donnellys as opposed to the true image of them. Reaney evokes these opposites visually when people form lines to represent the different factions, when some carry sticks and others carry stones. The overall effect is to show the Donnellys becoming more isolated as the action develops and left more and more to their own resources, so that by the end of the play they have emerged alone but determined, and aware of their strength and lonely destiny. 'I am proud to be a Donnelly against all the contempt of the world,' Jennie proclaims, and by this point the Donnellys have taken on a cosmic dimension and are opposed by all their world. This is the magic Reaney had worked in the play whereby the local situation of an unlettered family in a small community in Ontario has been transformed into that of tragic man facing a hostile world which will surely destroy him but will not break his will. This is what gives *Sticks and Stones* the universality that we associate with all enduring drama.

The notion of the Donnellys as tragic figures caught in the web of fate is reinforced by many of the images in the play. The series of opposing forces noted above contribute to this. So do the ladders, which are the most frequent prop used in the play. As Reaney says in one of his illuminating stage directions:

This is one of the most important design images of the story, a man caught between the lines of his neighbours, caught in a ladder, and the big dance at the end of the play will emphasize this quality of the Donnellys being planted in rows of people they can't get away from.

The idea of being trapped by such people is suggested again and again. The Ghost of Mrs. Donnelly tells her: 'There were ladders with certain rungs, Judith, you could have avoided, you know,' and her living self laments. 'Oh, if we could get out of the pound we're locked in—it's like a house with twisty windows.' The tragic fact that the Donnellys will be no freer in Biddulph than they were in Tipperary is brought out in the survey scene during which all the actors but the surveyor and the boy 'return to their lines stage right and stage left to make Jacob's ladders, or cats' cradles.' These children's games give visual immediacy to the message of this scene illustrating how the Donnellys will be trapped in the web of the roads of Biddulph on Concession Six, Lot Eighteen. The image is repeated at the end of the sequence where we see the actors 'using ropes and making cats' cradles (Jacob's ladders) out of them and their bodies; fates with string entangling people's lives':

Wild lands   wild lands   wild lands
Cut into concessions   cut into farms
Canada West   Canada West
In the new world   the new world   the new world

The imagery of the Donnellys as grain is the source of some of the finest poetry in the play. The Barley Corn Ballad sets the tone for this, but there are many other examples. Like grain the Donnellys are 'planted in rows of people they can't get away from'; their enemies

Harvested me and my sons like sheaves and stood
Us to die upon our ground
Where now nothing will ever grow.

After Mrs. Donnelly saves Donegan from mutilation at the hands of Cassleigh she uses the same imagery to condemn the whole community:

There's fields of grain to garner with bread for you all and you'd rather be thorns to each other. There's tables of food for you to eat and you won't come and sit down at them.

When Donnelly gives himself up he says: 'If they decide, Mr. Howard, to choke me off, there are seven men there under the blankets waiting to sprout up and show the world that I live,' and when he is returning from jail his wife commands the boys: 'Bring sheaves with you when you've finished the field. Your father will want to see what his farm's been doing.' They do, in the harvest moon, and 'We see sheaves through the shirts and the seven boys partly through them.' The identification of the family with the grain is complete when the father rejoices: 'Mrs. Donnelly, I was thinking what fair seed we have sown and I have come back at last to harvest.'

Rural imagery, too, is used to contrast the Donnellys and their enemies. It reminds us of the centrality in Reaney's work of the sounds and sights of his origins on a farm near Stratford, Ontario. Thus, as Mrs. Donnelly awaits news of her husband's commutation of sentence, we hear 'the cicadas strumming away with the heat.' In the church scene where Father Crinnon demands to know the murderer of the man he found killed in bed, 'there is silence filled with the buzzing of a fly against the window,' another image of the way in which people in Biddulph have become trapped in their own wickedness. When Will Donnelly is on trial for stealing six fleeces of wool 'the courtroom audience react with loud heehaws.' Mrs. Donnelly attacks Mrs. Ryan for laying charges against her for receiving the wool as stolen goods in these images:

You'd even gore your own ox to goad me, wouldn't you?... Anything goes, I see, if you can plunge your horn into me, into us—up to the very last wrinkle.

Mrs. Ryan becomes the focus of much of the scorn heaped upon the Donnelly foes, as in the lines recited by James and John as they are taking down her fence:

Why is our father's farm so narrow? Because he was cheated by the farrow. Of the pig and the sow, the fat woman who now snores as the moon lights our labours.

When Mrs. Ryan drops her sword over the fence Mrs. Donnelly returns it in language again from the animal world:

I shall throw the sword over the fence and I am shamed to see that glory used to chop turnips, but the fox has so long fouled the badger's den I shouldn't be surprised.

That 'glory' becomes an emblem of the heroic world in which the Donnellys live as contrasted to the earthbound, material one inhabited by their neighbours. The sword has its origins in the legendary past for Maggie says, referring to her own Grandmother: 'Her father's father found it on the battlefield a hundred years ago.' The lively scene in which she and Will, taking turns, play the fiddle and then dance with the sword is followed by the scolding she receives from her aunt, the Fat Woman: 'When I needed it to chop up turnips for the pigs, where were you with that old sword?' As Mrs. Ryan starts to sharpen the sword to chop the turnips Maggie vainly protests. 'You'll grind off the old writing that way, Aunt Theresa.' The insensitive reply is, 'What writing?' at which Will, shocked by the desecration, covers his face. At the fleece trial Stub laughs:

Will, this is like the story you told about the old sword that disappeared for a while on your road. When it was found again it was seen to be nothing but a rusty turnip knife.

This contrast between the Donnellys' awareness of beauty and glory and the dullness and insensitivity of their enemies is highlighted by other images such as Will's skill at fiddling, his giving the Indian Chief the more exalted title of 'King of the Indians,' and his desire to buy a horse from the King. The horse he eventually does get is appropriately called—and this is true historically—Lord Byron.

As in his earlier plays, Reaney makes effective use of popular song and verse. The most obvious example of this in *Sticks and Stones* is the Barley Corn Ballad, which opens and closes the play. It is a moving song in itself and has that combination of simplicity and lightness as well as fatality and strength that characterizes the play as a whole. In the Tarragon production the actors were singing this ballad in the lobby as the audience walked in before the play began on stage. The combination of lilting melody and sad tale served to underline the seriousness of the play and to give it a strength free of any sentimentalism. The ballad is so fitting to illustrate the fate of the Donnellys that if you substitute 'Donnelly' for 'barley grain' you have the story of the Donnellys told in ballad form. This association with the old ballad form is another way in which Reaney gives heroic stature to the Donnellys. Every possible effort is made to suppress the life and growth of the barley corn, but in the final, slightly vulgar, stanza that is 'said, not sung,' it, like the Donnellys, always emerges defiant and triumphant, just as they will at the end of the trilogy. Typical of these attempts is the stanza:

Then they sold me to the brewer
And he brewed me on the pan
But when I got into the jug
I was the strongest man.

This penultimate stanza, the only one used in Act Two of the play, gives an ominous closing to the act and fits in perfectly with the declaration of Donnelly to his wife at that point: 'Mrs. Donnelly, I was thinking what fair seed we have sown and I have come back at last to harvest.' The heavy accents of the fourth line of the verse resemble much of the poetic prose of *Sticks and Stones*, in passages already quoted, such as: 'Donnellys don't kneel,' and 'Your father and I will never leave Biddulph.'

The Barley Corn Ballad underlines the opening sequences of the play that remind us of the background of the Donnelly story. During the action each verse is repeated until the scene shifts from Ireland to Canada. As a ballad which originated in Ireland, it serves to emphasize the old world origins of the feud that will take its toll in the new land. When the recital of the ballad ends and the action of the play proper begins, the first stage direction is: 'Now the stage turns the deep green of a primeval forest; someone imitates the whistle of a deep forest bird.' Later in the act, as the last stanza begins and the old world sequence ends, Mrs. Donnelly 'turns from us and they leave the forest,' as the Donnellys left Ireland, but not before we are reminded of the price that must be paid by 'the strongest man' when she says: 'If you're afraid you should be... If you're not you'll live,' which 'fills the whole theatre.'

Names become an important strand in the fibre of the play. In this regard the title itself is a stroke of poetic insight. It recalls the child's world that for Reaney is always threatening as well as gay. The irony of the verses from which the title is taken is seen when Mrs. Donnelly says: 'there's a proverb that sticks and stones may hurt my bones, but names will never harm them,' and, in one of the key speeches in the play, her husband replies:

Not true, Mrs. Donnelly. Not true at all. If only he'd hit us with a stone or a stick, but ever since that day you told me they'd been calling our son that in the churchyard it's as if a thousand little tiny pebbles keep batting up against the windows in my mind just when it's a house that's about to sleep.

Names and lists of names are repeated throughout the play: names of families, names of the road lines in Biddulph, names of the Donnelly children, names for the census taker, names for the surveyor, names of people being prosecuted by the law. In a play for children entitled *Names and Nicknames* Reaney showed the devastating effect of a bad name on children and adults alike, and this same awareness is at the heart of the present play. It is emphasized chillingly in the sign left over the Donnellys' spring: 'No Water for Blackfeet.' The title of the original one part version of the trilogy was simply *Donnelly,* without the article, which again highlights the crucial importance of the name. *Sticks and Stones* thus becomes the struggle for a name, and by the end we are aware that one name stands above all other names and opposing names in the play—the name Donnelly.

Finally, the theatre itself becomes a metaphor in the play to suggest, paradoxically, both the evanescent quality of the lives of those depicted in the play and the permanence which the dramatic work will confer on these same lives. The evanescence is emphasized when Donnelly turns to the audience with a handful of dust and says, anticipating his murder:

Now my body belongs to its dust
Which dust once belonged to me.
As it is blown away I forget
Concession Six Lot Eighteen
South Half or North Half which was mine?
We are blown away and both lost
——————Like actors' words.

Earlier, in response to the catechism question: 'Who are punished in Hell?' Mr. Donnelly replies:

Not I. No, not James Donnelly. I'm not in Hell though my friends in Biddulph thought to send me there, but after thirty-five years in Biddulph who would find Hell any bigger a fire than that fire I died in. I'm not in Hell for I'm in a play.

The jauntiness of that final remark, like the barley corn that keeps reappearing in spite of repeated attempts to kill it, is an example of the combination of lightness and seriousness that runs throughout the play. Of course Donnelly can't be in Hell if he's in a play; but the play itself is the means whereby he will achieve immortality. And Reaney is deadly serious in his intention to confer permanence on the Donnellys by the trilogy he has written about them. *The Donnellys* is his *magnum opus* to date; all the preceding plays were preparations for this one. Through the drama he has conferred the kind of immortality on the Donnellys that is the accomplishment of great art.

This essay has pointed out some of the reasons why *Sticks and*

Stones is a drama of the highest order and, along with the two other parts of the Donnelly trilogy, probably the finest dramatic work ever written in English Canada. From its roots in the soil of our own history, Reaney has created a genuine Canadian myth that will endure even if future historians and lawyers ever answer the many questions that remain about the Donnellys and their times. Uniting as never before his gifts as poet and dramatist Reaney has given us a play that, while coming to life fully only on stage, can be studied as literature on the many levels of symbolism, metaphor, and irony that give *Sticks and Stones* such a rich texture. At the end of Part One of the trilogy a new name—Donnelly—has been added to our mythology. It is a name which neither sticks nor stones nor any other power on earth will be able to blacken again.

Chronology of Important Dates

(Note: This is an historical-literary chronology of events particular relevance to *The Donnellys.* I have compiled it mainly from Orlo Miller's book *The Donnellys Must Die* (Toronto:Macmillan, 1962), Reaney's own research, and the trilogy itself. A small number of changes in historical fact, including names of some people associated with the Donnellys, have been made in the plays for purposes of the drama.—J. Noonan)

The Donnelly Family

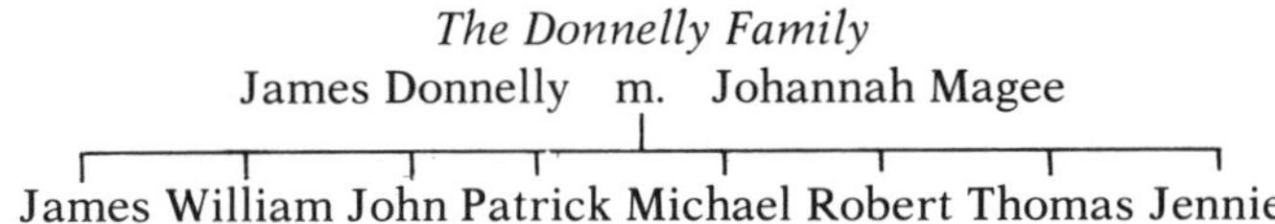

1761—the Whiteboys movement and name originates in Tipperary

1766—feud between the Whitefeet and Blackfeet Irish in Tipperary begins—it is conveniently dated from March 15, the day on which Father Nicholas Sheehy, parish priest of Clogheen, Tipperary, is hanged, drawn and quartered for complicity in the murder of an informer against the Whiteboys—this day became known as 'Sheehy's Day' to the Tipperary Irish in both Ireland and Canada, especially in Biddulph township where many of them settled

1816 – March 7 – James Donnelly, Senior, born in Tipperary
1823 – September 22 – Johannah (al.Judith or Julia) Magee born in Tipperary
1830 – refugee Negro slaves from the United States establish the settlement of Wilberforce in Biddulph township, near the site of Lucan, Ont. – shortly afterwards Irish settlers arrive in Biddulph – some of them petition the government not to allow more Negroes to settle there – many Negroes move away
1834 – survey of Biddulph township
1841 – James Donnelly marries Johannah Magee
1842 – James Donnelly, Junior,born
1844 – the Donnellys sail from Ireland to Canada
1845 – January – William Donnelly born
1847 – spring – Donnelly family settles on a piece of vacant land of about 100 acres on lot 18, concession 6, on the Roman line in the township of Biddulph near the village of Lucan, Ontario, formerly named Marysville
– September 16 – John Donnelly born
– George Stub burns Negroes' barns
1848 – census of Canada West is taken, in which the Donnellys are included
– Patrick Donnelly born
1850 – November – Michael Donnelly born
1853 – Robert Donnelly born
1854 – August 30 – Thomas Donnelly born
1855 – fall – Mr. and Mrs. Michael Ryan (al.'Fats') and Mr. and Mrs. Patrick Farrell move to the Roman line
1856 – Mr. and Mrs. Ryan buy the south half of the Donnelly farm
1857 – James Donnelly is awarded 50 acres of the land on which he squatted
– Feb.6 – Richard Brimmacombe, an English Protestant cattle drover from a neighbouring township, is killed near the Roman line – Patrick Marksey is named a suspect and Tom Cassleigh an accomplice – the murderer is never brought to justice
– June 25 – Mulowney's logging bee at which Donnelly strikes Farrel with a handspike; Farrell dies three days later – Donnelly goes into hiding
– December – Canadian elections – in the local riding Holmes (the Liberal and Protestant candidate) defeats Cayley (the Conservative and Roman Catholic candidate) – Donnellys and Keefes invariably vote Liberal
– Christmas Eve – in a post-election incident Andrew Keefe's

tavern is attacked by Protestants—George Stub, recently appointed Justice of the Peace, knocks down Keefe's signpost during the attack—no convictions are made

END OF ACT ONE OF STICKS AND STONES

1858—Reprisal by Roman Catholics on Keefe by burning his stables—10 horses are burned to death—no convictions
—Donnelly gives himself up and is convicted of the murder of Patrick Farrell—Sept. 17 is set as the day on which he is to be executed
—July 7—Mrs. Donnelly presents a petition for clemency to Governor-General Edmund Head at Goderich, Ont.
—July 28—Donnelly's sentence is commuted to seven years' imprisonment—he is sent immediately to Kingston Penitentiary
—Jennie (al.Jane) Donnelly born, the last of the Donnelly children and the only girl
1860—the Ryans move away, but Mrs. Donnelly can't afford to buy the half of the farm which the Ryans owned
1861—Will accused of stealing 6 fleeces of wool—the case is heard before Magistrate Stub—Mrs. Donnelly accused of receiving the fleece as stolen goods
1862—the indictments against Will and Mrs. Donnelly are withdrawn
—raising bee at Gallagher's at which Mrs. Donnelly prevents Cassleigh and others from torturing Donegan, brother of Patrick Farrell's widow Sarah, now Mrs. Flannery
—Donegan is found in bed by Father Crinnon, the parish priest, the flesh burnt off his bones—Father Crinnon later becomes Bishop of Hamilton
1863—Tom Donnelly and Jim Feeney swear fidelity in blood
1865—July 27—Donnelly released from prison
—Sept. 12—body of Patrick Marksey, the suspect in Brimmacombe's death, is found decapitated and mutilated

END OF ACT TWO OF STICKS AND STONES

1866—Quinns' barn is burnt out—they leave the township—Cassleigh buys their property
—the other half of the Donnelly property is for sale, but is bought by Mrs. Ryan with the help of her family
1867—July 1—Canada becomes a Dominion
—fall—persons unknown burn Donnellys' barn while they are at

a wedding dance—they also break their water pump: 'No water for Blackfeet'
—Donnelly buys the Mulowney property across the road from his farm
—Keefe's cheese factory is burnt—he leaves the township
—Cassleigh is made Justice of the Peace, the first Catholic judge in the township
—Donnellys decide never to leave Biddulph

END OF STICKS AND STONES: THE DONNELLYS, PART I

1870—Will becomes a driver for Hugh McPhee's stagecoach company, one of the three companies on the London-Exeter line
1872—Jan.1—Lucan becomes incorporated as a village
1873—May—Will buys out McPhee's company and operates the stage himself—May 27, Queen Victoria's birthday, is the official inauguration of the line—all members of the Donnelly family attend
1874—Jan.9—Will and friends go looking for Maggie Donovan, without success—she is prevented from marrying him because of her father's objections
—Jan.30—Will and friends take part in a violent 'shivaree' for William Donovan, Junior, and his bride—they don't find Maggie at William's either
—June—Will and four others are tried for assault on William Donovan, Senior, on the occasion of the search for Maggie—they are found not guilty—shortly aferward Maggie is married to the man of her father's choice
1875—Sept.—Will's stage collides with one of Finnegan's stages on the Proof Line Road, a few miles north of London
1876—Vigilance Committee formed
—Feb.—Committee hires a Hamilton detective, Hugh McKinnon, to build cases against the Donnellys
—March—at the Middlesex Spring Assizes all the Donnelly boys except Robert and Mike face charges—James, Will, and John receive sentences of nine, three, and nine months respectively
—Will marries Nora McDonald and moves to a farm three miles away at Whalen's Corners in Usborne township
1877—May 15—James, Junior, dies in Lucan, probably of inflammation of the lungs—'one down and eight to go'
—Bob works in Glencoe, 40 miles south of Lucan

–Mike works for the Canada South Railway, is married to Nellie Heins, and rents a house in Lucan
–Pat runs a blacksmith shop in Thorold, Ont.
–John and Tom live at home
–members of the Donnelly family buy property near Bad Axe, Michigan, perhaps with a view to moving there

1878–April 1–Bob convicted of assault with intent to do grievous bodily harm and sentenced to two years in Kingston Penitentiary–'two down and seven to go'
–Sept. 17–Federal general election–in Biddulph Tim Coughlin (Conservative and Roman Catholic candidate) is elected over Colin Scatcherd (Liberal and Protestant) as Sir John A. Macdonald and the Conservatives win the election

1879–February–Father John Connolly, who has been working in a parish in Quebec, is appointed parish priest of St. Patrick's, Biddulph, by Bishop John Walsh of the diocese of London
–June–Provincial election–in the North Middlesex riding John Waters (Liberal) defeats J. McDougall (Conservative)–Father Connolly gets parishoners to sign pledge to aid him 'in the discovery and putting down of crime'
–Bridget Donnelly, aged 21, niece of Mr. Donnelly, arrives from Tipperary, Ireland, and comes to live with the Donnellys
–Sept. 20–James Carroll appointed county constable at the urging of the Vigilance Committee
–late summer–members of the Committee search and upset the Donnelly home looking for William Donovan's lost cow–they then go to Will's and are driven away as he plays the fiddle–a number are charged with trespass, destruction of property, and assault, but all charges are thrown out
–Dec.9–Mike Donnelly stabbed to death in a bar-room in Slaught's Hotel in Waterford, Ont., by William Lewis, who is punished with suspicious lightness for the murder–'three down and six to go'–Mike leaves a wife and two children living in St. Thomas, Ont.
–Martin McLoughlin, a member of the Committee is appointed magistrate

END OF THE ST. NICHOLAS HOTEL: THE DONNELLYS, PART II

1880–Jan. 10–Bob returns home from Kingston Penitentiary, then leaves for St. Thomas and Glencoe

—Jan. 15—Pat Ryder's barns and stables are burned down—warrants issued for the arrest of Mr. and Mrs. Donnelly—Mrs. Donnelly is visiting Jennie, now Mrs. Currie, who lives in St. Thomas, when James Carroll arrests her—after four adjournments, Mr. and Mrs. Donnelly are to appear before Magistrate Tom Cassleigh on Feb. 4 in Granton, Ont.

The Fateful Week:

—Sunday, February 1

—Father Connolly preaches against depredation in the parish

—the Donnellys have not attended his church since John was refused Confession the previous April

—Monday, February 2

—the feast of Candlemas—candles are blessed on this day

—Tuesday, February 3

—feast of St. Blaise, on which parishoners have their throats blessed with candles

—Mr. Donnelly writes a letter to the *St. Mary Argus* declaring innocence in the Ryder fire, mails it, buys some things in the village and picks up 11 year old Johnny O'Connor to take care of the farm next day when he and Johannah will be in Granton —John goes to Will's to get the cutter for their journey and decides to stay there the night

—Will attends a dance in the evening

—about 10 pm Jim Feeheley visits the Donnellys, then leaves his coat there while he goes to the Ryders'—the door is left unlatched for him to return for it—and for the Vigilance Committee to enter the house

—Wednesday, February 4

—five Donnellys are murdered

—shortly after midnight a mob of about forty members of the Vigilance Committee led by James Carroll enter the Donnelly home, kill and mutilate James and Johannah as well as Tom and Bridget Donnelly, and then burn them and their home—Johnny O'Connor hides under a bed during the massacre

—1:30am—Johnny O'Connor, the sole witness of the murders, arrives at the home of Pat Whalen across the road

—2:15am—the mob arrives at Will's home, shoots and kills his brother, John, thinking it is Will—they start for Jim Keefe's home but disperse before arriving there—'six down and three to go'—the other three (Will, Pat and Bob) all die natural deaths

—Thursday, February 5, 7:00 pm

– inquest opens at the town hall of Lucan
– Friday, February 6
– funeral is held in St. Patrick's Church for the five murdered Donnellys – Pat, Bob and Jennie return for the funeral – two coffins are needed: one for John and one for the remains of the other four – Father Connolly says the Funeral Mass and preaches the sermon
– Wed., Feb 11 – Ash Wednesday, the beginning of Lent
– March 13 – preliminary hearing ends at London – six men are committed for trial: James Carroll, John Kennedy, Martin McLoughlin, James and Thomas Ryder, and John Purtell
– April 12 – trial of the six opens at London – then it is postponed to the fall assizes
– Late Sept. – fall assizes open in the Middlesex County Courthouse in London – all six prisoners plead not guilty – the defence is granted a severance of trials
– Oct. 4 – trial of James Carroll, the first of the prisoners to be tried, opens – W.R. Meredith is the defence lawyer; Aemilius Irving is the Crown lawyer; Mr. Justice Armour hears the case before a jury
– Oct. 9 – the divided jury is unable to decide on the guilt of the accused – a new trial is required

1881 – late Jan. – second trial of James Carroll begins, this time before two judges: Matthew Cameron and Featherston Osler
– Jan. 29 – ninth day of the trial – jury returns their verdict: 'not guilty of murder'
– the same day, after eleven jurors are sworn in for the trial of Thomas Ryder and John Purtell, Irving requests that their and the other three cases be tried at the next assizes – all the prisoners are granted bail. No further trial of them or of anyone else is ever held for the murder of the five Donnellys killed on Feb. 4, 1880.
– summer – Will, Pat and Bob leave Lucan – Pat returns to Thorold; Bob goes to Glencoe; Will settles in Appin, Ont., and runs the St. Nicholas Hotel

1897 – March 7 – Will dies at home in Appin
– Bob returns to Lucan and runs the Western Hotel
– Father Connolly dies at Ingersoll, Ont.

1860 – June 14 – Bob dies in Lucan

1914 – May 18 – Pat dies in Thorold

1917 – Jennie dies in Glencoe and is buried in Wardsville, Ont.; she was the last surviving member of the Donnelly family

1937 – Feb. 25 – Will's wife Nora dies in London, Ont., aged 85

James Noonan

Glossary of Terms

Angelus—daily prayer recited in honour of the Virgin Mary

avourneen—an Irish term of endearment

bee—a gathering of neighbours in a community for some combined work, e.g., a logging bee

Blackfeet—Irishmen from Tipperary, or their descendants, who would not join in the activities of the Whitefeet (q.v.) against the English landlords

bolster—a long, narrow pillow or cushion that extends from side to side of a bed

Canada West—the name given to what is now the Province of Ontario after it had been called Upper Canada

cats' cradles—patterns made in a children's game in which string is wound and intertwined around the fingers. The game is also known as Jacob's ladders or sewing fingers.

the Company—the Canada Land Company, which administered the sale of farmland in Biddulph township in the early 1900's

Confirmation ticket—a card held by a candidate for identification in the administration of the sacrament of Confirmation

Confiteor—a Latin prayer for the confession of sins

curtilage—a private yard attached to a house

cutter—a one-horse sleigh used as a means of transportation in the winter

et aliter—and others
fleece—the quantity of wool shorn from a sheep at one time
Grand Guignol—sensational and exaggerated, from a particular style of drama
grogboss—the man in charge of the liquor at a bee
an information—in law, a charge or complaint lodged with a court or magistrate
Jacob's ladders—cf. cats' cradles
Keeper's Hill—the name given to the location of the Donnellys' home in Tipperary, Ireland
larrup—to beat soundly
neat cattle—cattle of the ox kind, as distinguished from horses, sheep, and goats
return of convictions—formal report of convictions made by a court
severance of trials—separation of the trials of several people accused of the same crime, a process followed in the case of the six men accused in the massacre of the Donnellys
shivaree—a mock and often disorderly welcome by a group for a newly married couple
squatter—one who takes unauthorized possession of unoccupied land
Temple House reel—a particular type of Irish dance
the War—the Crimean War, 1854–56
white gloves of his lordship—gloves worn by a judge when there are no trials during a particluar session of the court
Whitefeet (also known as Whitefoot Society or Whiteboys' movement)—members and descendants of a secret society in Tipperary, Ireland, sworn to attack their English landlords

James Noonan